The Origins of the Liturgical Year

Thomas J. Talley

The Origins
of the Liturgical Year

Second, Emended Edition

A PUEBLO BOOK

The Liturgical Press   Collegeville, Minnesota

Design: Frank Kacmarcik

The author and publishers gratefully acknowledge permission to reprint portions of the copyrighted works listed in the acknowledgement section.

Scriptural pericopes quoted from the Revised Standard Version.

ISBN: 0-8146-6075-4

Printed in the United States of America

To my father,
my first and best mentor

Contents

Preface

The work presented here has developed over the past seven years, although it rests upon a much older fascination with the liturgical year and with the liturgical articulation of time in general. My original intention was simply to provide an updated replacement for Allan McArthur's *Evolution of the Christian Year*, a very helpful volume which has long been out of print. As the work progressed, however, it became increasingly clear that it would differ from the positions adopted by McArthur at many points, and the final result is, I fear, at variance with much that has come to be considered established.

At one point, however, McArthur suggested a bold hypothesis of his own, and the principal point of that hypothesis, the beginning of the course reading of the fourth gospel from the Epiphany at Ephesus in the second century, has, with slight alteration, been embraced and expanded upon here, suggesting (albeit hypothetically) much earlier roots for the liturgical year than have been proposed in most manuals of liturgical history. At the same time, the more commonly reported explanations have been presented and examined, and, I hope, most of the more important texts presented.

Since the Old Testament assumed by the liturgical documents examined was the Septuagint, its numbering of psalms has been retained in most cases, the Hebrew numbering appearing in brackets or else explicitly indicated.

I am grateful to the publishers for their acceptance of my manuscript and for guiding it into print. I would also like to express my thanks to students who have come forward with helpful suggestions and observations, especially the Revs. Robin Smith, Neil Alexander, Arshen Aivazian, and a former student, now a respected colleague, John Baldovin, S.J. Gratitude is due as well to a number of other colleagues who have offered not only helpful suggestions but bibliographical resources and even texts from their own libraries. From a much larger field of such cooperative scholars, I would like to thank especially Professors René-Georges Coquin of L'École Pratique des Hautes Études in Paris; Lawrence Hoffman of the Jewish Institute of Religion of Hebrew Union College; Aidan Kavanagh, O.S.B., of Yale University; John Koenig of the General Theological Seminary; Thomas Mathews of New York University; Niels Rasmussen, O.P., of the University of Notre Dame; Morton Smith of Columbia University; and Robert Taft, S.J., of Pontificio Istituto Orientale in Rome. From these and others too numerous to name here I have received a renewed appreciation of the essentially collegial character of our scholarly enterprise. Finally, my thanks are due to my assistant, Mr. Angus Davis, whose diligence and persistence have vastly eased my task and expedited its completion. These deserve my deep gratitude; responsibility for whatever is still amiss in the work is, of course, mine alone.

*   *   *

I am grateful to the publisher for the opportunity to offer in this slightly emended edition reference to some significant research not reported in the original, as well as to correct details in my own work. Thanks are due also to the many readers — students, colleagues, and others — whose kind criticism has brought to my attention the need for such corrections. I regret that the number of these correspondents precludes individual recognition of them. Not every shortcoming noted has been addressed adequately, but it is hoped that this edition will more nearly warrant the generous reception accorded the original publication.

T. J. T.

Abbreviations

ALW   *Archiv für Liturgiewissenschaft.*
ANF   A. Cleveland Coxe, ed., *The Ante-Nicene Fathers.*
Botte   Bernard Botte, *Les Origines de la Noël et de l'Épiphanie, étude historique. Textes et études liturgiques,* 1 (Louvain 1932).
CC Lat.   *Corpus Christianorum, Series Latina.*
CSCO   *Corpus Scriptorum Christianorum Orientalium.*
CSEL   *Corpus Scriptorum Ecclesiasticarum Latinorum.*
DACL   Fernand Cabrol, Henri Leclerq, eds., *Dictionnaire d'archéologie chrétienne et de liturgie* (Paris 1924–1953).
Egeria   Aet. Franceschini, R. Weber, eds., "Itinerarivm Egeriae," *Itineraria et Alia Geographica. CC Lat. CLXXV* (Turnhout 1965); English translation from John Wilkinson, *Egeria's Travels,* rev. ed. (Jerusalem and Warminster 1981).
GCS   *Die griechischen christlichen Schriftsteller der ersten Jahrhunderte.*
HE   *Historia Ecclesiastica.*
IDB   George A. Buttrick, ed., *The Interpreter's Dictionary of the Bible* (New York and Nashville 1962).
JLW   *Jahrbuch für Liturgiewissenschaft.*
JTS   *Journal of Theological Studies.*
LQF   *Liturgiewissenschaftliche Quellen und Forschungen.*
Mansi   J. D. Mansi, *Sacrorum Conciliorum Nova et Amplissima Collectio* (Florence 1759–1798).
Mateos, Le Typikon   Juan Mateos, *Le Typikon de la grande Église. Ms. Saint-Croix n° 40, Xᵉ siècle. Introduction, texte critique et notes. Tome I, Le cycle des douze mois.*

OCA 165 (Rome 1962); *Tome II, Le cycle des fêtes mobiles.* OCA 166 (Rome 1963).

Mus   *Le Muséon, Revue d'Etudes Orientales.*

NPNF   Philip Schaff, ed., *Nicene and Post-Nicene Fathers of the Christian Church*, Series I and II (photo-lithographic reprint, Grand Rapids, Mich. 1952).

OCA   *Orientalia Christiana Analecta.*

OCP   *Orientalia Christiana Periodica.*

PG   J.P. Migne, ed., *Patrologia Graeca.*

PL   J.P. Migne, ed., *Patrologia Latina.*

PO   F. Graffin, ed., *Patrologia Orientalis.*

Renoux,
Le Codex   Athanase Renoux, *Le Codex arménien Jérusalem 121. I. Introduction aux origines de la liturgie hiéro-solymitaine, lumières nouvelles.* PO XXXV.1. N° 163 (Turnhout 1969); *II. Edition comparée du texte et de deux autres manuscrits.* PO XXXVI.2. N° 168 (Turnhout 1971).

SC   *Sources Chrétiennes.*

TDNT   Gerhard Kittel, ed., Geoffrey W. Bromiley, trans., *Theological Dictionary of the New Testament* (Grand Rapids, Mich. 1964).

TL   *Theologische Literaturzeitung.*

TU   *Texte und Untersuchungen zur Geschichte der altchrist-lichen Literatur, begründet von O. von Gebhardt und A. Harnack.*

Part One

Pascha, the Center of the Liturgical Year

When Israel came out of Egypt, the core of the festival known as *Pascha* in Christian tradition was already central to the religious life of the people. The term itself is the transliteration of the Aramaic form of the Hebrew *pesach*. While the original meaning of *pesach* remains obscure, in biblical tradition it refers to the passage of the angel of death over the houses of the Hebrews marked with the blood of the sacrificed lamb, and for that reason it is regularly translated "Passover" in the Old Testament and in the New. Passover refers to the feast as a whole and also to the sacrifice itself. Further, in the New Testament period, Passover can refer to the whole complex of the spring festival, both the Passover and the feast of Unleavened Bread, and references to the latter feast can include Passover. It is generally agreed, however, that such usage represents the elision of what were originally two separate festivities: Passover, a spring sacrifice by nomadic shepherds, and Unleavened Bread, a Canaanite agricultural festival adopted by the Hebrews only after their settlement in the land. Passover itself, again, may well be much older than the Exodus, which provides its biblical content. It has commonly been identified as the feast to God in the wilderness for the observance of which Moses asked the Pharaoh's permission (Ex 5.1; 10.9).

The feast of Unleavened Bread was one of three agricultural festivals adopted by Israel in Canaan. With the feast of Weeks (at other times known as Harvest or Pentecost) and that of Tabernacles (Ingathering in the earlier documents), Unleavened Bread was observed as a festival of the people, a public cultic phenomenon, whereas Passover itself seems rather to have been a domestic ritual meal, although still of a sacrificial character. The three agricultural festivals were assemblies of the people at a sanctuary and thus served as important occasions for the renewal of their bonds within the covenant. From the time of Josiah, in the seventh century B.C., Jerusalem was designated as the sole sanctuary of the nation, and it was there alone that these pilgrim festivals were to be observed. That same reform, most would agree today, brought about the union of Passover with the feast of Unleavened Bread. From that time, at least, Passover was the great public festival of Israel's redemption out of slavery in Egypt, the feast of national liberation for which, it has been estimated, as many as 100,000 pilgrims converged on Jerusalem in the first century of our era.[1]

1. PASSOVER IN THE FIRST CENTURY

The domestic character of Passover was retained in that the feast was eaten in families or other companies, yet this was bound to the public observance by the sacrifice of the lambs for the feast by the temple priests. This, together with the putting away of the leaven, took place on the eve of the feast itself and so on 14 Nisan. The present practice of the Samaritans at Nablus may represent an older usage, viz., the slaughter of the lambs (at the foot of Mount Gerizim) only at sundown, the beginning of 15 Nisan, but it seems clear that the large number of animals to be dressed at Jerusalem in the first century of our era required the beginning of the Passover sacrifice at an earlier hour. In the afternoon, the time signaled by a triple trumpet blast, the slaughtering and dressing of the lambs began. The priests caught the blood in gold or silver basins and splashed it against the altar where the fat of the lambs was being burned, while levites sang the Hallel, Psalms 113–118 (Heb.). The dressed lambs were returned to the worshipers who had brought them and were carried away to be roasted for the feast.[2]

In the first century as still today, the nocturnal feast was the occasion for the remembrance of Israel's redemption out of slavery. However, in much of rabbinic tradition, that feast was also occasion for the sharpening of the hope for final redemption. Messianic expectation in the first century was focused on Passover when the redemption inaugurated by the slaying of Egypt's firstborn, "while all things were in quiet silence and that night was in the midst of her swift course," was expected to be brought to fulfillment at midnight. That hour, remembered in Wisdom 18.14, marked the conclusion of the Passover celebration. This expectation of final redemption at Passover was the tradition associated with R. Joshua and his followers. (We shall see later, however, that this was not the sole tradition.)

The deliverance out of Egypt and the expected coming of Messiah reflect the meeting of memory and hope in this festival. Two other themes further enriched the Passover early in the common era, but precise dating is impossible. The Palestinian Targum on Exodus contains a "Poem of the Four Nights," which assigns four events to Passover: the creation of the world, the binding (*akedah*) of Isaac, the deliverance from Egypt, and the coming of the Messiah.[3] These, as we shall see, had significant impact on the Christian themeology of Pascha.

Such a Passover provided the cultic context for the last supper of Jesus with his disciples, his arrest, trial, passion, and crucifixion. It was within the eight days of this paschal festivity that he rose from the dead on the first day of the week. It is such a Passover, indeed, that the Church has celebrated from the time of our earliest liturgical records as the central feast of the liturgical year. Yet, the precise relationship between the Christian Pascha and the Passover of the Law is riddled with questions. In the New Testament itself it is uncertain whether the last supper was such a Passover meal.

The testimony of the synoptic gospels seems clear enough. Jesus sends his disciples to prepare a room for the Passover (Mk 14.14; Mt 26.18; Lk 22.8). In Luke 22.15 he says, "I have earnestly desired to eat this passover with you before I suffer." An ambiguity in the account of Mark (Mk 14.21) that seems to confuse "the first day of Unleavened Bread" (actually 15 Nisan) with the day "when they sacrificed the passover lamb" (14 Nisan) is probably to be explained by an error in rendering an Aramaic phrase. The preparation for the festival in the synoptics is surely 14 Nisan and the supper eaten in the night is the Passover feast. Jesus, in this chronology, is crucified on 15 Nisan.

For the fourth gospel, on the other hand, the crucifixion itself occurs on 14 Nisan, at the time of the slaying of the lambs for the feast, and John 19.32-36 associates the failure of the soldiers to break Jesus' legs with the provision of the law (Ex 12.46) that no bone of the Passover lamb shall be broken. This identification of Jesus as the Passover lamb of the New Covenant is reflected already in St. Paul (1 Cor 5.7). While it has been easy at times in the past to dismiss this Johannine chronology as conscious theologizing of little historical merit, more recent exegetical opinion has been less inclined to reject the historicity of the Johannine chronology. It seems safe to say that 1 Corinthians 5.7 reflects Paul's familiarity with a tradition in the primitive Church predicated upon the chronology that we know as Johannine. Indeed, as we shall see, the early celebration of Pascha by Christians seems to presuppose that chronology.

The question of the time from which Christians began to observe Pascha probably presupposes too formal a Christian institution. Many have pointed out that 1 Corinthians 5.7 seems to indicate that such an observance was already common to Christians, but other exegetes are doubtful. To decide the matter would require the resolution of more questions than can have responsible attention here. Therefore, we must satisfy ourselves with a few observations that may, at least, set the question in context.

Paul writes around A.D. 55 from Ephesus in Asia Minor, a city with whose synagogue he had an extended relationship (Acts 19.8). Writing, possibly, from around the time of Passover, he tells the Corinthians that he intends to remain in Ephesus until Pentecost (1 Cor 16.8). His references to Passover and Pentecost show that these times were significant for him, and he seems to assume that they have a definite meaning for the Corinthians to whom he writes. While in this year he made no evident attempt to observe either festival in Jerusalem, at a later time Acts 20.16 shows him "hastening to be at Jerusalem, if possible, on the day of Pentecost." All this suggests that Paul had by no means cut himself off from the liturgical festivals of Judaism. Nothing tells us how he observed Passover in Ephesus around the time of his writing of 1 Corinthians 5.7, but it is clear that already the festival had for him a new meaning established on the Cross.

One could wish to know how his Passover supper in Ephesus in that year related to the eucharist that he discusses in chapter 11. However, even if Paul observed Passover in a form that would constitute a proclamation of "the Lord's death until he comes", it is clear that for him this new meaning of Passover was not limited to the annual festival, for in 11.26 he says that the memorial of Christ's death is made "as often as" the eucharist is celebrated. If Passover was transformed by the Cross, the very universality of

4

the Cross could point away from the distinctiveness of that night unlike every other night. While Paul's correction of the "foolish Galatians" is sometimes addressed not to Judaizing tendencies but to pagan residues, such texts as Galatians 4.10 suggest nonetheless that the promulgation of annual festivals had little place in the agenda of the Gentile mission.

On the other hand, ambivalence toward annual festivals (and other cultic aspects of the Law) such as we see in Paul makes it difficult to account for the Christian adoption of Pascha except as a continuity with Passover. There would have been less diffidence toward that continuity in the primitive community at Jerusalem, and there, we can believe, the observance of Passover continued, its ancient theme of redemption transformed by the triumph of the Paschal Lamb of the Covenant renewed.

2. THE QUARTODECIMAN PASCHA

Clear testimony to the Christian observance of Pascha appears only in the second century, but that testimony suggests that the Christian observance was a gradual modulation of the Passover as it continued to be observed by the primitive community, rather than an adoption of characteristics and themes from Passover and their application to a new Christian celebration of the resurrection. Indeed, there is little indication that the primitive Pascha was focused primarily on the resurrection, even though that theme was certainly included in the festival's celebration of our total redemption in Christ. The earliest textual evidence, from the second half of the second century, is called *Epistula Apostolorum*, a text written in all probability somewhere in Asia Minor. Originally in Greek, it is preserved complete only in Ethiopic, with a mutilated and occasionally variant version in Coptic and a single leaf in a Latin palimpsest. Chapter 15 of the Ethiopic version presents the following address of the risen Christ to the apostles:

"As for you, make the commemoration of my death, that is to say, the Passover. It is then that one among you who stand by me will be thrown into prison because of my name; he will be very sad and cast down, for while you keep the Passover he is in prison and does not keep it with you. But I will send my Power in the form of my angel, and the doors of the prison will be opened, and he will come to you to watch and rest with you. Then at cockcrow, when you have completed my agape and my commemoration, he will be taken again and cast into prison for a testimony, until he comes out to preach, as I have commanded you."[4]

Here Passover, surely kept in the night from 14 to 15 Nisan, is the memorial of the death of Jesus. In other second-century documents from Asia Minor, it becomes clear that this death is not seen as merely one incident in an extended Holy Week scenario. Rather, the content of the celebration is the entire work of redemption: the incarnation, the passion, the resurrection and glorification, all focused upon the Cross as locus of Christ's triumph. The observance is described as a watch, a vigil, and is kept past the midnight hour, which terminated the Jewish Passover, extending to cockcrow when it was concluded with "my agape and my commemoration," an expression that must be understood to include the eucharist.

This extension of the vigil ("night-watch" in the Coptic version) to cockcrow will be encountered again and again in the literature and seems to be a characteristic that distinguishes the Christian observance from the Jewish. The reason for this extension of the vigil is not evident, and it may mean only that the Christians chose to delay their time of rejoicing until after the termination of the feasting of the Jews, an early instance of the concern, repeatedly encountered in the later literature, that the Christian Pascha must come after that of the Jews. None of the texts seems to associate a particular event with the hour of cockcrow, neither Peter's betrayal nor the resurrection nor any other. It may be that the time just prior to dawn carried a particularly strong eschatological significance, but discussion of the relation of expectation of the *parousia* to festivals must wait for the following part of our study. Nonetheless, the references to watching and vigil in *Epistula Apostolorum* must surely have grown out of some element of expectation of Messiah in connection with the paschal night.

Just after the passage cited above from chapter 15 (26) of *Epistula Apostolorum*, the apostles put to the Lord a question suggesting that the author of the work was familiar with a dispute regarding the propriety of a Christian observance of Passover such as *Epistula Apostolorum* reflects. Following the command to "celebrate the remembrance of my death", the apostles ask, "O Lord, have not you yourself drunk the Passover definitively? As for us, do we have to do it anew?" Jesus responds to the apostles' question, "Yes, until I return from the Father with my wounds."[5] It seems that this reflects the author's awareness of a dispute over the necessity for the Christian celebration of Passover, and so would be in accord with the ambivalence that we noted in Paul, an ambivalence that, we can imagine, grew with the success of the mission to the Gentiles. We shall examine below a possible context for such an assertion of a dominical command to continue to observe Passover. Such a continuity with Passover can easily be assumed to have existed in the primitive community in Jerusalem. Most of that community was dispersed during the time of troubles attending the destruction of the temple in A.D. 70 and in the wake of the Bar Cochba rebellion. Those Christians who were "of the circumcision" settled elsewhere, and among those centers of resettlement we should include the seven churches of Asia addressed in the Apocalypse. In any case, in the second century it is in Asia Minor especially that we encounter a flourishing Quartodecimanism that, there or elsewhere in the diaspora, would face problems of computation in connection with the observance of Passover.

The inadequacy of the Jewish calendar, whose twelve lunar months did not equal a solar year, presented difficulties for the maintenance of uniform practice. This was a problem even for Jews in the diaspora, since in the second century no system was yet established for the intercalation of an added month when the disparity with the solar year became too great, and necessary adjustments were made ad hoc. In the second century a letter was sent out from the sages of Palestine to Jews in the diaspora ordering an additional month for that year, "the doves being still young, the lambs still weak, and the (barley) grain not yet ripened."[6] Nonetheless, such measures often failed to preserve unity of observance. Whatever problem the date of Passover presented for Jews, it must have been even more of a problem for Asian Christians who believed that they must observe Pascha on the fourteenth day of the first month. Christians were separated from the synagogues by the end of the first century, and were thereafter independent of the rabbinical authorities who determined the adjustment of the calendar by the periodic addition of an intercalary month. Apart from that authority, Christians could not know which month was first. Further, they lived in a culture that followed the solar Julian calendar and had done so since 9 B.C.

What was fundamental for Quartodecimanism, however, was the observance of the fast on "the very day" of Christ's passion, that is, the anniversary commemoration of the crucifixion on the fourteenth day of the first month. Therefore, Asian Christians gave up the lunar calendar regulated by the Palestinian rabbinical authorities in favor of the Asian recension of the Julian solar calendar. Sozomen (HE VII.18) notes that the Montanists of Asia Minor set the Pascha on April 6, following a solar calendar.

"They blame those who regulate the time of observing the feast according to the course of the moon, and affirm that it is right to attend exclusively to the cycles of the sun. . . . For they compute the day of the creation of the sun, mentioned in Sacred Writ, to have been the fourteenth day of the moon, occurring after the ninth day before the calends of the month of April, and answering to the eighth day prior to the ides of the same month" (NPNF II.II, p. 389).

Such a date would be perfectly understandable as a conversion of 14 Nisan to the Julian calendar in its Asian recension. When the Julian calendar was adopted in Asia in 9 B.C., it took its civil beginning from the birthday of Augustus, September 23, or, in Roman reckoning, IX Kalendarum Octobris. To that month, Kaisarios, was assigned the number of days in the Roman October, and the same was true of each successive month, although each began nine days earlier than its Roman equivalent, that is, on the ninth of the kalends. The first month of spring, Artemisios, therefore, began on the ninth of the kalends of April, March 24. The fourteenth day of Artemisios, then, would be equivalent to April 6, the Quartodeciman Pascha in that solar calendar. The establishment of the capital at Constantinople brought the adoption of the Roman calendar and translation of dates into its designations. Sozomen, writing in the fifth century, seems unaware of that earlier Asian calendar, although Constantinople in Sozomen's days still observed September 23 as the beginning of the year.[7] Although for him that paschal date of April 6, the old Asian 14 Artemisios, was peculiar to a Montanist group, there is every reason to believe that the early Quartodeciman Christians in Asia had observed the same date, because the indeterminacy of the lunar calendar demanded their acceptance of a solar computation for the all-important paschal date, the fourteenth day of the first month. August Strobel has given particular attention to this solar Quartodecimanism, although he, too, seems unaware of the structure of the Asian recension of the Julian calendar.[8]

Such an establishment of the fourteenth day of the first spring month as equivalent to the fourteenth day of the moon would, of course, disregard the lunar cycle itself, but that disregard for the lunar cycle was by no means unknown in early Jewish calendrical practice, as is shown by the solar calendar of the Essenes at Qumran, a calendar whose impact on Christianity we shall have occasion to examine later. Suffice it to say at this point that the Qumran calendar did not employ the Babylonian month names used in the lunar calendar, but only referred to the months by number, Passover being eaten in the night from the fourteenth to the fifteenth of the first month, that designation of the month of Passover as "first" being established by Exodus 12.2.[9]

By the third century, however, we encounter computations that aim at determining the Julian dates on which the fourteenth day of the moon occurred in the various years, with the result that the Julian date of Christ's passion was set on March 25. A statue discovered in Rome in 1551 near Porta Tiburtina was identified as that of the Roman theologian Hippolytus because a catalogue of his works is inscribed on the right rear corner of the chair in which the figure sits. Each of the side panels of that chair bears tables for the computation of the paschal date. In the table on the left side of the chair, the first column gives the Julian dates on which the fourteenth day of the moon should fall. The last entry in that column assigns Christ's passion to the eighth of the kalends of April, March 25.[10] That Hippolytus did indeed take that date to be also the fourteenth of the moon, and therefore the Preparation of the Passover, is clear in two texts from his writings cited by the Byzantine author of the *Chronicon Paschale*. These texts (one from the *Syntagma adversus haereses* and the other from the *Peri Pascha*)[11] show clearly that Hippolytus presumed the Johannine chronology, which set the passion of Christ at the time of the slaying of the lambs for Passover. As the second of those texts says of Christ at that Passover, "he did not eat it, but suffered it."

This same identification of March 25 with 14 Nisan in the year of our Lord's passion is found in a work usually attributed to Tertullian, *Adversus Iudaeos*. However, other writings of Tertullian suggest that he, as other North African writers of his time and later, accepted the synoptic chronology, which identified Jesus' last supper with his disciples as the Passover feast.[12] In *Adversus Iudaeos*, by contrast, the passion of the Lord is set on the day of the slaying of the lambs, although, as in Mark 14.2 and Matthew 25.17, that day is erroneously called "the first day of unleavened bread." That aside, it is clear that *Adversus Iudaeos* VIII.18 puts the passion on March 25 and relates that to the sacrifice of the lambs on 14 Nisan.

"The passion of Christ was perfected within the time of seventy hebdomads under Tiberius Caesar, in the consulates of Rubellius Geminus and Fufius Geminus in the month of March at the time of Passover, on the eighth of the Kalends of April, the first day of unleavened bread, on which they killed the lamb at even as Moses had taught."[13]

From these texts, it is clear that these western (and perhaps Roman) writers believed that in the year of our Lord's passion the Preparation of the Passover, 14 Nisan, fell on the Julian March 25. That Julian date happened to coincide with the date assigned to the spring equinox in the Julian calendar, and that coincidence would prove important in the future. In the third century, however, there seems to have been no concern to shift the paschal date to the equinox itself, since the Hippolytan tables establish the Julian equivalents for 14 Nisan in every year and show no concern to make the paschal celebration fall on the spring equinox in every year.

What is particularly significant in these texts is that they represent an acceptance of the Johannine chronology of the passion in contrast with the synoptic chronology, which makes the last supper the Passover, setting the passion on 15 Nisan, the first day of Unleavened Bread. We have mentioned the adoption of that synoptic chronology in North Africa. In *Adversus Marcionem* IV.40.1–3,

Tertullian argues for the institution of the eucharist at the Passover feast, and similar insistence that Jesus ate the Passover with his disciples before his passion is found in Cyprian and in the anonymous *De Pascha computus*.[14] This alternative chronology was already the subject of modest dispute in the second century and was spoken against by both Apollinaris of Hierapolis and Clement of Alexandria, according to the author of the *Chronicon paschale*.[15] Belief in the conjunction of the fourteenth day of Nisan with March 25 in the year of our Lord's passion and the adoption of that day as the historical date of the passion was not limited to Rome, however. Such a paschal date has been noted in Egypt by A. Jacoby[16] and it constitutes the basis for an important Latin work commonly called *De solstitiis et aequinoctiis*.[17] No clear date has been established for this work, although it seems unlikely that it could have originated before the fourth century. As its title suggests, it no longer views the coincidence of the Julian equivalent to 14 Nisan (March 25) and the established date for the spring equinox as accidental, but makes the equinox itself the occasion of the passion.

In the fourth and fifth centuries, still other texts focus on the March 25 date, but treat it as the original date of the resurrection rather than of the passion.[18] These, too, attach great significance to the spring equinox as the first day of creation and as the day of the new creation represented by the resurrection. Behind this lies the rabbinic teaching that Passover was the first day of creation, and the creation theme is encountered as well in texts that view March 25 as the date of the passion. This shift from memorial of the death to celebration of the resurrection, however, also manifests a shift in the nuance of Pascha from its original association with the day of the passion to the Sunday observance that was, in every week, the day of the resurrection. In most of the texts that speak of March 25 as the date of the passion, from Hippolytus forward, we are dealing with situations in which already the annual observance of Pascha is restricted to the night between Saturday and Sunday. Even so, Epiphanius reports a group of Quartodecimans in Asia Minor who take March 25 to be the true date of the passion and celebrate Pascha always on that date (by contrast to the Montanist date of April 6), appealing to the apocryphal *Acta Pilati*.[19]

We cannot know how early that difference in solar Quartodeciman dating appeared in Asia Minor, but it is possible that this was among the conflicts at issue in the controversy at Laodicea mentioned by Melito as recorded by Eusebius (HE IV.26.3). A. Strobel has suggested that such a Quartodeciman Pascha on March 25 was known also in Spain, Gaul, northern Italy, and perhaps in Syria.[20]

Those texts that assign the resurrection, rather than the passion, to March 25 clearly represent a secondary stratum, an adjustment to the shifting content of Pascha. The older and more constant current in the tradition assigns the passion to that date and sees it as a coincidence of the Julian date with 14 Nisan, the Preparation of the Passover, following the Johannine passion chronology. That tradition even treated the term *Pascha* itself as expressing the passion of the Lord. The *Peri Pascha* of Melito of Sardis, a paschal homily from around 165, maintains that the term is derived from the Greek verb *paschein*, meaning "to suffer."

"What is the Pasch? Its name is derived from what happened, from the verb 'to suffer,' to be suffering: learn then who it was who suffered, and who suffered along with the sufferer, and why the Lord is present on the earth. It is so that in the vesture of one who has suffered he may be taken up to the highest heavens."[21]

Here it is clear that the Lord's passion is not considered an event distinct from his glorification, as later developments will tend to distinguish Good Friday and Easter. Rather, as Melito makes clear, the primitive Pascha celebrated the memorial of the death of Jesus as a total festival of our redemption in Christ, including not only his glorification but also the incarnation. So it is that Melito says later in that magnificent homily:

"He came on earth from heaven for suffering man, becoming incarnate in a virgin's womb from which he came forth as man; he took on himself the sufferings of suffering man through a body capable of suffering, and put an end to the sufferings of the flesh, and through his spirit incapable of death he became the death of death which is destructive of man. . . . this is he who in the virgin was made incarnate, on the cross was suspended, in the earth was buried, from the dead was resurrected, to the heights of heaven was lifted up."[22]

From this, it should be clear that the Quartodeciman Pascha carried a much broader meaning than only a dysphoric response to the death of Jesus. An important concern in this focus on his death, as is also true of the phrase *sub Pontio Pilato* in later credal formulae, was to keep a firm hand on the *historicity* of our redemption, in opposition to the gnostic dehistoricization of the scheme of salvation. Nonetheless, the content of the celebration went beyond the death itself to proclaim the total mystery of the Cross in all its dimensions, from incarnation to parousia.

While that coming of Messiah in triumph remained a future expectation, the eucharist that broke the paschal fast was increasingly recognized as a prolepsis of that consummation. As in the encounter on the road to Emmaus, participants in the eucharist found the risen Lord present to them and with them in the breaking of the bread. The daily table fellowship of the primitive community continued the meal fellowship of the resurrection appearances, and this continuity perdured even when the growing numbers of believers made such daily assembly impracticable and gave rise to the weekly eucharistic observance.

By around A.D. 55, 1 Corinthians 11 shows how that cultic meal had begun to attain independence from any ordinary need for physical nourishment, and was acknowledged as encounter with Christ, the Supper of the Lord, *kyriakon deipnon* (1 Cor 11.20). This eucharist, too, spoke of the paschal mystery, "For as often as you eat this bread and drink the cup, you proclaim the Lord's death until he comes." While for Gentile Christians that weekly assembly may considerably antedate any annual festival, it would eventually have a profound impact on the annual Pascha, demanding that the day of that celebration, the celebration that closed the paschal fast, should be no other day in the week than that of the Lord's resurrection, the day of the weekly *kyriakon deipnon*, which the Church, perhaps for that reason, called *kyriakē hēmera*.

3. THE CHRISTIAN WEEK AND THE SUNDAY PASCHA

The phrase, *kyriakē hēmera*, first occurs in Apocalypse 1.10, and has commonly been identified with the Christian observance of the first day of the week, the day assigned to the sun in the planetary week, as the day of worship celebrating the resurrection of Christ. While some recent writers have regarded the text as reference to an eschatological "day of Jahweh" without calendrical precision, or to

Passover itself, there can be no doubt that the similar phrase in *Didache* 14, *kata kyriakēn de kyriou*, refers to the weekly Christian assembly. More recent studies in *Didache* might lead us to wonder whether that reference is not as ancient as the Apocalypse.[23] In any case, it is a matter of general consensus that the observance of the first day of the week by Christians reaches back into the apostolic period, and, an interesting essay of Samuele Bacchiocchi[24] to the contrary notwithstanding, there is wide agreement that that observance reaches back to the primitive Jerusalem community itself. Even so, however, there is less agreement about the relationship between that Christian observance of the first day of the week and the Jewish Sabbath observance.

A focus of that disagreement is the account in Acts 20 of a synaxis in Troas, "on the first day of the week, when we were gathered together to break bread." There Paul, "intending to depart on the morrow (*epaurion*)," preached until midnight. Still later, after the fall and restoration of the hapless Eutychus, the apostle broke bread with the gathering and continued with them until daybreak, at which time he departed according to his plan.

The disagreement about this text has to do with whether the night in question is that from Saturday to Sunday or that from Sunday to Monday. According to standard Jewish reckoning of the day in the first century, the first day of the week would begin with sunset on Saturday and conclude at sunset on the following day, such reckoning of the day from sunset to sunset being characteristic of cultures that follow a primarily lunar calendar. Greeks, on the other hand, reckoned the day from dawn to dawn, while the Roman *dies civilis* was, as is our own custom today, reckoned from midnight to midnight.

Since the dawn following the pernocturnal synaxis is referred to in Acts 20 as "the morrow," one might conclude that either the Greek or the Roman reckoning is intended, in which case this evening gathering "on the first day of the week" would be on what we would consider Sunday night, and so would have no close connection with the Sabbath, which had come to its conclusion twenty-four hours earlier.

Although he admits that the case cannot be made on the basis of the text alone, Willi Rordorf finally concludes that the author of Acts 20 had in mind the Roman way of reckoning and, therefore, the night in question is that from Sunday to Monday.[25] This is consistent with Rordorf's identification of the postresurrection appearances of Christ on the evening following the resurrection (Jn 20.19) and again eight days later (Jn 20.26) as the foundation for the continuing observance of the first day of the week by the primitive community. It is consistent as well with his general interpretation of Sunday as a deliberate substitution for and repudiation of the Sabbath in the early Church. This attitude toward the Sabbath was based, Rordorf believes, on the understanding of Jesus' infringements of the Sabbath as carrying Messianic claims. While Rordorf's argument is impressive and has enjoyed a wide following, his work is less strong in attempting to account for the evidence of Sabbath observance in Christianity from the second century.

The retention of Sabbath observance as well as the keeping of Sunday as a day of worship is understandable, at least in strongly Jewish-Christian circles, if we suppose that the Christian eucharistic assembly followed closely upon the conclusion of the Sabbath, that is, in the evening from Saturday to Sunday. Massey H. Shepherd hypothesizes that such a gathering after the close of the Sabbath was closely related to the concentration of the Church's evangelistic mission on the synagogues.

"We may suppose that the early Christian missionaries, after gathering a nucleus of converts from Jews and Gentile god-fearers who attended the synagogue Sabbath worship, assembled them in the house-churches on Saturday evening, when the Sabbath was over, for their peculiar Christian supper-rite. Thus Jewish converts would remain undisturbed in their accustomed way of observing the Sabbath. And Gentiles, who reckoned the day not from sunset to sunset but from sunrise to sunrise, might still view the Saturday evening meeting as in some sense a sharing in the Sabbath observance."[26]

A similar view of the origins of the Sunday observance has been taken more recently by Corrado Mosna. Mosna also understands the author of Acts 20 to be using the Jewish reckoning of the day, in contrast to Rordorf's assumption that he used Roman reckoning. If those are the alternatives, and if, as both he and Rordorf argue forcefully, the text makes a strong point of the affinity between the first day of the week and the celebration of the eucharist, then

Mosna may well argue that Rordorf's reconstruction violates that affinity since it is only after midnight that Paul actually breaks bread. If the determination of Sunday as the time for the eucharist is central to the author's purpose, and if, as Rordorf argued, this meeting at Troas was on the evening of a Sunday that had begun the previous midnight, then the author of Acts 20 has failed in his aim, since the eucharistic rite itself occurs, by his account, only in the early hours of Monday morning, i.e., after the midnight between Sunday and Monday.[27]

That may, however, be much too close a reading of the text. In any case, neither Rordorf nor Mosna takes account (as does Shepherd) of yet a third reckoning of the day, the common Hellenistic reckoning from dawn to dawn. If we take that popular way of speaking as the alternative to the Jewish reckoning from sunset to sunset, then Mosna's argument fails and we could as well suppose that the gathering was in the night from Sunday to Monday as from Saturday to Sunday. In point of fact, if we consider the Church's wider experience, which would go far beyond this single account of a meeting at Troas, it may very well be that both time patterns were practiced. Even if we read Acts 20.7 as does Rordorf, we are not justified in moving from that to the more general thesis that Sunday was, from the outset, such a substitution for the Sabbath as would make all Christians consciously and deliberately anti-sabbatarian.

The celebration of the eucharist as the distinctive characteristic of the Sunday observance established from the outset a close correspondence between the content of that day's celebration and that of the annual Pascha. Such a similarity in content between Sunday and Pascha poses, of course, the question of the relationship between them. It has been popular to speak of Sunday as a "little Easter," and patristic tradition spoke of the fifty-day paschal time as the "Great Sunday." The assumption common to both expressions is the celebration of Pascha on Sunday, by contrast to the Quartodeciman practice described above, which continued the celebration of Passover in the night from 14 to 15 Nisan, its form modified by its new Christian content, but still without regard for the day of the week on which it might fall. The establishment of Sunday, or more precisely, the night from Saturday to Sunday, as the only time for the termination of the paschal fast was a development of vast importance for the history of the liturgical year, and it is not surprising, therefore, that the circumstances of that development have been the subject of much dispute.

In the matter of the establishment of the Sunday Pascha, it has become customary to describe as "traditional" the assignment of that development to Rome in the apostolic age, and the authorities of Peter and Paul are not uncommonly invoked. Such a tradition, however, is less securely grounded than one might wish. Eusebius' testimony, for example, is rather modest. Having described the Quartodeciman practice, he says:

"But it was not the custom of the churches in the rest of the world to end it [the fast] at this time, as they observed the practice which, from apostolic tradition, has prevailed to the present time, of terminating the fast on no other day than on that of the resurrection of our Saviour."[28]

He makes no attempt to associate this tradition with Rome, nor does the reference to a tradition from the apostles in the letter that he quotes from the Palestinian synod (V.22) identify Rome as its source. Eusebius himself, it would seem, gives us no reason to think of the dominical Pascha as of Roman origin. Socrates, the fifth-century historian who built upon the work of Eusebius, does report the assertion, but he is far from credulous in the matter.

". . . the Quartodecimans affirm that the observance of the fourteenth day was delivered to them by the apostle John: while the Romans and those in the Western parts assure us that their usage originated with the apostles Peter and Paul. Neither of these parties however can produce any written testimony in confirmation of what they assert."[29]

Socrates' younger contemporary, Sozomen, however, is somewhat more bold, if nothing else.

"It appears to me that Victor, bishop of Rome, and Polycarp, bishop of Smyrna, came to a very wise decision on the controversy that had arisen between them. For as the bishops of the West did not deem it necessary to dishonor the tradition handed down to them by Peter and Paul, and as, on the other hand, the Asiatic bishops persisted in following the rules laid down by John the evangelist, they unanimously agreed to continue in the observance of the festival according to their respective customs, without separation from communion with each other."[30]

This account, while it is fairly strong in asserting a western tradition running back to Peter and Paul, is so insecure in matters of more verifiable history that it is difficult to be impressed with its testimony to the first century. The conflict whose amicable settlement Sozomen describes was not between Victor and Polycarp at all, but between Victor and Polycrates, bishop of Ephesus, and that conflict issued in Victor's hardly amicable excommunication of the province of Asia. There had been an earlier and evidently amicable resolution of certain difficulties between Anicetus, bishop of Rome, and Polycarp. However, whether that dispute regarded different *ways* of observing Pascha is itself open to dispute.

4. THE PASCHAL CONTROVERSY

The famous paschal controversy of the second century, which has occasioned such an extensive literature, certainly involved in the first instance the attempt initiated in the time of Victor of Rome to make the termination of the paschal fast on Sunday the universal practice of the Church. Our primary source for that controversy is Eusebius and the letters preserved by him in the fifth book of his *Ecclesiastical History* (chaps. 23–25). In view of Victor's subsequent prominence in the matter, the initiative in the marshaling of pressure against the Quartodecimans is commonly assigned to him, and, as we shall see, he may have had peculiar reason to take such a lead. However, Eusebius only tells us that synods and assemblies were held in various ecclesiastical areas to deal with the paschal question, reporting their progress toward common agreement on the dominical Pascha by exchanges of correspondence. That Victor had a central role in the matter is suggested by the fact that it was to him that Polycrates, bishop of Ephesus, addressed the Quartodeciman demurrer against what had emerged as an otherwise catholic consensus. If a tradition for the dominical Pascha reaching back to Peter and Paul is shadowy and indistinct, the same can hardly be said of the tradition claimed by Polycrates. His epistle to Victor, written around the beginning of the final decade of the second century, is as specific as it is forceful, and deserves quotation.

"We observe the exact day; neither adding, nor taking away. For in Asia also great lights have fallen asleep, which shall rise again on the day of the Lord's coming, when he shall come with glory from heaven, and shall seek out all the saints. Among these are Philip, one of the twelve apostles, who fell asleep in Hierapolis; and his two aged virgin daughters, and another daughter, who lived in the Holy Spirit and now rests at Ephesus; and, moreover, John, who was both a witness and a teacher, who reclined upon the bosom of the Lord, and, being a priest, wore the sacerdotal plate. He fell asleep at Ephesus. And Polycarp in Smyrna, who was a bishop and martyr; and Thraseus, bishop and martyr from Eumenia, who fell asleep in Smyrna. Why need I mention the bishop and martyr Sagaris who fell asleep in Laodicea, or the blessed Papirius, or Melito the Eunuch who lived altogether in the Holy Spirit, and who lies in Sardis, awaiting the episcopate from heaven, when he shall rise from the dead? All these observed the fourteenth day of the passover according to the Gospel, deviating in no respect, but following the rule of faith. And I also, Polycrates, the least of you all, do according to the tradition of my relatives, some of whom I have closely followed. For seven of my relatives were bishops; and I am the eighth. And my relatives always observed the day when the people put away the leaven. I, therefore, brethren, who have lived sixty-five years in the Lord, and have met with the brethren throughout the world, and have gone through every Holy Scripture, am not affrighted by terrifying words. For those greater than I have said, 'We ought to obey God rather than man.' "[31]

Polycrates' advanced years, his ecclesiastical family, which included seven other bishops, some evidently preceding him, his citation of the practice of Polycarp, an important link to the apostolic period, and his ability to refer to two "apostles" (one of them Philip the evangelist, not one of the twelve) and the places of their depositions—all this makes his letter, preserved by Eusebius, an important testimony to the strength of the claim of the Quartodeciman practice to be, indeed, apostolic in origin. We possess no such detailed pedigree for the apostolicity that, since the fourth century, has been claimed for the Sunday Pascha.

Upon receipt of this letter, nonetheless, Victor issued letters to all the Church, excommunicating the entire province of Asia (an area considerably larger than the diocese of Asia fixed by Diocletian later). Eusebius tells us that many bishops sharply opposed Victor's precipitate reaction, and provides us with excerpts from the invaluable, if difficult, response of Irenaeus of Lyons, who had presided over the synod in Gaul that declared for the dominical Pascha. Before attempting to comment on that letter, it will be well to have the text before us. Irenaeus writes to urge Victor to moderation.

"For the controversy is not only concerning the day, but also concerning the very manner of the fast. For some think that they should fast one day, others, two, yet others more; some, moreover, count their day as consisting of forty hours day and night. And this variety in its observance has not originated in our time; but long before in that of our ancestors. It is likely that they did not hold to strict accuracy, and thus formed a custom for their posterity according to their own simplicity and peculiar mode. Yet all of these lived nonetheless in peace, and we also live in peace with one another; and the disagreement in regard to the fast confirms the agreement in the faith. [Here Eusebius himself writes, "He (Irenaeus) adds to this the following account, which I may properly insert:"] Among these were the presbyters before Soter, who presided over the church which thou now rulest. We mean Anicetus, and Pius, and Hyginus, and Telesphorus, and Xystus. They neither observed themselves nor did they permit those after them to do so. And yet though not observing, they were nonetheless at peace with those who came to them from the parishes which observed, although this observance was more opposed to those who did not observe. But none were ever cast out on account of this form; but the presbyters before thee who did not observe sent the eucharist to those of other parishes who observed. And when the blessed Polycarp was at Rome in the time of Anicetus, and they disagreed a little about certain other things, they immediately made peace with one another, not caring to quarrel over this matter. For neither could Anicetus persuade Polycarp not to observe what he had always observed with John the disciple of our Lord, and the other apostles with whom he had associated; neither could Polycarp persuade Anicetus to observe, as he said that he ought to follow the customs of the presbyters that had preceded him. But though matters were in this shape, they communed together, and Anicetus conceded the administration of the eucharist in the church to Polycarp, manifestly as a mark of respect. And they parted from each other in peace, both those who observed, and those who did not, maintaining the peace of the whole church."[32]

The difficulties in the interpretation of this letter center upon two matters. First, Irenaeus refers to the Quartodecimans as those who "observe" (*tērein*) and contrasts them to those who do not "observe," without saying precisely what it is that is or is not observed. Since it is central to the entire matter that the opponents of the Quartodeciman practice hold that the paschal fast should be terminated only on the Lord's Day, it has commonly been held that the object of that verb, "observe," is "the fourteenth day of the moon," or some other expression denoting the Quartodeciman Pascha as contrasted to the dominical Pascha; it is not unusual to find some such phrase supplied in notes or even, within brackets, in the text. However, since Irenaeus does not apply this *tērein/mē tērein* distinction to the contemporary situation, but only to Victor's predecessors prior to Soter (A.D. 165), it has seemed to some that the object of that verb, "observe," is simply the Pascha itself.

The second difficulty in this extract is related to the first. Why does Irenaeus say that the Quartodeciman practice was "more opposed" to the practice of Victor's predecessors from Xystus through Anicetus (from, i.e., ca. 117 to the accession of Soter in 165) than it was in the situation confronting Victor? One who takes the observance in question to be only the termination of the fast on the fourteenth day of the moon, Christine Mohrmann,[33] explains that the operative consideration is Irenaeus' reference to the hospitality accorded to visiting Quartodecimans in Rome itself. At that point, Quartodecimanism was no longer just the practice of the church in Asia Minor, but that variant practice was confronted directly in Rome. Therefore, her argument goes, Irenaeus urged Victor to be as tolerant as were his predecessors toward those who brought Quartodecimanism right to Rome itself, a more difficult situation than the current observance of the fourteenth of the moon far away in Asia Minor.

Others, however, have pointed out that Quartodecimanism may well have been found in Rome in Victor's day also. George

LaPiana, in an important essay in 1925,[34] argued impressively that Victor's apparently precipitate action, while excessive, was not simply a matter of Roman pretension seeking to extend its power over a foreign church, but had to do rather with a local Roman pastoral problem, into which a foreign ecclesiastical authority was intruding. The ecclesiastical constitution of Rome in the second century, according to LaPiana, was hardly that of a modern diocese, but was rather a loose collection of different communities, drawn to Rome from many parts of the empire, all living in more or less close relationship with the native Roman community, while maintaining contact as well with the communities in other parts from which they derived. One such Roman subgroup, LaPiana argues, was a Quartodeciman community with strong ties to the church of Asia, and especially to Ephesus. Victor's attempt to establish a single paschal observance for Rome was resisted by the local Quartodecimans, and Polycrates, LaPiana believes, took their part against the local bishop. It was, then, this intrusion into Victor's sphere of pastoral responsibility that provoked his strong response.

While LaPiana did not question the observance of the Sunday Pascha by the Roman church itself prior to Soter, his reconstruction, if followed, would disallow Mohrmann's explanation of Irenaeus' assertion that the difference between the bishops of Rome and the Quartodecimans was more severe prior to Soter than it was in the time of Victor. That assertion of Irenaeus has led several important writers in this century to the more radical conclusion that prior to Soter the annual Pascha was not celebrated by the Roman church at all. Irenaeus' references to those who "observed" does mean, indeed, those who observed the Pascha on the traditional date of Passover. Those who did not "observe," however, did not observe the Pascha on the traditional date of Passover *or at any other time.* Such a conclusion would mean that for Rome the weekly liturgical cycle was the only liturgical articulation of the calendar, and that there was no annual festival that distinguished one Sunday from another until A.D. 165, around which time the dominical Pascha was established there by Soter.

Proposed by Karl Holl in 1927,[35] this reading of the letter of Irenaeus to Victor was followed by Hans Lietzmann in the second volume of his history of the early Church.[36] More recently, this argument was renewed in 1961 by Marcel Richard,[37] and several later writers have appealed to his presentation of the argument. A. Hamman, for example, suggested in 1971 that Richard's understanding of the history of Pascha at Rome might throw valuable light on the otherwise inexplicable silence of Justin Martyr with regard to the Christian observance of Pascha.[38]

Justin's *Dialogue with Trypho, the Jew* was based on a formal disputation held at Ephesus. It was only some twenty years later, however, that it was issued in written form. This was at Rome during the episcopate of Anicetus, the last of the "presbyters before Soter" of whom Irenaeus spoke. It was during Anicetus' episcopate that Polycarp of Smyrna made the visit to Rome described by Irenaeus in the passage just quoted from Eusebius. There Irenaeus tells us that the two bishops disputed about several things and finally agreed to disagree about the Pascha. Anicetus was unable to persuade Polycarp "not to observe what he had always observed with John the disciple of our Lord, and the other apostles with whom he had associated," and Polycarp was unable to persuade Anicetus to observe as he had, the Roman declaring that "he ought to follow the customs of the presbyters that had preceded him."

Given the authorities cited for Polycarp by Irenaeus, it is inexplicable that he reports no similar claim to apostolic tradition on Anicetus' part if, in Irenaeus' mind, Anicetus was speaking in defense of a tradition of the Sunday Pascha with apostolic roots. This passage, however, is perfectly clear if we accept the position of Holl and so recognize that the discussion between Polycarp and Anicetus had to do not with *when* one should observe the Pascha, but *whether* one should observe it. That, as Irenaeus suggested to Victor, was a more serious difference than the question of the day on which the fast should be terminated, whatever pastoral difficulty that might present. The disagreement between Anicetus and Polycarp represented yet another dimension of the still resolving difference of attitude toward Jewish roots held by the then-dispersed Jerusalem community, on the one hand, and the Gentile mission, on the other. It was simply the question of the importance of Christians continuing to observe Passover, the very question, incidentally, that the writer of *Epistula Apostolorum* 15 put on the lips of the apostles and to which they received the Lord's affirmative reply. That work, it will be remembered, was written in Asia Minor around the middle of the second century, although no firm dating is possible. The visit of the distinguished Asian bishop, Polycarp, to Anicetus was in 154. In the light of that coincidence, one might suppose that *Epistula Apostolorum* at that point adds its voice (and the authority of the risen Christ!) to the disagreement between the Roman and Asian bishops, however amicably Anicetus and Polycarp resolved their difference.

While the foregoing interpretation of the evidence provided by Irenaeus' letter to Victor suggests that Pascha was, indeed, introduced at Rome by Soter around 165, that surely was not the origin of the Sunday Pascha. Holl also drew attention to a notice of Epiphanius (*Panarion* 70.9), which asserted that the controversies over the date of Pascha began only after bishops at Jerusalem were no longer "of the circumcision," that is, only after the departure of the original Jewish-Christian hierarchy and their replacement by Greco-Roman bishops representative of the Gentile mission. While many Jews, and perhaps many Christians as well, may have fled the city in the time of conflict leading to Titus' destruction of the temple, surely all the circumcised were forbidden to enter Aelia, the unwalled Roman city built around 132 upon the rubble of Hadrian's destruction of Jerusalem. Christians of Gentile background, however, were allowed into the city, and we may date the Gentile-Christian hierarchy at Jerusalem from that time. Eusebius thus concludes his account of the Bar Cochba rebellion:

"And thus, when the city had been emptied of the Jewish nation and had suffered the total destruction of its ancient inhabitants, it was colonized by a different race, and the Roman city which subsequently arose changed its name and was called Aelia, in honor of the emperor Aelius Adrian. And as the church there was now composed of Gentiles, the first one to assume the government of it after the bishops of the circumcision was Marcus."[39]

Over half a century after the establishment of the Greek hierarchy in Jerusalem, the synod on the paschal question was held that brought together the bishops of Caesarea, Jerusalem, Tyre, and Ptolemais. In their letter to the other churches, according to Eusebius, "having stated many things respecting the tradition concerning the passover which had come to them in succession from the apostles," they added the following:

"Endeavor to send copies of our letter to every church, that we
may not furnish occasion to those who easily deceive their souls.
We show you indeed that also in Alexandria they keep it on the
same day that we do. For letters are carried from us to them and
from them to us, so that in the same manner and at the same time
we keep the sacred day.[40]"

Unfortunately, Eusebius does not detail the contents of the tradition that the gathered bishops had received "in succession from
the apostles," and we cannot know, therefore, whether that tradition had to do with the observance on Sunday, which, by the time
of the synod, was well established among them. Given that silence, we have no reason to reject the testimony of Epiphanius that
controversy over the time of Pascha only appeared after the establishment of the Greek hierarchy at Jerusalem. Was the establishment of the Sunday Pascha the work of these Greek bishops, and,
if so, did that development represent the accommodation of a Gentile hierarchy, which had known only a weekly liturgical cycle, to
the vestiges of the observance of the annual festival by the Jerusalem community? That is a possible conclusion from our data, but
not the only possible conclusion. What does seem clear is that such
a Sunday Pascha was established in Palestine and at Alexandria
well before the paschal controversy of 190, and that those churches
were careful to celebrate it on the same day, without reference to
Rome. Indeed, as the data become available in the following century, we find that the principles for the computation of that Sunday differed between Rome and Alexandria. At Rome the feast
could not fall before the sixteenth day of the moon, while at Alexandria the earliest date was the fifteenth, that is, the Sunday following or coinciding with Passover.[41] This latter stands, it would
seem, much closer to the original Quartodeciman determination
than does the Roman dating system in the time of Hippolytus,
which, taking the fourteenth day of the moon to be the date of the
passion, understands the sixteenth day to be the day of the resurrection and therefore the earliest date for Easter Sunday.
    Still, however we understand the relative ages of the Sunday
Pascha at Jerusalem and Rome, it is probable that both the observance of the first day of the week as occasion of eucharistic assembly
and the annual observance of Pascha both reach back to apostolic

times, the one growing out of a Christian assembly following the close of the Sabbath and the other a less universally observed continuation and modulation of the annual Passover. Most writers today would accord some measure of historical priority to the Quartodeciman observance of Pascha, and thus allow that Easter Sunday represents an adjustment of that custom to the independently established weekly Sunday.

It is significant that as that conflation occurred, it did not alter the content of the original Pascha, a total celebration of our redemption commemorating the passion of Christ. So Tertullian speaks of paschal baptism: "The Passover provides the day of most solemnity for baptism, for then was accomplished our Lord's passion. . . ."[42] Origen, as well, in his fifth Homily on Isaiah states: "There is now a multitude of people on account of the Preparation day, and especially on the Sunday which commemorates Christ's passion. For the resurrection is not celebrated only once in the year, but also every eighth day."[43] Even, then, where the Pascha was observed in the night from Saturday to Sunday, its content was the same as the Quartodeciman observance, and that was rooted in Passover itself, that Passover of which Jesus Christ had become the paschal lamb of a covenant renewed. Origen, indeed, while continuing the traditional description of Pascha as commemoration of the passion, did make it clear that the term was not derived from *paschein*. He is the first Christian writer to define Pascha as "passage," *transitus*, and to apply that understanding to Christ's passage into the kingdom.[44] Considerably later, however, Augustine would still oppose that understanding to the false but durable etymology of the early Quartodecimans.[45]

Before turning from the paschal controversy in the second century, there is yet a third interpretation of Irenaeus' letter that seeks to acknowledge the change that came about with the accession of Soter, and still to hold to an earlier observance of the Sunday Pascha at Rome. This is the suggestion of Hans von Campenhausen that the object of Irenaeus' "observe/not observe" distinction is the paschal fast, not the feast that concluded that fast, a suggestion made earlier by Theodore Zahn.[46] Surely, Irenaeus' letter does discuss the fast, but that itself only testifies to the fact that the fast was integral to Pascha. The form of the paschal question, indeed, was whether the fast should be terminated on the old date of Passover or, instead, on the day of the resurrection (Sunday). It is difficult to know what a Sunday Pascha without a preceding fast would consist of. In what respect would that differ from any other Sunday? What can be said, and must now be examined, is that the accommodation of the annual Pascha to the structure of the week did have an impact on the duration and, eventually, the character of that paschal fast.

5. THE PASCHAL FAST

The *Mishnah* required a fast from all food from the time of the offering of the evening sacrifice that preceded the sacrifice of lambs for Passover. While this daily evening offering was normally completed around 3 P.M., on the Preparation of the Passover the hour was advanced somewhat to allow more time for the slaughter and offering of the paschal lambs. This fast was not broken until nightfall, and then only with the eating of the Passover.[47] It was such a fast, however modest in its extent, that would be the germ of the Christian paschal fast. For Christians, however, that fast was progressively extended. As the Christian Pascha emerged it would not, as memorial of Christ's death, share in the festivity of the Jews. Therefore, the Christian fast was extended through the hours of the rejoicing accompanying Passover, past the midnight conclusion of that festivity. *Epistula Apostolorum* and other texts show that this vigil, and presumably the fast, was extended to cockcrow, the hour for the sacramental consummation of the vigil. The established Quartodeciman practice is generally regarded as having extended the fast through the day of 14 Nisan to cockcrow of 15 Nisan.

The establishment of the dominical Pascha, however, would situate the preceding fast on the Sabbath, and both Jewish and Christian disciplines forbade fasting on the Sabbath under normal circumstances. Western, especially Roman, tradition made occasional exceptions to this prohibition from as early as the third century. Tertullian in his Montanist period castigated these Sabbath fasts, insisting that fasting is never to be allowed on any other Sabbath than that of Pascha.[48] Such an exception to a general rule (still maintained in eastern traditions) suggests again that the dominical Pascha is derivative from the Quartodeciman, not a parallel development. Such a fast on the eve of Pascha, however, would find itself juxtaposed to another fast day of great antiquity. From as early as *Didache* 8.1, Wednesday and Friday of each week were designated as fast days, specifically contrasted to the Monday and Thursday fasts of pious Jews, and especially the Pharisees.

Those fasts of the Pharisees, referred to in Luke 18.10, presumed a week centered upon the Sabbath and were concerned to avoid further religious obligation on either the preparation of the Sabbath, Friday, or the morrow of it, Sunday. Otherwise, the two weekly fast days were as widely separated from one another as possible, viz., on Thursday and Monday. The prescription of *Didache*, however, does not seem to have the same concern. A pattern analogous to that of the Pharisees, but taking Sunday as the center of the week, would call for fasting on Tuesday and Friday, the days following the Monday and Thursday fasts of the "hypocrites," as the text calls the Pharisees. While some have supposed on the basis of that castigation that the concern was primarily one of dissociation from Judaism, more recent studies have suggested repeatedly that Christian liturgical origins, although they diverge from the contemporary development of Judaism in the second century, are seldom motivated by deliberate dissociation from inherited patterns. On the contrary, our growing familiarity with sectarian Judaism in the earliest period has suggested at several points a cultural context for what once seemed only Christian peculiarities.

In spite of the manifest dangers of overstatement, it is at least valuable to see this problem of the weekly fasts in *Didache* in the context of the valorization of the days of the week occasioned by the unusual structure of the calendar of the Essenes at Qumran. This calendar, meticulously reconstructed by Annie Jaubert from the sources in which it is imbedded,[49] represents a liturgical ideal that must have involved serious practical problems. The year has only 364 days and we are still in the dark as to how it might have been intercalated without destroying its most characteristic feature: so fundamental an emphasis on the week as to make every date in every month fall every year on the same day of the week. The 364 days are divided into four completely symmetrical quarters of 91 days each, each quarter divided into two months of 30 days each and a third month of 31 days. The first day of the first month, however, does not fall on the first day of the week, but on the fourth day, the day of the creation of the heavenly lights, according to Genesis 1.14–19. So the first days of the first, fourth, seventh, and tenth months are all Wednesdays. Those of the second, fifth, eighth, and eleventh months are Fridays. The first days of the third, sixth, ninth, and twelfth months are Sundays. Passover, the fifteenth day of the first month, falls always on Wednesday, placing the Passover celebration in the night from Tuesday to Wednesday. The Feast of Weeks, kept on the fifteenth day of the third month at Qumran, fell always on Sunday. The Day of Atonement, the tenth day of the seventh month, was always a Friday, and the feast of Tabernacles, the fifteenth day of that month, a Wednesday. Thus, all of the major cultically significant days assigned to fixed month dates fell on Sunday, Wednesday, or Friday.

Jaubert, having reconstructed this calendar, offered the hypothesis that the Passover eaten by Jesus and his disciples according to the synoptic tradition was observed at the beginning of the fifteenth day of the first month as determined by this sectarian calendar, that is, in the night from Tuesday to Wednesday, so that the arrest of Jesus took place early Wednesday morning. The crucifixion fell on Friday, the Preparation of the Passover according to the temple calendar, as the fourth gospel asserts. This suggestion of two Passover dates would therefore harmonize the synoptic and Johannine traditions.

While few exegetes have found such radically revised chronology of the passion convincing, it did have its adherents in the early Church. This chronology is found in *Didascalia Apostolorum* in the first half of the third century,[50] and is presented as well in a letter of Epiphanius.[51] In *Didascalia* Judas' treasonous compact is made on Monday, the last supper with the disciples on Tuesday evening, the arrest of Jesus and his appearance before Caiaphas on Wednesday, the appearances before Pilate and Herod on Thursday, and the final condemnation and crucifixion on Friday. Thus in the *Panarion*, Epiphanius explains the weekly fast days: "Wednesday and Friday are days of fasting up to the ninth hour because, as Wednesday began, the Lord was arrested and on Friday he was crucified."[52]

In ordinary weeks these days were commonly fasted only to the ninth hour, as Epiphanius noted. But the juxtaposition of that Friday fast to the one day of the paschal fast, Saturday in the case of the dominical Pascha, led to the extension of the fast to two days in many places, as was noted already by Irenaeus.[53] However, in Syria the extension of the fast from one day to two was but the first stage in the lengthening of the fast. In *Didascalia Apostolorum* we find those two days observed by a total fast from all nourishment, but the first four days of the week, Monday through Thursday, are kept with a lighter fast in which bread, salt, and water are allowed at the ninth hour.[54]

This further extension can be understood as a function of the chronology that put Judas' compact with the priests on Monday. Because the writer of *Didascalia* accepts the chronology predicated on the Essene date for Passover (the night from Tuesday to Wednesday), he placed the treason of Judas on Monday, and began the fast of the passion then. The *week* of the passion, as opposed to the ancient *triduum*, I would suggest, represents, as do (perhaps more remotely) the Wednesday and Friday weekly fasts, an influence from the Qumran calendar in early Christianity. In the first half of the third century, however, such an extension of the fast to six days was not limited to Syria, for we find a similar six-day fast in Alexandria, in a letter of Dionysius often referred to as the first of the extant "festal letters." There no distinction is made between the fast of the last two days and that of the first four days, but there are tantalizing suggestions of that Essene Passover date in ancient Egyptian tradition as well.[55]

Somewhat earlier in the third century, presumably at Rome, the paschal fast consisted of only the two days before Pascha, but the *Apostolic Tradition* makes provision for the infirm to observe only one day:

"At the Pascha no one may eat before the offering is made. If anyone does so, it does not count for him as fasting. Anyone who is pregnant or ill, and cannot fast for two days, should fast [only] on the Saturday on account of their necessity, confining themselves to bread and water. Anyone who was at sea or found himself in some necessity, and did not know the day, when he has learned of it, shall observe the fast after Pentecost. For the type has passed away: that is why it ended in the second month; and when he has learned the truth, he should observe the fast."[56]

30

This insistence that the Saturday be fasted if only one day is possible shows again the strength of the original one-day fast of the Quartodecimans. In other writings Hippolytus shows a strong opposition to fasting on Sabbath or Sunday,[57] but this day before the Pascha must be kept as a fast. If, as now seems generally supposed, the baptismal liturgy in *Apostolic Tradition* was employed at Pascha, then we may be sure that the fast of the baptizands, begun on Friday, was extended through Saturday, even though the text does not make this explicit.

The third-century extension of the paschal fast to six days in *Didascalia Apostolorum* and in the first of the Alexandrian festal letters that we have from Dionysius marks the complete extension of the fast to Holy Week as we know it. Many commentaries have considered the six weeks of Lent to be a still further extension of the paschal fast, but that seems to be a serious oversimplification. In the West we are accustomed today to a six-week Lent of which the final week is Holy Week, and our tendency is to see that as only the last and most solemn week of the longer fast season. Such a total of six weeks was urged also at Alexandria in the time of Athanasius, but it is clear from his festal letters, of which we possess a great many, that his church understood the final week of the six to be distinct. Some of those letters, such as the first, announce only the beginning of the six-day fast and the date of Easter; but all his festal letters that give dates for the beginning of the fast of forty days and for Easter give as well a separate date for the beginning of the paschal fast of six days.[58] Indeed, *Apostolic Constitutions* V.13 calls for a complete separation of the lenten fast of forty days from the paschal fast by an interval of two festal days, Saturday and Sunday.[59] The significance of this will be examined further in Part Three. It is sufficient here to note that, whatever we are to make of Lent, the later third-century fast of six days represents the full extension of the paschal fast as such, the fast which later ages will know as the Great and Holy Week.

6. THE LITURGY OF PASCHA BEFORE NICEA

The texts remaining to us from the second and third centuries afford little information concerning the liturgical arrangements for those days, save for the vigil itself. We have seen already in *Epis-*

tula Apostolorum that the paschal vigil is integral to the celebration of Pascha from as early as the middle of the second century. From perhaps a bit later, around 165, the *Peri Pascha* of Melito of Sardis assures us that at that vigil the Passover charter narrative from Exodus had a significant place. There the slaying of the lamb and the marking of the doorposts of the houses in chapter 12 is central, not the passage through the Red Sea two chapters later. Throughout, Melito's homily is a celebration of Christ as Redeemer, the Paschal Lamb of the New Covenant, whose death and resurrection has fulfilled the Passover; there is little focus on our deliverance from bondage. Apart from the opening testimony to the reading of Exodus 12, however, Melito's sermon betrays nothing of the liturgy of the vigil. We may be sure, nonetheless, that it reached its conclusion, like the vigil in *Epistula Apostolorum*, in a celebration of the eucharist. Such is clearly the case in a paschal homily formerly ascribed to (or supposed to be influenced by) Hippolytus, but which Raniero Cantalamessa has shown to come from the same Quartodeciman matrix as the *Peri Pascha* of Melito. In this homily, also, the exegesis is focused on Exodus 12.[60]

Early in the following century, the *Apostolic Tradition* speaks of a vigil through the night kept by the candidates for baptism, but this is hardly more helpful. After describing a final exorcism by the bishop on Saturday, the author says: "And they shall spend the whole night in vigil; they shall be read to and instructed. Those who are to be baptized shall not bring with them any other thing, except what each brings for the eucharist."[61] It is worthy of note, however, that the baptism itself begins with the blessing of the font at cockcrow, the hour assigned for the eucharist in *Epistula Apostolorum*, and the baptism is followed by the presentation of the neophytes to the bishop and to the congregation, who must also, therefore, have participated in the vigil.[62] Of the content of that vigil, however, we know nothing in detail.

In Syria, somewhat later in the first half of the third century, *Didascalia Apostolorum* affords a slightly fuller picture of that vigil. After ordering the complete fast on Friday and Saturday, which was noted above, the text continues:

"You shall come together and watch and keep vigil all the night with prayers and intercessions, and with reading of the Prophets, and with supplication, until the third hour in the night after the Sabbath; and then break your fasts. For thus did we also fast, when our Lord suffered, for a testimony of the three days; and we were keeping vigil and praying and interceding for the destruction of the People, because that they erred and confessed not the Saviour. So do you also pray that the Lord may not remember their guilt against them unto the end for the guile which they used against our Lord, but may grant them a place of repentance and conversion, and forgiveness of their wickedness."[63]

There is no explicit mention of Exodus 12 here, such as we noted in the second-century documents from Asia Minor. Still, the description does list the elements that will be found in later and more developed liturgies. Again, the breaking of the fast is set at the hour of cockcrow, three o'clock in the morning. Until then the people are occupied in prayers and intercessions for the repentance of the People (a concern mentioned as the motive for the fast), and in scripture readings, including psalms. More interesting here is the absence of any reference to baptism in connection with the paschal liturgy, although the work does speak elsewhere of baptism. Given the importance assigned to the baptismal focus of the paschal liturgy later, it is necessary now to examine the roots of that tradition.

7. PASCHAL BAPTISM

To deal here with the complex issues of baptism in the New Testament would take us much too far afield, nor can we deal responsibly even with the total question of baptismal practice in the early Church. We can at least point out that one of our richest sources for a paschal understanding of baptism is the sixth chapter of Paul's letter to the Romans, written from Corinth. We have already suggested reasons for doubting the observance of Pascha at so early a period in the church to which that letter was addressed. Still other New Testament books (one thinks immediately of 1 Peter and the Apocalypse) have seemed to some to present baptism in the context of the Pascha.[64] If baptism was administered in the first century without regard for the time of year, then there is no reason to exclude its administration at Pascha, where that was observed by Christians. Indeed, such a theology of baptism as that expounded by Paul and the author of 1 Peter might make Pascha seem a particularly appropriate time, as clearly it did later. It would be a mistake, however, to suppose that the paschal theology of baptism derived from the general observance of the annual Christian Pascha as the occasion par excellence for the conferral of baptism in the apostolic period.

There is no suggestion of baptism in *Epistula Apostolorum*, but that is perhaps not surprising, given the character of that work. More problematical, perhaps, is the silence regarding baptism in the *Peri Pascha* of Melito. As noted above, that homily dwells heavily on the institution of Passover as recounted in Exodus 12, but there is no allusion to the crossing of the Red Sea in Exodus 14, a baptismal type already in 1 Corinthians 10.2. Ottmar Perler has argued that Melito's frequent references to the smearing of the blood of the lamb upon the doorposts as an "anointing" of them does, in fact, constitute a baptismal allusion and does suggest that baptism was one dimension of the paschal vigil at which the homily was delivered.[65] There is clearer reference to baptism in the homily *In S. Pascha*, which Cantalamessa considers to belong to the same milieu as that of Melito. However, after prudent examination of both texts, Cantalamessa concludes that we cannot document the administration of baptism at the Quartodeciman paschal vigil in the second century.[66]

Our earliest definite reference to paschal baptism is the text in Tertullian's *De Baptismo* 19, from around the beginning of the third century. The complete text, to which reference has been made above, reads as follows:

"The Passover provides the day of most solemnity for baptism, for then was accomplished our Lord's passion into which we are baptized. Nor is it incongruently interpreted in a figure that when the Lord was about to celebrate the last Passover, he said to the disciples who were sent to prepare, 'you will meet a man bearing water.' He indicates the place for the celebration of Passover by the sign of water. After that, Pentecost is a most joyful period (*laetissimum spatium*) for arranging baptisms, in which also the resurrection of the Lord was frequently made known to the disciples, and the grace of the Holy Spirit first given, and the hope of the coming of the Lord was indirectly revealed, in that then, when he had been received back into the heavens, the angels said to the apostles that he would come in the same manner in which he had ascended into the heavens, certainly at Pentecost. Moreover, when Jeremiah says, 'And I will gather them together from the extremities of the land in the feast day,' he signifies the day of Passover and Pentecost, which is properly a festal day.''[67]

Tertullian's reference to Passover here is less ambiguous than it might seem at first glance. He elsewhere uses the term to refer to the day of the paschal fast. Cantalamessa suggests that the "Passover" in this passage is, in fact, the Friday of the passion. While that might well be the case, we have noted that in the *Apostolic Tradition* the principal day of the paschal fast was the Saturday that ended in the paschal vigil. In any case, it is by no means clear that Tertullian is speaking of baptism in the course of that vigil, nor does his reference to Pentecost suggest a very definite time. For him, the Pentecost is the fifty-day period initiated by the Sunday of the resurrection, and in spite of his urging of the appropriateness of baptism in that *laetissimum spatium*, Tertullian proceeds at once to insist that any other time will do: "For all that, every day is a Lord's day; any hour, any season, is suitable for baptism. If there is a difference of solemnity, it makes no difference to the grace." This qualification and his focus of interest on the entire paschal period rather than the paschal vigil itself (to which Tertullian testifies in *Ad uxorem* 2.4.2 without mentioning baptism) might well lead us to wonder whether this text does not represent a recent association of the annual Pascha with baptism, an association just emerging around the turn of the second to the third century. While it has been suggested that the African testimony might well be an influence from the Quartodecimans of Asia Minor and might continue a tradition brought from the primitive Jerusalem community,[68] Raniero Cantalamessa has raised serious questions about such early association of baptism with Pascha.[69]

In the following century, beyond the testimony of Tertullian, Hippolytus' *Commentary on Daniel* clearly presents Pascha as an appropriate day for baptism.[70] This might lend greater strength to the common supposition that the baptismal vigil described in the *Apostolic Tradition* is, indeed, the paschal vigil. Even so, however, it is clear that this is not the only time at which Hippolytus envisioned the administration of baptism. This is why Cantalamessa doubts that the rites of initiation described in the *Apostolic Tradition* were peculiar to the paschal vigil. He suggests, in fact, that the vigil described there is not specifically paschal, but that such a vigil would have accompanied the administration of baptism at whatever time those unable to be baptized at Pascha were initiated.[71]

The silence of *Didascalia Apostolorum* regarding paschal baptism is perhaps more serious. This work does refer to baptism, and yet there is no suggestion that the rites of initiation were focused on the Pascha. The detailed treatment of the paschal fast and the relatively detailed description of the vigil make no reference whatsoever to baptism. There seems, in fact, to be good reason to doubt a very early tradition of paschal baptism in the Syrian milieu of *Didascalia Apostolorum*. It has frequently been argued that the Syrian baptismal tradition represented in that document was not shaped by such a paschal interpretation of baptism as we see in Romans 6, but was rather a rite whose themeology was focused on birth and adoptive sonship. Indeed, it has been argued that the evangelical model of the Syrian baptismal tradition was more that of Christ's baptism in the Jordan than that of his death and resurrection.[72]

In the fourth century it is clear that at Rome, Pascha and Pentecost were considered the sole appropriate times for solemn baptism, and Milan in the days of Ambrose seems to have limited the rite to Pascha alone.[73] Pascha appears as the chief occasion for solemn baptism throughout the Church by the end of the fourth century. However, it is less clear that this was the sole occasion for baptism. The letter of the Roman bishop Siricius to Himerius of Tarragona in A.D. 385, condemning the administration of baptism there at such times as Christmas and Epiphany and "innumerable festivals of apostles and martyrs,"[74] might well prepare us for the fact that at the same time baptism at the paschal vigil was unknown in Alexandria. There, as we shall see later, baptism came into close relationship with Pascha only during the patriarchate of Theophilus, Siricius' contemporary, and even then baptism was not an aspect of the paschal vigil.[75]

Although baptism became central to the paschal vigil itself and to the times leading to it and following it, the present state of our evidence seems to point to a development in the course of the third century that became the common standard only in the fourth century. Of that development the testimonies of Tertullian (*De baptismo* 19) and Hippolytus (*Comm. in Danielem* 1.16.2) are our earliest evidence. Justin Martyr, half a century earlier, presumably speaking of Rome, carefully described the rites of initiation as distinct from the regular Sunday assembly.[76] He does not assign that initiatory rite to a particular time in the year, however, nor does he suggest that is occurs only once in the year. Indeed, as we have noted already, A. Hamman (following Holl and Richard) argues that the annual Pascha was not yet observed at Rome in the time of Justin.

Still earlier, while the first converts were probably baptized without regard to any special time for that rite, we might expect that baptism would soon be limited to those times when the community assembled, so that the initiation could be consummated in the eucharist. Therefore, we may agree with Rordorf that baptism came to be performed on Sunday once that day had become the established occasion of the eucharistic assembly,[77] although there is no reason to suppose that baptism occurred on every Sunday or even on most Sundays. Only with time would the development of the catechetical process limit baptism to but a few occasions in the year. It should not be at all surprising that Pascha became the principal occasion in much of the Church during the third century. It would be somewhat more surprising to learn that it had been so universally from the end of the apostolic age.

8. THE LITURGY AT JERUSALEM IN THE FOURTH CENTURY

However imprecise the picture of the paschal vigil afforded by the documents preserved to us from the second and third centuries, they tell us even less regarding liturgical exercises, if such there were, on the earlier days of Holy Week. For a picture of the liturgical articulation of the entirety of Holy Week we must wait for the developed liturgy of Jerusalem in the fourth century.

The documents for the Holy City are sufficiently plentiful and detailed to afford a rich opportunity to observe liturgical evolution over a considerable period. We possess a full set of lenten catechetical lectures delivered by Cyril, first a presbyter and later bishop of

Jerusalem, and an evidently separate set of mystagogia, probably from the same Cyril as bishop.[78] Two fourth-century accounts of pilgrimages are preserved, the first by an anonymous pilgrim from Bordeaux in 333.[79] Much more valuable is the account by a female pilgrim whose home is most frequently today taken to be either Galicia or Aquitaine. Her name and the dates of her sojourn in Jerusalem have also varied in the literature, but modern scholarship knows her as Egeria and dates her knowledge of Jerusalem to the years 381–384. More precisely, the year for which she gives a more or less continuous account of the Jerusalem liturgy has been shown to be 383.[80] While she seldom indicates details of scriptural readings, it was long customary to complement the picture she gives by reference to the so-called "Old Armenian Lectionary" published by Conybeare in his *Rituale Armenorum*.[81] The value of that work, based on *Paris arm. 44*, was vastly expanded by Athanase Renoux's edition of another manuscript of the same work. He presented that more recently discovered manuscript, *Jerusalem 121* (of the Armenian patriarchate), in a comparative edition with that of Paris, using yet a third, less valuable manuscript as control.[82] Both the Jerusalem and Paris manuscripts reflect the liturgical order of Jerusalem as it was in the period between 417 and 439, but the two manuscripts translate different originals and therefore reflect two stages in the development of the hagiopolitan liturgy in the early fifth century. Of the two, *Jer. 121* is closer to the state of affairs reported by Egeria in the late fourth century.

A picture of still later development of the Jerusalem liturgy is afforded by the lectionaries in Georgian, edited by Tarchnischvili.[83] These carry our information from the fifth century to the eighth. Finally, the rites of Holy Week are described in the tenth-century *Typikon of the Anastasis*.[84] To all these may be added a great deal of other material, homiletical or historical, which informs the more strictly liturgical sources to provide an unusually complete picture of the liturgical tradition of the church of Jerusalem from the fourth to the eleventh centuries. With the latter centuries of that tradition we shall not be concerned, but no other Christian see offers us such a controlled view of liturgical development in the first years of Christendom.

That rich documentation, however, has frequently seduced scholars into assigning to Jerusalem a larger and more innovative role in liturgical development than can be supported. It has, for example, been argued frequently, and especially by Gregory Dix,[85] that fourth-century Jerusalem was the stage for a liturgical development that marked the rise of a new historical consciousness in the Church, transforming if not displacing an original eschatological outlook. More recent and more precise study of the sources has shown this to be a false dichotomy.[86]

Historical commemoration and eschatological expectation go hand in hand and have done so from the Passover piety of the first century. The first three centuries were by no means unconcerned with historical questions, and the date of Pascha was accorded high importance as the anniversary of Christ's triumph, whatever weight we give to the emphasis on expectation of the parousia at Pascha on the part of B. Lohse and A. Strobel. The original unitive celebration of the whole of the Christian mystery at Pascha was refracted, in time, to yield a series of discrete commemorations, and that sense of progression through the historical events of Holy Week has been noted already in Syria in the first half of the third century in *Didascalia Apostolorum*. Odo Casel rightly observed that the Sunday Pascha continued the unitive character of the Quartodeciman observance, but the accommodation of the annual celebration to the structure of the week—the termination of the fast on the day of the resurrection, and the extension of the fast so as to begin on Friday, the day of the crucifixion—contained the seeds that would eventually yield the refraction of the single mystery of redemption into a series of commemorations of discrete historical moments in that mystery.

Already in the writings of Tertullian, as mentioned above, a discernible distinction is made between Pascha and the Pentecost, between the memorial of the passion and rejoicing in the resurrection. As we shall see, the later fourth century saw the division of the fifty days by the feast of the Ascension, with fasts after or even before it, but the accommodation of the unbroken paschal rejoicing to the chronology implied in Acts was no initiative of the liturgy of the Holy City. Jerusalem was much more conservative and resisted such partition of the paschal season into the fifth century. We shall be concerned to argue later that many fourth-century observances that have been considered innovations at Jerusalem are better accounted for as responses to the expectations of pilgrims who had learned in their home churches to associate certain events in the life of Christ with particular days in the liturgical year. In many instances, the special visits to the scenes of events mentioned in the gospels tell us more about the liturgical year elsewhere than they do of the native Jerusalem liturgy.

9. THE SETTING OF THE JERUSALEM LITURGY

It is true, however, that the recovery of the tomb of Christ following the Council of Nicea and the Constantinian building program in Jerusalem and environs did add much to the way in which liturgical events were celebrated. In many cases the native Jerusalem tradition was expanded by added functions associated with particular locations. These practices, together with visits to the sites of events celebrated in other liturgical traditions, gave to the earlier Jerusalem liturgy a sort of paraliturgical overlay, which had lasting effects on the liturgy of that city and, eventually, the Church at large.

Central to the whole liturgy of Jerusalem was the complex built by Constantine at Calvary. This complex focused on the tomb of Christ, unearthed from the rubble that formed the foundation of the Forum of Hadrian until the Christian building program was instituted. At the time of Constantine's death (337), the tomb, separated from the stone of the hill into which it had originally been carved, stood in an open space; as the removal of the surrounding hill proceeded, however, the mass of dressed stone blocks was assembled from which would be built the vast rotunda around the tomb that remains today, the building that Egeria calls the Anastasis.

Across the remainder of the open space before this rotunda was the apse of the basilica known as the Martyrium. This basilica stretched toward the east, and a further atrium to its east terminated in the *propylaea* on the Cardo Maximus.

At the southwest corner of the Martyrium, sharing a wall with it, stood the smaller church of Golgotha, its apse in the east, unlike the basilica. Outside this, in the southeast corner of the courtyard before the rotunda, was a large cross. Therefore, Egeria refers to the courtyard as "before the Cross," and speaks of the church at Golgotha as "the chapel behind the Cross." Southward from the rotunda stretched the wing containing the three chambers of the baptismal complex, the vestibule on the south end, the chamber with the font in the center, and, nearest the rotunda and the tomb, the chamber where the chrismation was performed.[87]

After that complex at Calvary, perhaps the most important of the churches of Jerusalem was that which Egeria calls Sion. No longer extant, this "upper church," as Cyril called it (probably from its location in Sion, the upper part of the city), was identified as the spot where stood the house in whose "upper room" the disciples were gathered on Pentecost. Epiphanius reports that a church was there when Hadrian visited the ruined city in 130.[88] John Wilkinson has argued that the church that Egeria knew was built between 336 and 348,[89] but it is clear that it still embodied the old traditions of the "upper room" of Acts 1.13 and, by association, the "one place" of Acts 2.1. It seems likely that the Jerusalem church's headquarters was here prior to the Constantinian building program.

In addition to the "most holy cave" of the tomb, Eusebius records that Constantine "discovered other places, venerable as being the localities of two sacred caves."[90] These were in Bethlehem and on the Mount of Olives and had been venerated since at least the third century as the sites, respectively, of the nativity and the ascension. The site on the Mount of Olives, which Egeria calls "Eleona," was by her time distinguished from the place of the ascension, Imbomon, a short distance away. The Eleona (of which only vestiges remain) has its sanctuary built over a cave in which, Egeria says, "the Lord used to teach." She speaks of this as the place of our Lord's discourse with his disciples in the night before his passion, an association made earlier by the Pilgrim of Bordeaux and continued in following centuries. Shortly after 314, however, Eusebius identified it rather as the place of our Lord's final discourse before the ascension, a tradition whose roots seem to run back to the *Acts of John* in the third century.[91] In Egeria's time, it was the customary place of burial of the bishops of Jerusalem. Constantine built the church over the cave, but the nearby hillock, Imbomon, did not have a church in Egeria's time, although we know that one was built there by the end of the century, because Jerome mentioned it in 392.[92]

Somewhat further along the high ground on that side of the Valley of Kidron lies Bethany and the tomb of Lazarus, some two

miles from the city in Egeria's description. This area atop the
Mount of Olives was important for the events of the Saturday and
Sunday preceding the week of the paschal fast and needs to be
mentioned here, even though our discussion of those days must be
postponed until our treatment of Lent. Already in the time of
Egeria the Sunday preceding the paschal fast was considered by
her to be the beginning of Great Week, and, as the first day of the
week, it clearly is that. Nonetheless, it will be easier to understand
the emergence of those as two festal days, the Saturday of Lazarus
and Palm Sunday, if we see them not as the beginning of Holy
Week, but as the conclusion of Lent. This is clearly their character
in Byzantine tradition.

Such were the principal churches of Jerusalem and environs
around which the liturgy was celebrated in the time of Egeria: the
old church of Sion (although probably a relatively new building),
the complex at Calvary (the Anastasis with the cave of the tomb,
the great basilica called Martyrium, the smaller church of Golgotha
or the "chapel behind the Cross," and the three-chambered baptistry running south from the Anastasis), and finally the Mount of
Olives across the Valley of Kidron, its principal church being the
Eleona, but with the place of the ascension (Imbomon) and Bethany lying close by, and Gethsemane lying nearer the foot of the
mount toward Jerusalem. More distant from Jerusalem itself but
nonetheless important for the city's liturgy was the basilica over
the cave of the nativity in Bethlehem. Against such a topographical
backdrop, we may be able to visualize Jerusalem's liturgy in the
later fourth century.

10. GREAT WEEK AT JERUSALEM

We noted earlier in discussing the extension of the paschal fast that
a distinction was drawn in *Didascalia Apostolorum* between the first
four days of the fast and the complete fast of the Friday and Saturday. That same sort of distinction is visible in the liturgy of Jerusalem in the later fourth century. The first four days of Great Week,
while exhibiting their own peculiarities, are nonetheless, as Egeria
notes, very much like other days in Lent at least up to noon. The
distinctive functions fall in the afternoon, usually at the ninth
hour, when there is a service of readings that extends to and most

often connects with the evening office, Lucernare, which is not celebrated until around seven in the evening.

In the fifth-century orders preserved in Armenian, there has been a considerable conflation of the services described by Egeria. The hour of the afternoon gathering has been advanced to four o'clock and is no longer a service of readings prior to Lucernare, but (an expanded?) Lucernare itself. On Tuesday, for example, whereas Egeria described a nocturnal visit to Eleona, following Lucernare and the customary final visit to the Anastasis, the lectionary in *Jer. arm. 121* makes Eleona the station for Lucernare, beginning at the tenth hour.[93] At that evening office the gospel reading is the one that Egeria's description assigned to the added nocturnal visit to "the cave where the Lord used to teach his disciples," Matthew 24.1–26.2, the eschatological discourse of Jesus that ends, "You know that after two days the Passover is coming, and the Son of man will be delivered up to be crucified."

By the time of the ordo represented in *Paris arm. 44*, the gospels for the evening office on Wednesday in the two principal Armenian manuscripts reveal a decay in the principle of course reading. For that office, *Jerusalem 121* appoints Matthew 26.3–16, the account of Jesus' anointing in Bethany, which concludes with a brief account of the visit of Judas to the chief priests and his treasonous compact with them. By the later time represented by *Paris 44*, however, it is only the treason of Judas that constitutes the gospel (Mt 26.14–16), and the account of the anointing at Bethany is omitted.[94] Renoux has suggested that the reason for this radical abbreviation is the desire of the redactor of *Paris arm. 44* to avoid redundancy, given the reading of the Johannine account of that anointing in Bethany on the preceding Saturday, a matter to which we must give closer attention in Part Three.[95] Similar departures from the principle of course reading are found in the gospels in *Paris 44* for the second oblation at the end of the paschal vigil, on Easter Day, and on Easter Monday. On these three occasions the resurrection accounts of John, Mark, and Luke are read, respectively. However, while *Jer. 121* takes up each one at the point at which it was broken off in the readings on Good Friday, and thus includes their accounts of the burial, *Paris 44* has omitted the verses pertaining to the burial and begins each reading with the resurrection itself. Here we can see how a vestige of the unitive Pascha has come, as late as the fifth century, to give way to a reduction of the content of the feast to the resurrection alone.[96]

Throughout the Armenian documents it is clear that the gospel of preference is that of Matthew. It is this gospel that forms the basis of the Great Week services and, in fact, the same priority can be seen underlying the entire liturgical tradition of the Holy City. Again and again it will be seen that those occasions that are oldest in the calendar take the reading for their principal service from Matthew. By contrast, the functions added in view of the Constantinian building program and the waves of pilgrims attracted in the second half of the fourth century are more likely to employ one of the other gospels. Surely this was not the only factor affecting the evangelical repertoire. Still, a careful reading of the fifth-century lectionaries leaves one with a strong impression that behind the richness of the Jerusalem liturgy of the later fourth and early fifth centuries, with all its visits to sacred sites, lies vestigially visible the cursus of the liturgical year of ante-Nicene Jerusalem based on the course reading of the gospel of Matthew.

The last of the first four days of Great Week, what we think of as Maundy Thursday, is distinguished from those that preceded it in that the afternoon synaxis, normally at the ninth hour, includes the eucharist and begins an hour earlier. While Egeria notes that this is because the dismissal must take place earlier than usual, she does not give a reason for that. It is surely, however, only to allow time for the people to eat what will be their last meal for some time. More difficult to understand is why, when the archdeacon has announced the gathering at Eleona for that evening and the dismissal has been pronounced in the Martyrium, the people do not, in fact, depart. Instead, all go immediately to the church of Golgotha, the chapel behind the Cross, and there a second oblation of the eucharist is made at which the general distribution of communion occurs. Egeria tells us that this is the only occasion in the year for the celebration of the eucharist there, but gives no explanation of that.[97]

In the Armenian documents of the following century, this second eucharist no longer takes place in the chapel but rather in the courtyard before the Cross. By that time still a third celebration of the eucharist is held, this one at Sion, now identified also, no doubt, with the "upper room" of the institution of the eucharist.[98]

44

The celebration there has the same psalm and epistle as were used at the first celebration at the Martyrium: Psalm 22 [23] and 1 Corinthians 11.23–32. Here at Sion, however, Mark's account of the institution replaces that of Matthew read at the Martyrium. This makes it clear that the second celebration at Golgotha did not have as its purpose a special commemoration of the institution of the eucharist. That second celebration had no readings at all, and was clearly an appendage to the liturgy that had just been concluded in the Martyrium. The reason for the second oblation remains a mystery.

The dismissal from the Martyrium came, Egeria says, at four o'clock in the afternoon. Here it will perhaps be helpful to recall that for Jerusalem's order predicated upon the Matthean chronology, this is the Preparation of the Passover, the hour of the slaying of the lambs for the feast. This Thursday is called "the Thursday of the old Passover" in the Armenian lectionaries, an identification familiar as well to Egeria.[99] While Jerusalem will keep watch with Christ in his agony throughout this night, and will observe his passion on the morrow, here at Golgotha at the hour of the slaying of the lambs for the feast at the temple, that is, at the place and time (relative to the temple calendar) of the death of Christ in the Johannine tradition, there is an added celebration of the eucharist without readings but with general communion. Can it be that this second celebration at Calvary represents in some way (however confused) a concession to pilgrims out of the Johannine tradition, which associated the death of the Lord with the hour of the slaying of the lambs? It is on this day alone in the year that the eucharist is celebrated here, and it will be in the same place on the following morning that the wood of the Cross will be venerated.

The third celebration of the eucharist at Sion reported in the lectionaries forges a connection between the afternoon service and a vigil stretching through the entire night. In the fourth century, however, the service of Thursday was separated by a few hours from the beginning of the observance of Good Friday after sunset. As suggested above, it was perhaps because the vigil through the night from Thursday to Friday of Great Week was more unusual to Egeria than the paschal vigil itself that she was so clearly impressed with its rigor.

Rigorous it surely was. All gathered at Eleona around 7 P.M., after a hurried and evidently nonreligious meal at whatever lodging one had found. At Eleona there were hymns and antiphons and readings, "appropriate to the day and the place," as Egeria always says, until around 11 P.M. The Johannine discourse (John 13.16–18.1, according to the Armenian lectionaries) was read, and, at around midnight, there was a procession with hymns to the Imbomon nearby. Here there were more readings and hymns and antiphons and prayers, until the cocks began to crow. Then, with singing, there was a further procession down to the place where the Lord prayed, and the gospel account of his urging the disciples to "watch, lest ye enter into temptation" was read. Then, with candles, the crowd began the perilous descent to Gethsemane. At the church there the account of Jesus' arrest was read. Finally, after this night of prayer and vigil, the crowd moved back across the bottom of the valley into the city, reaching the gate, as Egeria says, only at the time when they could recognize one another in the emerging light. By the time the procession arrived at the courtyard between the Anastasis and the Martyrium, "before the Cross," the light was almost full. There, after words of encouragement from the bishop, they were dismissed until the next gathering around 8 A.M.

In fact, it is not clear that there was a general assembly of all the people at that hour on Good Friday morning. Rather, the people seem to have passed through the church of Golgotha, "the chapel behind the Cross," which had been the station for the second celebration of the eucharist and the distribution of communion on the previous afternoon. There, from eight in the morning until noon, the wood of the Cross was exhibited and venerated, the element of the Jerusalem observance of this day that has perhaps most strongly influenced western liturgical tradition.

At Rome from around A.D. 700 a large fragment of the Cross was venerated at the Church of the Holy Cross in Jerusalem at a function that, as at Jerusalem, preceded the service of readings; by the second half of the century, however, a simple cross is venerated in local churches in place of the relic of the wood. This veneration follows the prayers that conclude the word liturgy, preceding the distribution of communion.[100] This latter form of the rite, perhaps devised first for the *tituli*, became standard in the West.

In Egeria's Jerusalem, however, it was not a symbolic cross that was venerated, but what was taken to be the very wood of the historical Cross. In later years such veneration took place as well each September 14, on the second day of Encaenia, the eight-day festival for the dedication of the Martyrium.[101] On Good Friday the relic was held in its place on a table by the bishop and guarded by deacons as all the faithful filed past to venerate it until noon. From that hour until three in the afternoon there were readings (psalms, epistles, and each of the four passion narratives) in the courtyard before the Cross. At three o'clock the service of readings usual at that hour began in the Martyrium and, connected with that, the evening office. At the dismissal from the office, all went as usual to the Anastasis, and there was read, the pilgrim says, "the Gospel passage about Joseph asking Pilate for the Lord's body and placing it in a new tomb."[102] A prayer, blessings of catechumens and faithful, and the dismissal brought the day's observances to a close. Nonetheless, Egeria notes, a vigil was kept at the tomb by the clergy, and those who could do so took part in all or some of that vigil through the night from Friday to Saturday.

11. THE PASCHAL VIGIL AND ITS LATER DEVELOPMENT

Of the Saturday of Great Week, Egeria says, "they have normal services at the third and sixth hours, but the ninth hour is not kept on this sabbath because they prepare for the vigil in the Great Church" (38.1). This has led some commentators to suppose that the vigil began at that hour, but this seems unlikely. The paschal vigil opened, we may be sure, with the lighting of a lamp, the Lucernare which gave its name to the evening office. By the tenth century the light ceremony had acquired a much greater importance and was resituated to a point following the Old Testament readings, as is still the case in Jerusalem.[103] However, the light ceremony still precedes those readings in the Georgian lectionaries of the eighth century. In the fourth and fifth centuries the bishop lighted a taper from the lamp that burned constantly in the tomb in the Anastasis, and proceeded to the Martyrium, where he lighted one or more lamps. The clergy then began the vigil of readings.

Although Egeria does not detail the readings of the vigil in fourth-century Jerusalem, the stability that is discerned later suggests that they were substantially those encountered in the Armenian lectionaries (both the Paris and the Jerusalem manuscripts) and in the still later Jerusalem lectionaries in Georgian, although there is some lengthening of individual lessons by the eight century. From that point, there was a growing influence from Constantinople, an influence that becomes quite discernible in the tenth-century typikon for the Anastasis.[104] Documents prior to that typikon show such a constancy in the vigil reading appointments that it is safe to suppose that they reflect with some measure of accuracy the state of affairs in the later fourth century, and therefore give our earliest detailed picture of the specific content of the vigil.

The early Jerusalem usage shows a series of twelve lessons, each followed by prayer with genuflection (kneeling). Prior to the first lesson, Psalm 117 [118] was sung with the response, "This is the day which the Lord has made." Apart from that initial responsorial psalm, there is no indication of psalmody accompanying each reading. Nor, it should be noted, is there any period of prayer following the final reading. During the singing of the canticle that concludes that reading, the *Song of the Three Children*, the bishop leads the newly baptized into the church. Since the last reading is not followed by prayer, as are those preceding, some have thought it to have been understood originally as the Old Testament lesson of the eucharistic synaxis. It is clear, in any case, that upon the conclusion of that canticle (at midnight, according to the rubric), the prokeimenon of the eucharistic liturgy began at once. The scheme of the vigil, therefore, is: Psalm 117 [118]; eleven prophetic readings, each followed by prayer; and the final reading, leading into the *Song of the Three Children*.

Because this Jerusalem lesson series is the oldest known and because, evidently, it influenced other series so greatly, it deserves careful consideration. The twelve Old Testament readings appointed in the Armenian lectionary are:

1. Genesis 1.1–3.24 (the story of creation);
2. Genesis 22.1–18 (the binding of Isaac);
3. Exodus 12.1–24 (the Passover charter narrative);
4. Jonah 1.1–4.11 (the story of Jonah);
5. Exodus 14.24–15.21 (the passage through the sea);
6. Isaiah 60.1–13 (the promise to Jerusalem);

7. Job 38.2–28 (the Lord's answer to Job);
8. 2 Kings 2.1–22 (the assumption of Elijah);
9. Jeremiah 31.31–34 (the new covenant);
10. Joshua 1.1–9 (the command to possess the land);
11. Ezechiel 37.1–14 (the valley of dry bones);
12. Daniel 3.1–90 (the story of the three children).

The first three readings build directly on the themeology of Passover, as known in Judaism in the early centuries of the Common Era. This can be seen clearly in the previously mentioned "Poem of the Four Nights" in the *Targumim.* Of Passover, Targum Yerushalmi says:

"Four nights are there written in the Book of Memorial. Night first; when the Word of the Lord was revealed upon the world as it was created; when the world was without form and void, and darkness was spread upon the face of the deep, and the Word of the Lord illuminated and made it light; and he called it the first night. Night second; when the Word of the Lord was revealed unto Abraham between the divided parts; when Abraham was a son of a hundred years, and Sarah was a daughter of ninety years, and that which the Scripture saith was confirmed, — Abraham a hundred years, can he beget? And Sarah, ninety years old, can she bear? Was not our father Izhak a son of thirty and seven years, at the time he was offered upon the altar? The heavens were (then) bowed down and brought low, and Izhak saw their realities, and his eyes were blinded at the sight, and he called it the second night. The third night; when the Word of the Lord was revealed upon the Mizraee, at the dividing of the night; His right hand slew the firstborn of the Mizraee, and His right hand spared the firstborn of Israel; to fulfill what the Scripture hath said, Israel is My firstborn son. And he called it the third night. Night the fourth; when the end of the age will be accomplished, that it might be dissolved, the bands of wickedness destroyed, and the iron yoke broken. Mosheh came forth from the midst of the desert; but the King Meshiha (comes) from the midst of Roma. The Cloud preceded that, and the Cloud will go before this one; and the Word of the Lord will lead between both, and they shall proceed together. This is the night of the

Pascha before the Lord, to be observed and celebrated by the sons of Israel in all their generations."[105]

The third of these "nights," the deliverance from Egypt, hardly requires comment. The other three, however, are important for our understanding of the continuity between the Jewish celebration of Pascha and the Christian. The association of Passover with creation points to the cosmic importance attached to the Exodus; the event that constituted Israel was seen as the constitution of the world itself as well. In much of Israel's tradition, Nisan was treated as the first of the months of the year, and therefore the month in which creation occurred. This tradition stems from Israel's adoption of the Babylonian calendar in the seventh century B.C., but, as we shall see, that calendar reform never entirely displaced an earlier association of the turning of the year with the month of Tishri in the autumn. Nonetheless, as the Targum reveals, the great spring festival in Nisan was regularly perceived as the celebration of creation, and this association of creation with the paschal date is seen also in early Christian usage.

Similarly, the fourth theme, that of final redemption in the coming of Messiah, was associated by some with the month of Tishri and by others with Nisan. Here, however, the hope of final redemption is associated with the latter of these, and especially with the night of Passover. These associations of the coming of Messiah with Passover, on the one hand, and with the festivals of Tishri (from Rosh Hashanah to Sukkoth), on the other, should not be understood so narrowly as to preclude the perhaps more constant and widespread recognition that the time of the final redemption is known but to God. These associations speak more to the inherently eschatological character of festival than to eschatology itself.

The second theme of the poem relates the sacrifice of Isaac (Genesis 22) to Passover, an association found already in *Jubilees* (2nd cent. B.C.). The sacrifice of Isaac also has associations with Rosh Hashanah in Tishri, and, while it is agreed that it was a Passover theme before the framing of the Jerusalem lectionary, the time and significance of that association is hotly debated.[106]

The first three readings, then, thoroughly establish the Jerusalem vigil as the continuation of the Passover tradition in the New Covenant, and the following readings interpret the passage to that New

Covenant, a passage that was being accomplished sacramentally in the baptistry while the readings were being proclaimed in the Martyrium. It is in connection with the conferral of baptism that Egeria notes the only difference between the Jerusalem paschal vigil and that which she knew in the West, viz., that after all have been baptized and clothed, they go with the bishop to the Anastasis where, after a hymn, he says a prayer for them. Then he leads them into the Martyrium, she says, "where all the people are keeping the vigil in the usual way" (38.2). Here, topologically as well as sacramentally, the newborn are introduced into the Church having just stepped from the tomb of Christ.

Distressing as Egeria's omission of detail can often be, here her failure to find anything more noteworthy about the paschal vigil is precious information indeed. Such omission means that the Jerusalem practice concerning which we have such rich information was, for all practical purposes, just what was considered normal in her home country, Aquitaine or Gallicia, the area that the bishop of Edessa described as "the other end of the earth" (19.5). Neither in East nor West can we expect much liturgical uniformity from city to city in the fourth and following centuries, but as our earliest western evidence does appear it is interesting to observe that the paschal vigil often seems to have twelve readings, and many of them are common with Jerusalem. Something of that community of tradition can be indicated by comparison of lectionaries.

The following table lists in the left column the Jerusalem appointments (by book and chapter only) from *Jerusalem 121*. The other columns indicate the number of each Jerusalem reading in the series of lessons in five other documents, in which those readings are found at all. The five other documents are:

Syriac = *Early Syriac Lectionary System* of the late fifth century edited by Burkitt from Brit. Mus. add. 14528;

Mozarabic = the use of Toledo in the second half of the seventh century, from G. Morin, ed., *Liber Comicus;*

Gallican = the Lectionary of Luxeuil of the end of the seventh century, edited by P. Salmon from Paris, B.N. lat. 9427;

Murbach = the Comes of Murbach, a lesson list for use with the Gelasian Sacramentaries of the later eighth century; and

Tridentine = the *Missale Romanum* of Pius V.[107]

Jerusalem	Syriac	Mozarabic	Gallican	Murbach	Tridentine
Gn 1		1	(1?)	1	1
Gn 22	11	6	4	3	3
Ex 12		9	6	9	9
Jonah	4		11	10	10
Ex 14		5	7	4	4
Is 60	10				
Jb 38					
2 Kgs 2	7				
Jer 31					
Jos 1					
Ez 37	9	11	8	7	7
Dn 3	3	12	12	12	12

From such a schema, it seems altogether possible that Egeria already knew at her home a vigil that, like Jerusalem, had twelve readings, perhaps half of them common to both churches (if she could have been aware of that fact). In view of its constancy even in vigils of fewer or more than twelve readings, it seems quite likely that the first reading in the Lectionary of Luxeuil was the Genesis cosmogony, although the manuscript is defective at that point, resuming after the lacuna only in the course of the third reading, the story of the flood from Genesis, a story frequently encountered in western lectionaries, but not at Jerusalem. On the other hand, as will appear from the table, the sixth through the tenth readings at Jerusalem found no permanent place in the west, if they ever found place there at all. The first and the last readings of the Jerusalem series, however, are found in Spain and Gaul two centuries after our Armenian documents, and remained the first and last readings of the Roman paschal vigil from the end of the Middle Ages to the reforms of the present century.

The vigil of twelve lessons in the Missal of Pius V, preserved as an option in the *Lutheran Book of Worship* for North America, is as old as the eighth-century Comes of Murbach. Behind that lies the ten-lesson series of the old Gelasian Sacramentary, I.xliii, to which the Murbach Comes adds only Baruch 3.9ff. as the sixth reading and Jonah 3 as the tenth. The reading from Baruch appears to be of Roman origin, but the Jonah story had been read in Gaul since the lectionary of Luxeuil and at Jerusalem already in the Armenian lectionaries. Given the Gallican influences on even that old Gelasian tradition, it seems unlikely that we should take its series of ten readings to represent the situation in Rome. There the Gregorian reform evidently reduced a longer vigil to only four readings, and the vigil of Pentecost had the same number. Herman Schmidt has suggested that this short series resulted from a division of a longer seven-lesson vigil between the Easter and Pentecost vigils. It would have had seven rather than eight readings because the third in each Gregorian vigil is Isaiah 4. By Schmidt's hypothesis, the original Roman pattern (with the Gregorian reassignments) would have been:

1. Genesis 1 (Gregorian Easter Vigil);
2. Genesis 22 (Gregorian Pentecost Vigil);
3. Exodus 14 (Easter);
4. Deuteronomy 31 (Pentecost);
5. Isaiah 4 (Easter and Pentecost);
6. Isaiah 54 (Easter); and
7. Baruch 3 (Pentecost).

It may argue in favor of Schimdt's hypothesis that the Comes of Murbach added the reading from Baruch to the old Gelasian paschal vigil lessons. It seems more likely that the reading would have come from a pre-Gregorian paschal vigil than from the Gregorian Pentecost readings.

If we follow Schmidt, then, it would appear that Rome gave no place to the oldest reading at the paschal vigil, the Passover charter narrative in Exodus 12. Although that later forms the second reading of the synaxis on Good Friday, there is no indication that it was transferred to that point from the paschal vigil. The absence of that text from the earliest form of the Roman vigil would be yet another indication of Roman muting of continuity with Jewish institutions. Nor do we find in early Rome the lesson and canticle from Daniel 3, which greeted the neophytes coming from the baptistry and the tomb of Christ in Jerusalem, as it would greet neophytes also in Gaul and Constantinople. As the Constantinopolitan data become available, the number of readings is flexible (seven, to which another seven may be added as required), but to those is always added in last place the Daniel pericope, which leads into the *Song of the Three Children.*

At Jerusalem, the arrival of the neophytes was the occasion for the beginning of the eucharist that brought their baptism to its fulfillment. The Armenian lectionaries testify that, at the conclusion of the *Song of the Three Children*, Psalm 64 [65] was sung with verse 2 as refrain. The epistle, 1 Corinthians 15.1–11, followed at once. Alleluia was sung with Psalm 29 [30], and the gospel was Matthew 28.1–20. Neither Egeria nor the lectionaries give any further details of the eucharistic liturgy or the communion of the neophytes, nor do the *Mystagogical Catecheses* point to anything distinctive about this first communion of the newly baptized, such as the three cups in the *Apostolic Tradition*.

Both Egeria and the lectionaries, however, are concerned to point to one characteristic of the Jerusalem paschal celebration not mentioned in the Mystagogia, viz., a second celebration of the eucharist in the Anastasis immediately following the dismissal in the Martyrium. We have noted above such a duplication of the oblation on Thursday of Great Week, but on that occasion the second oblation was not preceded by readings. Here, by contrast, there is a gospel reading, John 19.38–20.18 in *Jerusalem 121*, but John 20.1–18 only in *Paris 44*. While the Georgian lectionaries later have only a single oblation of the eucharist (celebrated, like the entire vigil, in the Anastasis), that liturgy retains the Matthean gospel, the Johannine being read at matins following. This, we may suppose, is testimony to the priority regularly given to Matthew's gospel at Jerusalem, a fact that throws the second oblation of the eucharist with its Johannine gospel into higher relief. Here, once again, we must suppose, the celebrations that commemorate events at the very place of their occurrence represent a secondary stratum in the hagiopolitan liturgical tradition.

12. EASTER WEEK

"The eight days of Easter they celebrate till a late hour, like us," says Egeria, "and up to the eighth day of Easter they follow the same order as people do everywhere else." This custom of observing Pascha for a week may well have its ultimate roots in the Passover and the seven days of Unleavened Bread. For Christians, however, the testimony of the fourth gospel, with its accounts of the appearances of Jesus to his disciples in the evening of the day of the resurrection and again eight days later, surely played a large role in the extension of the festival throughout the week, from Sunday through Sunday.

In the fourth century a central feature of the liturgical arrangements of this week was the explanation of the mysteries to the newly baptized. These *Mystagogical Catecheses* constitute one of our richer sources of information regarding patterns of Christian initiation. Those representing the Jerusalem tradition have long been circulated under the name of Cyril, Bishop of Jerusalem from around 351 to 386. The attribution of the Jerusalem *Mystagogia* to Cyril, however, has been questioned, in part on the basis of supposed conflicts between those lectures and the series of catechetical lectures more securely assigned to Cyril. In the last of those, number 18, Cyril gives notice of the mystagogical lectures that will be given in Easter Week.[108]

"And after Easter's Holy Day of salvation, ye shall come on each successive day, beginning from the second day of the week, after the assembly into the Holy Place of the Resurrection, and there, if God permit, ye shall hear other Lectures in which ye shall again be taught the reasons of every thing which has been done. . . ."

This seems to imply clearly that there are to be such lectures on every day of Easter Week, therefore seven of them, the last on Sunday. Yet only five mystagogical lectures are in the series attributed to Cyril. For this reason, many have insisted that those manuscripts that attribute the *Mystagogia* to Cyril's successor, John, indicate the correct author. For our purposes, the question of authorship is of little importance, but the argument based on Catechetical Lecture 18 does point to an interesting area of the development of the Jerusalem liturgy in the fourth and fifth centuries. While Cyril in that earlier lecture does clearly imply that there should be daily lectures in Easter Week, he also makes the point that these are to be delivered in the Anastasis. Yet, in Egeria's time, the stational cursus for Easter Week puts the morning service for Wednesday at Eleona and that of Friday at Sion.[109] In the following century, however, the number of days on which the station is at the Calvary complex is still further diminished. After the invention of the relics of Stephen in 415, Tuesday had its station at the Martyrium of Stephen, Wednesday was at Sion, and Thursday at Eleona. Consequently, provision is made in the Armenian lectionaries for only four mystagogical lectures at the Anastasis: Monday, Friday, Saturday, and Sunday.[110] In Egeria's day there would have been five, evidently, just the number preserved to us under Cyril's name. Renoux, in 1965, having noticed this correspondence between the stations at Calvary and the number of mystagogical lectures, accepted the attribution to John on the basis of the dating of Egeria's visit during John's episcopate (386–417).[111] Two years later, however, Devos published in *Analecta Bollandiana* the revised dating for Egeria's visit, which has since enjoyed general acceptance, 381–384.[112] The picture she gives of the stational cursus does correspond to the number of the Jerusalem *Mystagogia*, and seems to belong to the last years of Cyril.

Renoux, in a careful study of the gospel appointments for Easter in the two principal manuscripts of the Armenian lectionary, was able to show that at the opening of the fifth century in Jerusalem the Pascha still retained vestiges of the original unitive celebration of the whole of our redemption in Christ.[113] The gospels of the second celebration at the vigil, of Easter Sunday morning, and of Easter Monday are drawn from John, Mark, and Luke, respectively. In *Jerusalem 121*, as noted above, these still contain elements of course reading, continuing from the point at which the reading of those gospels was terminated on Good Friday, and so include reference to the burial of Christ that had not been included in previous readings. In the later ordo of *Paris 44*, however, these readings have been abbreviated so as to contain nothing but the accounts of the resurrection. This development, we shall see, was affecting the latter part of the *laetissimum spatium* as well, although not first at Jerusalem.

Such an earlier, more unitive Pascha perdured in an especially pure form in the first half of the fourth century, as has been shown in Hansjörg Auf der Maur's study of the Easter homilies of Asterios Sophistes.[114] A Cappadocian writing probably between 335 and 341, Asterios reveals a paschal observance contained within the single week of Easter, a week begun with baptism during the vigil and given over to mystagogical catechesis, coming to its close on the following Sunday. There are in these Easter sermons some indications of a preceding fast, but we have no details as to its length. It cannot be excluded that Asterios' church knew such an extension of the paschal festivity for fifty days as we see elsewhere, but there is no mention at all of any such extension. Pascha itself is celebration of Christ's victorious passion and death, his resurrection and ascension, and the sending of the Spirit upon the Church. It is clear in these homilies that Asterios was well aware of the chronology of the ascension and mission of the Spirit in Acts, but that chronology still had no influence on the character of the paschal observance.[115] This is a deeply traditional source and shows that the primitive conception of Pascha as total celebration of our redemption was still being followed in the first half of the fourth century.

13. PENTECOST

Asterios' silence regarding the fifty days of paschal rejoicing need not, however, be read as a total absence of such an observance in his church. Indeed, given the Nicene prohibition against kneeling during that time (Canon 20), a total absence of sensitivity to the great fifty days would be well nigh impossible. That prohibition, of course, was nothing new, but simply the ecumenical establishment of a tradition that is visible at least as early as the later second century.

In that tradition, it is clearly the whole period that is of central importance to Christians, not simply its final day. That fact, however, presents a problem. The name regularly given to that *laetissimum spatium* is *pentekostē*, the ordinal form of the number fifty, "fiftieth." That this term is used rather than *pentekonta* (fifty) suggests a focus on the final, fiftieth day. *Pentekostē* is the term used in the LXX twice to indicate the Feast of Weeks (Tb 2.1; 2 Mc 12.32), and it is used with that same signification by Philo and Josephus. Such is its use, of course, in the New Testament as well. It is clear, therefore, that any understanding of the Christian references to Pentecost must begin from the understanding of the Feast of Weeks in the first century.

The "feast of harvest" of which Exodus 23.16 speaks is elsewhere and more commonly known as *Shabuoth*, "Weeks." It represents a period of seven weeks measured from the morrow of the "sabbath" of Passover, and the feast itself is kept on the same day of the week as that on which the period began to be counted.

Julius and Hildegard Levy considered such a period to be an extension from the seven-day week and hypothesized that a calendar so based on the seven-day cycle was the oldest West Asiatic calendar.[116] Based on the week, that calendar's next larger segment was a week of weeks (7 × 7) plus a festival day, thus a *pentecontad*, or fifty-day period. A week of pentecontads plus two weeks constituted the year. Evidence for the actual existence of such a calendar is lacking, but such a hypothesis would explain an oddity in the series of Babylonian "unlucky" days, the seventh, fourteenth, nineteenth, twenty-first, and twenty-eighth days of the month. These are, obviously, every seventh day, with the exception of the nineteenth. That exception, however, can be explained by the Levys' hypothesis as the day that concluded a week of weeks begun on the first of the preceding month (30 + 19 = 49 = 7 × 7).

Apart from such a hypothesis, the feast of Weeks in the Old Testament is presented primarily as bringing to a close the season of harvest begun with the feast of Unleavened Bread. In the first century the Pharisees understood the "sabbath," from the morrow of which the seven weeks were to be counted, as the first day of Unleavened Bread, 15 Nisan, on whatever day of the week it might fall. However, the Boethusians, a sect of the Sadducees, held it to be the weekly sabbath, in this case, the sabbath occurring within the seven days of Unleavened Bread. For them, then, the seven weeks were always counted from the first day of the week, the morrow of the sabbath, and the fiftieth day would always fall on Sunday. If we accept the Johannine chronology of the passion, 15 Nisan would have been on the weekly sabbath in that year, and the variance in computation would have made no difference. The Pentecost to which reference is made in Acts 2 fell on Sunday by both systems of computation. It should be noted as well that the Qumran calendar referred to above situated the feast of Weeks permanently on Sunday, but there it was counted from the morrow of the Sabbath following the seven days of Unleavened Bread. Today, the Jews of Ethiopia count the seven weeks from the seventh day of Unleavened Bread.

In all this welter of conflicting computations, what is uncertain is the day from which the counting is to begin, not the length of the period to be counted. This lends more than a little verisimilitude to the insistence of J. van Goudoever that, "the Counting of the

Omer, the counting of seven times seven days, cannot be a purely agricultural phenomenon."[117] Whatever one may make of the hypothetical calendar of J. and H. Levy, it is clear in Leviticus that this sort of computation was not limited to the determination of the date of the harvest festival; the same computations are applied to years to determine the year of Jubilee: "And you shall count seven weeks of years, seven times seven years, so that the time of the seven weeks of years shall be to you forty-nine years. . . . And you shall hallow the fiftieth year, and proclaim liberty throughout the land to all its inhabitants" (Lv 25.8, 10a).

The disputes over the day from which the week of weeks should be counted, and the concomitant absence of dispute regarding a particular date for the feast of Weeks, suggest that in the first century it was not simply the fiftieth day that was considered sacred, but the very period between that fiftieth day and the day from which it was counted, a day related in one way or another to Passover. Also, in contrast to Passover and the feast of Tabernacles, both of which were observed over a week, Pentecost was kept on a single day, although pilgrims assembled for it not only from Judea but from Galilee and other parts. This, again, suggests that Pentecost remained, at least vestigially, not so much a discrete observance as the solemn conclusion of a period begun at Passover (or, at least, at a point defined by Passover).

On the other hand, in the first century of our era there are clear signs that that fiftieth day was being regarded as a festival with its own proper content, not just the conclusion of a festal season. That, of course, had long been true of the ritual phenomena associated with the feast, but there emerges around the beginning of our era a distinct historical reference of the feast. No longer simply the conclusion of the time of harvest, it begins to celebrate the renewal of the covenant and, eventually, to commemorate the giving of the Law. This was already evident in the *Book of Jubilees* (ca. 140–100 B.C.).[118] There, however, not only is the covenant at Sinai commemorated in the third month, but also the covenants with Noah and Abraham. In the light of such associations, it is not surprising that in *Jubilees* the feast of Weeks is treated as a divinely instituted festival for the renewal of the covenant. Such was the feast observed on the fifteenth day of the third month at Qumran.

Evidence for such a commemoration of the giving of the Law in rabbinic Judaism is considerably later. E. Lohse, believing that the destruction of the temple in A.D. 70 occasioned the assignment of this commemorative theme to the festival, finds the earliest sure testimony to that development ascribed to Rabbi Jose ben Chalapta around the middle of the second century.[119] By the later third century this theme was more fully developed and is today taken for granted as the content of the feast.

To whatever time we assign the historicization of the festival in Judaism, it is clear that it was already a feast of covenant renewal at Qumran in the first century and, as such, included commemoration of the giving of the Law. It will be in connection with Pentecost that patristic preaching will understand Paul's contrast between the written code and the Spirit in 2 Corinthians 3.6, but when he refers explicity to Pentecost it is of the Jewish festival that he speaks, as for example in 1 Corinthians 16.8. In the preceding chapter (15.20 and 23) he speaks of Christ as "the first fruits," and exegetes regularly understand this as an allusion to the presentation of the first fruits of the harvest on Pentecost. As with his reference to Christ as "our paschal lamb" in 5.7, it is clear that he is conscious of the Jewish festal calendar and relates Christ to those festivals as to all else.

That Pentecost was still an important time of pilgrimage to Jerusalem is indicated by the description of the multitudes in Acts 2.9–11. In the sermon ascribed to Peter, with its eschatological citation of Joel 2.28–32, both the resurrection of Christ and the giving of the Spirit to the community are seen as preparing the way for the day of the Lord, the *parousia*. We may wonder whether the author of *Epistula Apostolorum* did not have access to this account when he wrote in chapter 17 of that work that the advent would come between Pentecost and Passover. The Stuttgart manuscript of *Epistula Apostolorum* places the coming of the Father "when the days of Passover and Pentecost are past."

This reading suggests at least that those days were regarded already as a distinct, continuous period. That is not suggested necessarily in the other manuscript material, which speaks rather of the time between Pentecost and Passover. Given the many variations in the manuscripts, and that only the Stuttgart uses that expression, it would seem imprudent to appeal to *Epistula Apostolorum* 17 for evidence of the Christian observance of the time from Passover to Pentecost as a period of uninterrupted rejoicing. By the end of the second century, however, the fifty-day period was so observed, fasting and kneeling in prayer being forbidden. The prohibition against bending the knee in prayer is reported from a lost work of Irenaeus by the *Quaestiones et Responsiones ad Orthodoxos* (PG 6.1364–1365). While the date of that work and the authenticity of its citation of Irenaeus remain uncertain, a more secure reference to the same phenomenon of paschal piety during Pentecost is given in the *Acts of Paul*, an Asian work contemporary with Irenaeus. It recounts Paul's condemnation to the arena, and then adds, "but, as it was the pentecost, the brethren did not weep nor did they bow the knee, but they prayed in joy."[120]

The Asian provenance of these *Acta Pauli* establishes, if *Epistula Apostolorum* does not, the observance of the *laetissimum spatium* among the Quartodecimans. We have no information on how the Pentecost was computed among those who kept Pascha on a fixed date. However, where Pascha was established on Sunday, the fifty days were counted from that day itself, and the fiftieth day was always the eighth Sunday. Nonetheless, in all the references it is clear that for both groups, the Pentecost was conceived as an unbroken period of rejoicing.

That it was so not only in the Gaul of Irenaeus and the Asia of the *Acta Pauli* but also in northern Africa is clear from the numerous references in the writings of Tertullian, beginning from around the turn of the second to the third century. In *De Oratione* 23 (CC Lat. 1.271–272) he writes:

"In the matter of kneeling also prayer is subject to diversity of observance, through the act of some few who abstain from kneeling on the Sabbath; and since this dissension is particularly on its trial before the churches, the Lord will give his grace that the dissentients may either yield, or else indulge their opinion without offence to others. We, however (just as we received), only on the day of the Lord's resurrection ought to guard not only against kneeling, but every posture and office of solicitude; deferring even our businesses lest we give any place to the devil. Similarly, too, in the period of Pentecost; which period we distinguish by the same solemnity of exultation" (ANF III., p. 689).

For Tertullian, indeed, this understanding of Pentecost as the *lae-tissimum spatium* is so strong as virtually to include the Sunday of Easter itself, assigning the term Pascha to the preceding fast day. Indeed, somewhat earlier in *De Oratione* 18 (CC Lat. 1.267), linking omission of the kiss of peace to fasting, Tertullian says, "on the day of the passover (*die Paschae*), when the religious observance of the fast is general and, as it were, public, we justly forego the kiss." The paschal solemnity that terminates that fast, the vigil through the night, also initiates the Pentecost. Indeed, one may say that for Tertullian, it is the Pentecost that celebrates the resurrection. Then, too, the advent of the Lord is promised, as we have noted already in *De Baptismo* 19, by the announcement of the angel that he would return as he had ascended.

That the content of the celebration of these fifty days is so richly manifold in the early experience of the Church is due, no doubt, to the variety of New Testament witness to the resurrection. Not even the gospel of Luke prepares us for the chronological precision that later times would predicate on Acts 1.3. Whatever the importance of the fifty days to the church to which Asterios preached his Easter homilies, we see in the content of Pascha as presented there the full, complex range of the celebration: Christ's death, resurrection, ascension into heaven, and the mission of the Spirit upon the Church. Still, by the time Asterios' sermons were delivered, that complex unitive celebration was beginning to disintegrate.

A synod at Elvira at the very opening of the fourth century, A.D. 300, shows that the fiftieth day itself is beginning to take on a new importance. The forty-third canon of that synod is concerned to correct, *iuxta auctoritatem Scripturarum*, an error that had arisen but that is not specified. The correction, however, is a reaffirmation of the importance of celebrating "the day of Pentecost" (*diem Pentecostes*). Other manuscripts of the acts of that synod make it clear that this reaffirmation is directed against the custom of some to close the Pentecost on the fortieth day. Cabié suggests that those condemned by this canon were resuming normal fast practice after the fortieth day, believing that it was then that the bridegroom was taken away.[121] If this reasoning is correct, Canon 43 of the Council of Elvira would reflect the first suggestion that the phrase in Acts 1.3, "during forty days" (*di' hēmerōn tessarakonta*), was beginning to be understood to give such precision to the time of the Ascension that it should control the paschal celebration. Further, the standard text of the canon is the first reference in Christian usage to Pentecost as a particular day, the final fiftieth day, rather than the fifty-day period. That such a change in the meaning of the term was not universal is clear from the twentieth canon of Nicea in 325. There it was decreed that prayer must be offered standing, not kneeling, on Sundays and in "the days of the Pentecost" (*tais tēs pentekostēs hēmerais*).[122]

Even so, it proved difficult to avoid any further articulation of that period, and J. van Goudoever has argued for the antiquity of a division of the Pentecost with a festival of "Mid-Pentecost."[123] Indeed, Peter Chrysologus, in the first half of the fifth century, claimed that such was a tradition from the apostolic fathers (PL 52.440–441). Related to that may be the times established for annual synods in Syria. *Apostolic Constitutions* VIII.47.37 orders synods of bishops twice in the year, the first of them being held in the fourth week of the Pentecost. This reiterates the order of an earlier council in Antioch, which specified that the synod should assemble, "in the third week of the feast of the Pascha, so that the synod may be concluded in the fourth week of the Pentecost."[124] This council was held in 341, and there can be little doubt that it gives local expression to the fifth canon of Nicea, sixteen years earlier, which ordered two synods each year, the first of them "before the fortieth" (*pro tēs tessarakostēs*). Although that text has often been taken to refer to the lenten fast, S. Salaville[125] argued early in this century that it refers rather to the fortieth day of the paschal rejoicing, since the canon speaks of a time when, "having put away all pettiness, the pure gift may be offered to God."[126] Such a statement seems to make no sense at all for the time preceding Lent, but it is understandable in terms of the paschal season. Salaville went beyond the evidence to conjecture that this is a reference to the Ascension, but Cabié is on surer ground in applying it only to the term before which the local synods should be convened in the latter half of the days of Pentecost, a position to which Salaville himself came in a later article.[127]

There is another mention of that fortieth day, which does not seem to refer to the Ascension, although the passage has had many interpretations. Egeria (42) writes of Jerusalem:

"The fortieth Day after Easter is a Thursday. On the previous day, Wednesday, everyone goes in the afternoon for the vigil service to Bethlehem, where it is held in the church containing the cave where the Lord was born. On the next day, the Thursday which is the Fortieth Day, they have the usual service, with the presbyters and the bishop preaching sermons suitable to the place and the day; and in the evening everyone returns to Jerusalem."

This is but one of a number of places in Egeria's narrative at which one would wish to ask, "how suitable?" What is the connection between this fortieth day after Easter Sunday and the basilica of the nativity in Bethlehem? The Armenian lectionary of the next century offers some help in this instance, however. There the fortieth day is kept at Imbomon as the feast of the Ascension, but there is at about the same time a station at Bethlehem that commemorates the slaughter of the innocents, although our two principal manuscripts do not agree on the date of that commemoration, *Jerusalem 121* making it May 9 and *Paris 44* making it May 18. Renoux, commenting on that discrepancy, offers the opinion that it reveals a concern to avoid the fortieth day, by that time kept at Imbomon as the Ascension.[128] Since that was not yet the case for Jerusalem in the time of Egeria, it is possible that the assembly she describes at Bethlehem really was on the fortieth day. Paul Devos has shown, in fact, that in 383 the date given for the feast of the Innocents in *Paris 44*, May 18, did fall on the fortieth day after Easter.[129] That leaves little room for doubt that this was the service described by Egeria. That she describes it as falling on the fortieth day after Easter may indicate that it was a day in the paschal time to which she had already learned to attach a special significance. However, if she already associated that day with the Ascension of Christ, she gives no indication of doing so, nor is there direct evidence for its celebration prior to her time in Jerusalem. She does describe an observance clearly related to the ascension, but that is on the fiftieth day, and vestiges of that observance are still visible in the Armenian lectionary after the adoption (from usages outside Jerusalem) of the feast of the Ascension ten days earlier. Patrick Regan has argued persuasively that the readings on the Mount of Olives reported by Egeria for the afternoon of the fiftieth day, "the

Gospel reading about the Lord's ascension, and then the reading from the Acts of the Apostles about the Lord ascending into heaven after the resurrection" (43.5), formed the readings for the new feast on the fortieth day in the fifth-century lectionaries.[130] Nonetheless, that assembly on the Mount of Olives on the afternoon of the fiftieth day continued in the fifth century, its gospel now John 16.5–14, "now I am going to him who sent me. . . ."

Still, such a commemoration of the ascension on the afternoon of the fiftieth day, full or vestigial, coexisted with the mission of the Spirit as the content of the celebration on the fiftieth day. In Egeria's account, in fact, the dismissal at the Martyrium on that Sunday morning is made somewhat earlier than usual, and all escort the bishop with singing to the old church of Sion, identified as the place of the assembly of the disciples on the occasion of the outpouring of the Spirit, so that all may arrive there by nine o'clock, the "third hour" of Acts 2.15 (Egeria, 43.1–3). That passage is read and there is an oblation of the eucharist. After the noonday meal, all climb the Mount of Olives and assemble at Imbomon, where a service of readings, hymns, and prayers focused on the ascension lasts until the ninth hour. All then repair to the nearby church of Eleona for Lucernare. More is involved, perhaps, in this station at Eleona for Lucernare than merely the fact that it was a church building in Egeria's day while Imbomon was not. It will be remembered that the cave over which the church of Eleona was built was reckoned in the third century to be the place from which the Lord ascended, an identification still made in the early fourth century by Eusebius.

In the Armenian lectionaries there is no longer any indication of this station at Eleona for Lucernare. Rather, in the evening there is a single assembly at Sion. In Egeria's account, however, that final meeting at Sion took place around midnight, and was the climax of a whole series of synaxes that filled every moment from the gathering at Imbomon in early afternoon. Such simplification of the rites in the fifth century sets in even higher relief the retention of the afternoon assembly at Imbomon at a time when the feast of the Ascension had been observed at the same place ten days earlier. This suggests that the Ascension of Jesus and the mission of the Spirit were still held together as the seal of the pentecost in the fifth century as they had been in the fourth. Cabié has noted several references to such an observance of the ascension on the fiftieth day, and those include the celebration of the mission of the Spirit.[131]

Georg Kretschmar has marshaled an impressive body of evidence that indicates that two traditions exist in the early Church regarding this fiftieth day.[132] One tradition focuses on the theme of the messianic community inaugurated by the gift of the tongues of all nations in Acts 2.5–13, a tradition that achieved particular importance as the mission of the Church spread into all lands. Alongside this is another tradition, identified especially with Palestine and the East, which treated the gift of the Spirit as a dimension of the glorification of Christ (as in John 20) and his messianic kingship (as in Peter's address in Acts 2.33ff.). In Ephesians 4.7–12, he believes, this latter tradition is brought into relation to a rabbinic tradition that applied the words of Psalm 68.18 (Heb.) to Moses' ascent of Sinai and his delivery of Torah to Israel, while altering those words from "received gifts" to "gave gifts." It is that rabbinic alteration of the psalm that appears in Ephesians 4.8, and Kretschmar suggests that this text represents a typological identification of Jesus' ascension with Moses' ascent of Sinai. This is the source of the liturgical tradition that situates the ascension on the Jewish Feast of Weeks with its celebration of the giving of the Law. That Palestinian tradition was still vestigially present in the Jerusalem liturgy in the early fifth century, although by then the Ascension had come to be celebrated primarily on the fortieth day under influences from other churches.

14. THE FORTIETH DAY OF THE ASCENSION

Moves to resume normal fast practice after the fortieth day seem to have begun, and to have been opposed, as early as the Council of Elvira in A.D. 300. If one may so conclude from a gloss on the text of one of the Elviran canons, it is certain that some, already, believed that the fortieth day marked the time at which "the bridegroom was taken away." That scriptural text (Mark 2.18–20 and parallels) was regularly appealed to as the ground for the prohibition of fasting during the Pentecost and for the resumption of fasting after that *laetissimum spatium*. While that early attempt to abbreviate the period of rejoicing was rejected by the Spanish synod of Elvira, the issue did not disappear forever, and by the later fourth century the feast of the Ascension of Christ was being celebrated on that fortieth day in many places, Jerusalem and Alexandria being significant exceptions.

The celebration of the Ascension on the fortieth day is explicitly mentioned in *Apostolic Constitutions* (V.20.2), but it is difficult to date that work securely. Although a date around 375 or 380 is frequently assigned to it, Funk argued from this list of festivals that even A.D. 400 must be taken as a *terminus post quem*. In fact, this passage of the constitutions shows the primitive Pentecost to be fully dismantled. The feast of Easter itself is to be celebrated afresh on the eighth day, the Ascension on the fortieth day, the outpouring of the Spirit on the fiftieth, and fasting is to be resumed only in the second week following that fiftieth day, the week following the fiftieth day itself being celebrated as a festal time. While neither this week nor Easter week is explicitly celebrated as an octave, that idea is clearly present. Given the absence here of any sense of the primitive fifty days of unbroken rejoicing, it is almost ironic to find, at the close of that chapter of the constitutions, a return to that primitive meaning of Pentecost: "for he will be guilty of sin who fasts on the Lord's day, being the day of the resurrection, or during the time of Pentecost."

Jean Daniélou[133] has argued that the first mention of the Ascension on the fortieth day is in a sermon of Gregory of Nyssa preached in 388, and that the separation of the Ascension theme from that of the mission of the Spirit resulted from the strong theological emphasis on the personhood of the Spirit in the Council of Constantinople's condemnation of Macedonianism in 381. Gregory's sermon was preached, according to the title given to it, "on the Ascension of Christ, which is called Episozomene according to the local custom of Cappadocia" (PG 46.689). The meaning of that term, *episozomene*, remains obscure, but it occurs again in the title of a sermon of Chrysostom, preached in 387, "for the Sunday of *episozomene*." There, however, it seems to have no reference to the ascension. Chrysostom, in the first of his homilies on Pentecost (PG 50.456), does refer to having celebrated the Ascension ten days earlier, but it seems impossible to assign to that sermon a more precise date than the time of his preaching at Antioch, 386 to 398 (although Dom Botte, as we shall see in Part Two, wished to assign it to the beginning of that period). Similar reference to the just-past celebration of the Ascension is made in the second of Chrysostom's Pentecost sermons (PG 50.463), and we have also a sermon that he preached on the Ascension itself (PG 50.441–452). If all these are, as Daniélou argues, later than Gregory of Nyssa's sermon of 388, they would seem to be so slightly later that the difference in time would not be of great significance for the history of the festival. The same may be said as well for a sermon preached on the feast by Chromatius, bishop of Aquileia from 388 to 407, a sermon in which the feast is commended with a zeal that could suggest it is of recent appearance.[134]

Nothing in any of these texts from Syria, Cappadocia, or Cisalpine Gaul from the latter dozen years of the fourth century, however, reveals such development as has been noted in *Apostolic Constitutions* V.20. On the other hand, still other evidence from northern Italy suggests that the assignment of a very much later date for the *Constitutions* should not rest on its more complete dismantling of the primitive Pentecost alone.

At Brescia we encounter a picture of the liturgical year that seems pivotal for the transition from the ancient understanding of the Pentecost to the familiar medieval western patterns. Filastrius, bishop of Brescia at the time of his death in 397, wrote ca. 385–391 the *Diversarum Hereseon Liber,* for which he is chiefly known. There, in a list of major festivals (*dies festivitatis maioris*), which he evidently meant to include only feasts of Christ, he named the Nativity, the Epiphany, Pascha and, finally, the Ascension, *in quo ascendit in caelum circa pentecosten.*[135] Such a description of that feast could well suggest that we have here such an observance on the fiftieth day as has been noted at Jerusalem. Such is not, however, the case. In another passage, chapter CXLIX (121), dealing with fasts, Filastrius states explicitly that the Ascension is on the fortieth day, *post pascham die quadragensimo.*[136] He observes that four times of fast are observed in the Church, at the Nativity, the quadragesima before Pascha, before the Ascension, and then from the Ascension to Pentecost. There, however, the text adds, *aut postea.* It is difficult to know just what is to be made of the fast "until Pentecost, or afterward." Evidently, Filastrius did know the traditional view regarding the resumption of fasting *ablato sponso*, but was aware of diversity regarding the time when the fasting was resumed. In his own church, it is clear that fasting was resumed from the Ascension on the fortieth day, but the phrase, *aut postea*, suggests that he was well aware of churches that did not resume the fast until after Pentecost.

Such was, in fact, the case at nearby Milan in Filastrius' day.[137] Cabié has shown the tenacity of the ancient Pentecost in Egypt,[138] and both Milan and Aquileia seem to have been open to Alexandrian influence at many points. It is not surprising, therefore, to find Ambrose maintaining the full fifty days of rejoicing. Such a practice was not only known to Filastrius, but seems to have had such authority that he found himself called upon to give a reason for fasting during the ten days intervening between the Ascension and Pentecost. Thus he speaks of the apostles praying and fasting in those days during which they waited for the gift of the Spirit.[139]

Behind this, of course, lies the question of the time when the bridegroom was taken away; but for Filastrius that was not the only reason for fasting, because he gives us for the first time the insertion of a preparatory fast prior to the Ascension. The text does not detail the length of that fast, but one might suspect that such a fast was already in place in Gaul when Mamertus instituted in Vienne the litanies on the three days before the Ascension in the following century.[140] Those rogations, however related to Filastrius' fast before the Ascension, formally established for Gaul the decadence of the primitive Pentecost. Around that same time, in the Syria of *Apostolic Constitutions,* the fiftieth day was observed with what seems to be at least the germ of an octave, normal fast practice being resumed only from the Sunday after Pentecost. Such an octave is encountered at Rome by the end of the seventh century, displacing the resumption of the fast.[141]

In these ways the unity of Tertullian's *laetissimum spatium,* a unity visible already in the second century, was sundered in much of the Church during roughly the last decade of the fourth century, although those developments were resisted at Jerusalem for a time and still longer at Alexandria. The classical fast after Pentecost was frequently reinstated in the West, and even in the ninth century some places still maintained a fast of forty days following Pentecost.[142] In our own day, renewed appreciation of the Pascha as central to the liturgical year and the fountainhead of all festival has carried with it, as inherent in it, a renewed emphasis on the integrity of this "Great Sunday" of paschal joy, the seventh part of the year, the time of harvest initiated, as Paul said, when Christ our Paschal Lamb was sacrificed for us, and brought to consummation when he, the firstfruits of the resurrection, ascending to the Father, led captivity captive, and gave to us the gift of life, the Holy Spirit of God.

If at the end of the fourth century in much of the Church the individual moments of that redemptive *transitus* were celebrated as distinct festivals, it would be wrong to suppose that this was because they were looked upon only as events in a departed past, to be recalled in our now distant present. It was of the Ascension, to be sure, but also of all the celebrations, whether of incarnation, or death, or burial, or resurrection, or mission of the Spirit, that Leo said, "all that was visible of the Redeemer has passed over into the sacraments."[143]

Not less than all of that was what it meant and means to "proclaim the Lord's death until he come." The Cross, the central symbol of Christian life, has been, ever since Jesus' renewal of the Passover, the sign of joy and of hope—joy for his passage (and that of our nature in him) into his kingdom, and, therefore, assured hope for his Lordship at the end. Until his coming again the Church rejoices at his presence, his parousia, in the sacraments—and not just baptism and eucharist, but the whole liturgical complex by which the richness of our salvation is articulated, the all-embracing mystery of worship. Yet, there lies deep within that mystery of faith the certainty that such paschal joy is not its own end. Almost from the beginning, it would seem, that rejoicing has issued and issues still into hope for the day of his triumphal advent, and watching for his parousia, until his coming again.

NOTES

1. So, e.g., Rylaarsdam in IDB, s.v., "Passover."
2. *Mishnah Pesachim* 5.
3. J. W. Etheridge, *The Targums of Onkelos and Jonathan ben Uzziel on the Pentateuch, with the Fragments of the Jerusalem Targum from the Chaldee* (New York 1968) pp. 479–481.
4. Translated from the French of L. Guerrier, PO XI, fasc. 3, p. 58. The Ethiopic text of *Epistula Apostolorum* is embedded in a version of *Testa-*

mentum Domini, its chapter 15 being chapter 26 of the compound document.

5. Ibid., p. 59.

6. E.J. Bickerman, *Chronology of the Ancient World* (London 1968) p. 26.

7. See Mateos, *Le Typikon,* Tome I, p. 55.

8. See August Strobel, *Ursprung und Geschichte des fr#christlichen Osterkalenders.* TU 121 (Berlin 1977) p. 373.

9. Ibid., pp. 440–449. Also A. Jaubert, *The Date of the Last Supper* (Staten Island, N.Y. 1965).

10. DACL, VI². 2423–2426.

11. *Chronicon Paschale ad exemplar Vaticanum recensuit Ludovicus Dindorfus,* I (Bonn 1832) p. 13.

12. See Vincenzo Loi, "Il 25 Marzo data pasquale e la cronologia Giovannea della passione in età patristica," *Ephemerides Liturgicae* 85 (1971) pp. 51f.

13. Tertullian, *Adversus Iudaeos,* VIII.18 (ANF III, p. 160).

14. Tertullian, *Adversus Marcionem* IV.40.1–3 (CC Lat., I.655f.) Cyprian, *Epistula LXIII.16.2* (Bayard, *Saint Cyprien. Correspondance,* II, pp. 210–211); Ps. Cyprian, *De Pascha computus,* 2 (ed. Hartel, CSEL III/3, p. 250).

15. *Chronicon paschale,* pp. 13f.

16. Cited by V. Loi, op. cit. (note 12 above), p. 59, n. 45. Unfortunately unavailable to this study, the work as cited by Loi is: A. Jacoby, *Ein bisher unbeachter apokrypher Bericht über die Taufe Christi* (Strassburg 1902) p. 15.

17. The standard text is that appended to Botte, pp. 88–105.

18. To the texts reported in Vincenzo Loi (op. cit., pp. 60ff.) may be added J. Forget, ed., *Synaxarium Alexandrinum* (CSCO, arab. III.19), pp. 51f.

19. Epiphanius, *Panarion* 50.1.8. The *Acta Pilati* are also appealed to by an anonymous Anatolian chronographer concerned to establish the date of Pascha in 387. He is also concerned to protect the identification of March 25 with 14 Nisan, and to that end argues that this date fell after the equinox. See F. Floeri and P. Nautin, *Homélies Pascales, III: Une homélie anatolienne sur la date de la Pâques en l'an 387.* SC 48 (Paris 1957) p. 127, 2.

20. Strobel, op. cit., pp. 370–371. Regarding the controversy at Laodicea, Pier Franco Beatrice, *La lavanda dei piedi* (Rome 1983), p. 33 and note 1, suggests that it had to do rather with synoptic vs. the Johannine chronology.

21. The translation is that of Thomas Halton from the French of A. Hamman, *The Paschal Mystery. Alba Patristic Library* 3 (Staten Island, N.Y. 1969) p. 31. For the Greek text, see O. Perler, *Méliton de Sardes, Sur la Pâques et fragments,* SC 123 (Paris 1966) sections 46f.

22. Ibid., pp. 33f. (Perler ed., sections 66, 70).

23. See especially J.-P. Audet, *La Didaché, instructions des apôtres* (Paris 1958).

24. S. Bacchiocchi, *From Sabbath to Sunday* (Rome 1977).

25. W. Rordorf, *Sunday* (London 1968) p. 205.

71

26. Massey Hamilton Shepherd, Jr., *The Paschal Liturgy and the Apocalypse* (Richmond, Va. 1960) p. 31.

27. C. S. Mosna, S.C.J., *Storia della domenica dalle origini fino agli inizi del V secolo* (Rome 1969) pp. 13f.

28. Eusebius, HE V.23.1. (NPNF II.I, p. 241).

29. Socrates, HE V.22. (NPNF II.II, p. 131).

30. Sozomen, HE VII.19. (NPNF II.II, p. 390).

31. Eusebius, HE V.24.1–7 (NPNF II.I, p. 242).

32. Ibid., V.24.12–17 (NPNF II.I, p. 243).

33. Christine Mohrmann, "Le conflict pascal au IIe siècle: note philologique," *Vigiliae Christianae* 16 (1962) p. 161.

34. George LaPiana, "The Roman Church at the End of the Second Century," *Harvard Theological Review* 18 (1925) pp. 201–277.

35. Karl Holl, "Ein Bruchstück aus einem bisher unbekannten Brief des Epiphanius," *Gesammelte Aufsätze zur Kirchengeschichte*. II: *Der Osten* (Tübingen 1927) pp. 204–224.

36. Hans Lietzmann, *A History of the Early Church*. II: *The Founding of the Church Universal* (Cleveland and New York 1961) pp. 135f.

37. Marcel Richard, "La question pascal au IIe siècle," *L'Orient Syrien* 6 (1961), pp. 179–212. Without reference to the work of Richard or those before him, I reached similar conclusions in "History and Eschatology in the Primitive Pascha," *Worship* 47 (1973) pp. 212–221.

38. A. Hamman, "Valeur et signification des reseignements liturgiques de Justin," *Studia Patristica* XIII.ii. TU 116 (Berlin 1975) pp. 364–374.

39. Eusebius, HE IV.6. (NPNF II.I, pp. 177 178).

40. Ibid., V.25. (NPNF II.I, p. 244).

41. See A. Strobel, op. cit. (note 8 above), p. 375.

42. *De baptismo* 19.1 (CC Lat. I.293).

43. *Hom. in Isa.* 5.2. GCS 33.

44. Origen, *De Pascha* (fragment, Papyrus Toura, ed. P. Nautin, *Sources Chrétiennes* 36 [Paris 1953] p. 35).

45. Augustine, *Enarrationes in Psalmos* 120.6. (CC Lat. 40.1791).

46. H. von Campenhausen, "Ostertermin oder Osterfasten? Zum Verständnis des Irenäusbriefs an Viktor," *Vigiliae Christianae* 28 (1974), pp. 114ff.

47. Tal. bab. Pes. 99b.

48. Tertullian, *De Ieiuniis*, 14.3.

49. A. Jaubert, *The Date of the Last Supper* (Staten Island, N.Y. 1965).

50. R. H. Connolly, *Didascalia Apostolorum* (Oxford 1929) pp. 181f.

51. K. Holl, "Ein Bruchstück aus einem bisher unbekannten Brief des Epiphanius," *Gesammelte Aufsätze zur Kirchengeschichte*, II. pp. 204–224. The text is on pp. 205–207.

52. Ibid., p. 212, n. 1.

53. Eusebius, HE V.24.

54. Connolly, *Didascalia Apostolorum* V.18, p. 189.

55. C. L. Feltoe, *The Letters and Other Remains of Dionysius of Alexandria* (Cambridge 1904) pp. 101f. Emmanuel Lanne, "Textes et rites de la liturgie pascale dans l'ancienne église copte," *L'Orient Syrien* 6 (1961) 279–300, has observed vestiges of a commemoration of the institution of the eucharist on Tuesday of Holy Week in Coptic tradition, but he does not relate these to the chronology found in *Didascalia*.

56. B. Botte, *La tradition apostolique de saint Hippolyte: essai de reconstitution*. LQF 39. Chapter 33, pp. 78–81.

57. Hippolytus, *Commentarium in Danielem* IV.20.3. GCS. *Hippolytus*, I (Leipzig 1897) p. 236.

58. *The Festal Letters of S. Athanasius* (Oxford 1854). An example of the separate date can be seen in the second letter, for 330, on p. 21.

59. Funk, *Didascalia et Constitutiones Apostolorum* (Paderborn 1905) p. 271.

60. Raniero Cantalamessa, *L'Omelia "in S. Pascha" dello Pseudo-Ippolito di Roma: Ricerche sulla Teologia dell'Asia Minore nella Seconda Metà del II Secolo. Pubblicazioni dell'Università Cattolica del Sacro Cuore, Contribuiti Serie III, Scienze filologiche e letteratura* 16 (Milan 1967) pp. 34–43.

61. Botte, op. cit. (note 56 above), p. 45.

62. Ibid., p. 55.

63. Connolly, *Didascalia Apostolorum*, p. 189.

64. So, e.g., F. L. Cross, *I Peter, A Paschal Liturgy* (London 1954); Massey H. Shepherd, Jr., *The Paschal Liturgy and the Apocalypse. Ecumenical Studies in Worship* 6 (London 1960).

65. O. Perler, *Méliton de Sardes. Sur la Pâques*. SC 123 (Paris 1966) pp. 144–146, 173.

66. R. Cantalamessa, op. cit. (n. 60 above), pp. 282–287. Cantalamessa does, however, agree with Perler on the baptismal significance of the anointing references in Melito.

67. Tertullian, *De baptismo* 19 (ANF III, p. 678).

68. G. Kretschmar, "Die Geschichte des Taufgottesdienstes in der alten Kirche," *Leiturgia*, Band V (Kassel 1970) pp. 137–140.

69. R. Cantalamessa, *Ostern in der alten Kirche. Traditio Christiana* IV (Bern 1981) p. 79, no. 48, n. 1.

70. *Commentarium in Danielem* 1.16.1–3. G. Bonwetsch, ed., GCS. *Hippolytus* I.1 (Leipzig 1897) pp. 26–27.

71. See note 69 above.

72. See, e.g., S. Brock, "Studies in the Early History of the Syrian Orthodox Baptismal Liturgy," JTS, n.s. 23 (1972) pp. 16–64; G. Winkler, "The Original Meaning of the Prebaptismal Anointing and its Implications," *Worship* 52 (1978) pp. 24–45.

73. J. Schmitz, *Gottesdienst im altchristlichen Mailand. Theophaneia* 25 (Köln/Bonn 1975) p. 4.

74. Mansi, III. 656B.

75. See G. Kretschmar, "Beiträge zur Geschichte der Liturgie, insbe-

sondere der Taufliturgie, in Aegypten," *Jahrbuch für Liturgik und Hymnologie*, Band 8 (1963) p. 51.

76. Justin, *Apology* I, cc. 65–67.

77. W. Rordorf, *Sunday*, pp. 264–271.

78. The question of the authorship of the *Mystagogical Catecheses* need not concern us here, but one dimension of that question has hinged on the date accorded to the time of Egeria's description. The present state of research makes the date of the mystagogia consistent with the closing years of the episcopate of Cyril.

79. CC Lat. CLXXV.1–26.

80. Paul Devos, "Egérie à Bethléem. Le 40e jour après Pâques à Jérusalem en 383," *Analecta Bollandiana* 86 (1968) pp. 87–108.

81. F. C. Conybeare, *Rituale Armenorum* (Oxford 1905) Appendix II, pp. 507–527.

82. Renoux, *Le codex.*

83. M. Tarchnischvili, *Le grand lectionnaire de l'Eglise de Jérusalem.* CSCO 188, *Scriptores Iberici* 9 (Louvain 1959).

84. A. Papadopoulos-Kerameus, "Typikon tēs en Hierosolymois ekklesias," *Analecta Hierosolymetikēs Stachyologias* II (St. Petersburg 1894) pp. 1–254. A useful English-language description of this and the other documents mentioned may be found in Gabriel Bertonière, *The Historical Development of the Easter Vigil and Related Services in the Greek Church.* OCA 193 (Rome 1972) pp. 7–20.

85. Gregory Dix, *The Shape of the Liturgy* (New York 1982) Chapter XI. The continuing impact of Dix's assessment of the central role of Cyril in the development of the liturgical year was still evident thirty years after the publication of his major work in the *Academisch Proefschrift* of Karel Deddens, *Annus Liturgicus? Een onderzoek naar de betekenis van Cyrillus van Jerusalem voor de ontwikkeling van het 'kerkelijk jaar'* (Goes 1975). The author is concerned there to oppose the liturgical year to the theology and spirituality of the New Testament and, on that ground, to resist ecumenically inspired initiatives to restore the liturgical year in the Reformed tradition.

86. T. Talley, "History and Eschatology in the Primitive Pascha," *Worship* 47 (1973) pp. 212–221; Robert Taft, "Historicism Revisited," *Liturgical Time: Papers Read at the 1981 Congress of Societas Liturgica* (Rotterdam 1982) pp. 97–109.

87. This description of the Constantinian constructions at Calvary follows the reconstruction of Charles Coüasnon, *The Church of the Holy Sepulchre in Jerusalem. The Schweich Lectures of the British Academy, 1972* (London 1974). See also E. D. Hunt, *Holy Land Pilgrimage in the Later Roman Empire, A.D. 312–460* (Oxford 1982) chapter 1.

88. Epiphanius, *De mensuris et ponderibus* 54c. PG 43.251. Syriac text ed. J. E. Dean (Chicago 1935) p. 30.

89. John Wilkinson, *Egeria's Travels to the Holy Land*, rev. ed. (Jerusalem 1981) p. 39.

90. Eusebius, *Vita Constantini* 9.41–42 (PG 20.1369f.).

91. Eusebius, *Demonstratio Evang.* 6.18 (PG 22.457). *The Acts of John* 97, 102, in M. R. James, *The Apocryphal New Testament* (Oxford 1924) pp. 254, 256.

92. J. Wilkinson, *Egeria's Travels to the Holy Land*, rev. ed. p. 51. Note 4 cities Jerome, *Comm. in Zeph.* 1.15. Cf. E. D. Hunt, op. cit. (note 87 above) p. 143 and n. 75.

93. Egeria, 33. Cf. Renoux, *Le codex*, II.XXXVI, p. 261.

94. Renoux, *Le codex*, II, p. 265.

95. Ibid., n. 3.

96. Ibid., p. 311, n. 8.

97. Egeria, 35.2.

98. Renoux, *Le codex*, II. XXXIX bis, p. 269. Note 1 reports that Hesychius is the oldest testimony to the association of Sion with the institution of the eucharist.

99. Ibid., XXXVIII, p. 265. Egeria, 29.6.

100. Hermanus Schmidt, *Hebdomada Sancta. Volumen Alterum* (Rome 1957) pp. 791–796.

101. Renoux, *Le codex*, II. p. 363.

102. Egeria, 37.8.

103. See Gabriel Bertonière, *The Historical Development of the Easter Vigil and Related Services in the Greek Church.* OCA 193 (Rome 1972) pp. 29–58; also Gabriele Winkler, "Einige Randbemerkungen zum österlichen Gottesdienst in Jerusalem vom 4. bis 8. Jahrhundert," OCP 39.2 (1973) pp. 483f.

104. Bertonière, op. cit., 59–62.

105. J. W. Etheridge, *The Targums of Onkelos and Jonathan ben Uzziel on the Pentateuch, with Fragments of the Jerusalem Targum* (New York 1968) pp. 480–481; cf. G. Vermes, *Scripture and Tradition in Judaism* (Leiden 1961) pp. 216–217.

106. *Jubilees* 18 puts the sacrifice of Isaac on the 15th day of the first month (and on Mount Zion), and the event is commemorated annually in a festival of seven days. On the basis of that and other texts, many writers have understood the haggadic tradition regarding the *Akedah* (Binding) of Isaac — a consummated expiatory sacrifice as basis of the entire temple cultus — to have been a prechristian model for Christian soteriology. For the *Akedah* tradition, see Sholem Spiegel, *The Last Trial* (New York 1967). For a critical review of the literature on the historical origins of that tradition (and argument for a date in the Amoraic period) see Bruce Chilton, "Isaac and the Second Night: A Consideration," *Biblica* 61 (1980) pp. 78–88. An early dating for the tradition is accepted by Robert J. Daly, *Christian Sacrifice. Studies in Christian Antiquity* 18 (Washington, D.C. 1978) pp. 175–186.

107. F. C. Burkitt, *The Early Syriac Lectionary System. Proceedings of the British Academy*, XI; G. Morin edited the *Liber Comicus* from Paris B.N., nouv. acq. lat. 2171 in the first volume of *Anecdota Maredsolana* in 1893, but

the appointments are presented more conveniently in DACL V².266; P. Salmon, *Le lectionnaire de Luxeuil* (Rome 1944). (Also in DACL V².275); the *Comes* of Murbach (Besançon, Municipal Library, ms. 184) was edited and studied by A. Wilmart in *Rev. bénédictine* 30 (1913) 25–96 (in DACL V².317f.).

108. Cat. Lect. 18.33 (NPNF, II. Vol. VII, 142).

109. Egeria, 39.2.

110. Renoux, *Le codex*, II. LII ter, p. 327.

111. A. Renoux, "Les catéchèses mystagogiques dans l'organisation liturgique hiérosolymitaine du IVe et du Ve siècle," Mus. 78 (1965) pp. 355–359.

112. P. Devos, "La date du voyage d'Egérie," *Analecta Bollandiana* 85 (1967) pp. 165–194. The following year Devos published a further paper (note 80 above), in which he shows that the liturgical year she describes was 383.

113. Renoux, *Le codex*, II. p. 311, n. 8.

114. Hansjörg Auf der Maur, *Die Osterhomilien des Asterios Sophistes. Trierer theologische Studien* 19 (Trier 1967) pp. 71–73.

115. Ibid., 26.

116. Julius and Hildegard Levy, "The Origin of the Week and the Oldest West Asiatic Calendar," *Hebrew Union College Annual* XVII (1942–1943) pp. 1–152.

117. J. van Goudoever, "The Significance of the Counting of the Omer," *Jewish Background of the New Testament* (Assen, Holland n.d.) pp. 64–86.

118. Jubilees VI.1–17; XIV.1–20.

119. E. Lohse, art., "Pentēkostē," TDNT VI, esp. pp. 48f.

120. W. Schubart and C. Schmidt, eds., *Praxeis Paulou* (Hamburg 1936) p. 1, 30–32. (Cited in Cabié, *La Pentecôte*, p. 38, n. 2).

121. R. Cabié, *La Pentecôte*, p. 182.

122. Cited in Cabié, op. cit., p. 183, n. 1.

123. J. van Goudoever, *Biblical Calendars* (Leiden 1959) pp. 130–138. This feast of Mid-Pentecost has been more thoroughly studied in an unpublished dissertation (No. 180) at *Pontificio Istituto Orientale* in Rome, to which the Secretary graciously afforded access: Georgius Gharib, *La Fête byzantine de la Mesopentecôte. Thèse de Doctorat in sciences Ecclésiastiques Orientales. Pontificium Institutum Orientalium Studiorum* (Roma 1964). That the feast had appeared by the end of the fourth century is shown by a Ps.-Chrysostomian homily now assigned to Amphilochius of Iconium (PG 60.763-766; PG 39.119-130).

124. Cabié, op. cit., p. 184. Note 1 gives the citation from Mansi, II.1316.

125. S. Salaville, "La *Tessarakosté* au Ve canon de Nicée," *Echos d'Orient* 13 (1910) pp. 65–72; 14 (1911) pp. 355–357; "La *Tessarakosté*, Ascension et Pentecôte au IVe siècle," *Echos d'Orient* 28 (1929) pp. 257–271.

126. Cabié, op. cit., p. 183, n. 2.

127. Ibid., p. 184.

128. A. Renoux, *Le codex*, I, pp. 72–73.

129. See note 80 above.

130. Patrick Regan, "The Fifty Days and the Fiftieth Day," *Worship* 55 (1981) pp. 194–218, esp. p. 210.

131. Cabié, *La Pentecôte*, pp. 133–142.

132. Georg Kretschmar, "Himmelfahrt und Pfingsten," *Zeitschrift für Kirchengeschichte*, Folge IV, Band 66.3 (1954–1955) pp. 209–253.

133. Jean Daniélou, "Grégoire de Nysse et l'origine de la fête de l'Ascension," *Kyriakon: Festschrift Johannes Quasten*,II (Münster Westfalen 1970) pp. 663–666.

134. Cited in Cabié, *La Pentecôte*, p. 188, from J. Lemarié, "Homélies inédites de saint Chromace d'Aquilée," *Revue bénédictine* 72 (1962) pp. 201–277.

135. CXL [112].2. CC Lat. IX, p. 304.

136. CXLIX [121].3. CC Lat. IX, p. 312.

137. J. Schmitz, *Gottesdienst im altchristlichen Mailand. Theophaneia* 25 (Köln/Bonn 1975) p. 236, and note 22.

138. *La Pentecôte*, chap. III.

139. CC Lat. IX, p. 312.

140. DACL 14², cols. 2459–2461.

141. Cabié, *La Pentecôte*, p. 255.

142. So, e.g., Canon 17 of the Synod of Tours in 567 (See K. Holl, "Die Entstehung der vier Fastenzeiten in der griechischen Kirche," *Gesammelte Aufsätze zur Kirchengeschichte, II*, pp. 191–192).

143. PL 54.398A.

Part Two

The Day of His Coming

Maranatha. That exclamation, transliterated from the Aramaic in
1 Corinthians 16.22, figured significantly in primitive Christian
spirituality, and, as is clear from its occurrence in *Didache* 10, in
primitive Christian liturgy as well. Like the Greek term, *parousia*, to
which it is closely related, it has a double meaning. The double
meaning of *parousia*, as we shall see, is simply a matter of interpretation. In the case of "maranatha," however, the problem is one of
grammar. The term as preserved in 1 Corinthians and in *Didache*,
transliterated into Greek characters, appears as a single, unbroken
word. In Aramaic (and Syriac) it is two words, *marana tha*, a form
of imperative force oriented toward the future, "Come, our Lord."
However, that Greek transliteration could as easily present the perfect form expressive of a completed event in the past, *maran atha*,
"our Lord has come." This dual meaning, examined closely by
Dom Botte at the liturgical week of the *Institut Saint-Serge* in 1965,[1]
is crucial for our understanding of the second pole of the liturgical year, the celebration/expectation of the coming of Christ,
a theme extended in current western liturgical practice over
the many weeks that comprise the Advent–Christmas–Epiphany
cycle.

In the closing weeks of the time after Pentecost in the western
Church today there is a growing emphasis on the consummation of
history, which comes to something of a climax on the final Sunday,
the feast of Christ the King. This leads into the season of Advent,
itself focused upon the coming of the Redeemer. The first of the
four Sundays of that season is concerned with the final parousia,
while the second and third focus on the Forerunner's promise of
Messiah's coming. In the recent reforms, the fourth Sunday is
given to the reading of accounts of the annunciation, followed in

the succeeding week by the festival of the nativity of the Redeemer. In the four weeks of Advent, in other words, the meaning of the coming of the Messiah shifts from the expectation of the consummation of history itself to preparation for the nativity of the Savior, a preparation expressed on the final Sunday in the reading of the account of the incarnation event itself, the taking of flesh in the womb of Mary, fulfilled in the celebration of his nativity on December 25. Twelve days later the Church celebrates the festival of the Epiphany, which has, as we shall see, an uncommonly rich themeology, and the name of the feast itself is closely linked with the notion of *parousia* (cf. 2 Thessalonians 2.8).

In all this, it is clear that the Advent/Epiphany complex is a time of beginning that carries with it a strong note of eschatological expectation. In ritual cycles, the beginning and end times meet, and the liturgical year is no exception. It is with the Sundays of Advent that our liturgical books have long begun the year, an extension of the earlier custom of placing liturgical provisions for the vigil of Christmas before those for the feast. At Rome in 336 it is clear that the nativity itself, December 25, was considered the beginning of the liturgical year, and still earlier in the eastern empire the same was true of the Epiphany.

While the earliest stratum of this Christian festal complex seems to be older than had been supposed in such works as those of Usener and Botte,[2] there can be no doubt that these festivals that mark the beginning of the year are secondary developments, subsequent to and (we shall be concerned to argue) dependent upon the original Christian annual observance, Pascha. As we observed in Part One, the expectation of the parousia was often wedded to the Christian Passover, as it had been to the Jewish.

Such eschatological expectation, however, should not be taken for simple prediction of the future. Rather, it was a dimension of Jewish chronology and of the understanding of festival as the fulcrum of the year. The notion of a "New Year" is always in fact more ambiguous than we suppose, and we recognize a number of points at which the year turns. The civil New Year's Day is January 1 now, although in England it was March 25 through the first half of the eighteenth century. In addition, there are many other points from which the year is measured, the fiscal year, the academic year, the liturgical year, the years of our lives measured from the day of our birth. Any of these is likely in certain respects to be considered an end time and a new beginning.

1. CREATION AND FINAL REDEMPTION IN JEWISH FESTIVAL

In Judaism at the beginning of our era, we have noted, two points were especially important as turnings of the year, the months of Nisan and Tishri, and both creation and eschatological expectation were associated with each and with the festivals that fell at the full moons of those months.

The New Testament assures us repeatedly that none can know the time of that final act of the mystery of redemption, and the rabbinic sources are equally cautious. Nonetheless, eschatological expectation appears as an important element in the content of festivals associated with the turning of the year, and it is as such that Passover was urged as the time of the parousia, expressed as the sure time of Messiah's coming.

Other rabbinic sources reveal the alternative time for that final redemption. Tractate *Rosh Hashanah* relates a dispute between Rabbi Eliezer and Rabbi Joshua around the beginning of the second century. R. Joshua held:

"In Nisan the world was created; in Nisan the Patriarchs were born; on Passover Isaac was born; on New Year Sarah, Rachel and Hannah were visited; on New Year Joseph went forth from prison; on New Year the bondage of our ancestors ceased in Egypt; and in Nisan they will be redeemed in time to come."[3]

R. Eliezer, by contrast, said:

"In Tishri the world was created; in Tishri the Patriarchs were born; in Tishri the Patriarchs died; on Passover Isaac was born; on New Year Sarah, Rachel and Hannah were visited; on New Year Joseph went forth from prison; on New Year the bondage of our ancestors in Egypt ceased; in Nisan they were redeemed and in Tishri they will be redeemed in the time to come."[4]

In the following text, R. Eliezer argues further to defend his view, point by point. There he further specifies his disagreement with R. Joshua, again placing the coming redemption in Tishri.

" 'On New Year the bondage of our ancestors ceased in Egypt.' It is written in one place, *And I will bring you out from under the burdens of the Egyptians,* and it is written in another place, *I removed his shoulder from the burden.* 'In Nisan they were delivered,' as Scripture recounts. 'In Tishri they will be delivered in the time to come.' This is learnt from the two occurrences of the word 'horn.' It is written in one place, *Blow the horn on the new moon,* and it is written in another place, *In that day a great horn shall be blown.*"

More is involved in all this discussion than simply the date of the coming redemption. The teaching here reveals two important matters: first, time is thought of as a series of integral years so that the day of creation and the day of final redemption are the same, and on that same basis the births and deaths of the patriarchs are placed on the same day; second, there is evident a disagreement about the month in which creation occurred, and therefore the month which marks the turning of the year. According to R. Eliezer, that turning of the year is in the autumn. For R. Joshua, on the other hand, creation began in the spring, whence Nisan had been called the first of the months of the year. *Rosh Hashanah* 12a suggests that R. Joshua's dating of the annual cycles from Nisan prevailed: "Our Rabbis taught: 'The wise men of Israel follow R. Eliezer in dating the Flood and R. Joshua in dating the annual cycles.' " In spite of that, again, the Mishnah under discussion in this first chapter of the tractate makes Tishri the month from which years are marked.

"There are four New Years. On the first of Nisan is the New Year for Kings and for festivals. On the first of Elul is the New Year for the tithe of cattle. R. Eleazar and R. Simeon, however, place this on the first of Tishri. On the first of Tishri is the New Year for years, for release and jubilee years, for plantation and for [tithe of] vegetables."

The designation of the first spring month as "Nisan" derives, as do the other month names, from the Babylonian calendar. Even before the adoption of that Babylonian name, however, the month with which spring began had been taken to be the first month of a year based on the Babylonian lunar calendar, its months numbered rather than named. That calendar was adopted in Israel, evidently, in the seventh century, but after the reign of Josiah. Deuteronomy 16.1 still uses the old Canaanite name for the opening month of spring, Abib.[5]

Prior to this seventh-century adoption of the Babylonian lunar calendar beginning in the spring, there is evidence of a turning of the year in the autumn, in the month later called Tishri. This was the month of the great feast of Ingathering, later to be called Tabernacles, Booths, or *Sukkoth*. Exodus 23.16 speaks of that festival as occurring at the "going out" of the year, and Exodus 34.22 also places the festival at the turning of the year (*tequphath hashshanah*). That was all changed, of course, by the adoption of the Babylonian calendar beginning in the spring, yet something of that ancient role of the month of Tishri continued, and it must be this tradition that is reflected in the teaching of R. Eliezer, teaching that continued to reflect the earlier preeminence of the feast of Tabernacles as the day of creation and the day on which the promised one would bring to completion the redemption of Israel, however strong the later tradition that bound those limits of history to the Passover in the month of Nisan. That disagreement lies beyond our concerns, but it is important that there was a significant alternative to paschal expectation of the parousia in the first centuries of the Common Era, and that the Jewish calendar beginning with the first day of Tishri bears continuing testimony to that alternative.

2. EXPECTATION OF THE PAROUSIA IN EARLY CHRISTIANITY

B. Lohse, in his significant study of the Quartodeciman Pascha,[6] argued that the difference between that form of paschal observance and the Sunday Pascha was that the latter was a celebration of the resurrection, while the Quartodeciman Pascha was focused entirely on eschatological expectation. That difference has been shown to be false, but his characterization of the Quartodeciman Pascha is also seriously oversimplified. His argument rested primarily on a somewhat contrived reconstruction of chapter 17 of *Epistula Apostolorum*, in which he sought to make the original form of that text announce the parousia at Passover. In fact, as is clear in the edition of Duensing (cited by Lohse on p. 15 of his study), Christ's an-

nouncement of the parousia places it between Pentecost and the
following Passover. The text of the Ethiopic version on which
Lohse (pp. 78f.) attempted to build his reconstruction of the original is itself erroneous due, evidently, to a misprint in the text as
presented by Wajnberg in the massive study of that document by
Carl Schmidt. Schmidt notes that one would expect the parousia
within the paschal Pentecost and says of the peculiarity of situating
that event outside the paschal period, "what motive has moved the
author to this time determination is his secret, as it remains generally unclear whether a more definite time was really in his mind."[7]

Nonetheless, in light of the ambiguity regarding the beginning
of the year that we have seen in the Judaism of the period, we
probably should not preclude the possibility that the writer of *Epistula Apostolorum* is reflecting in the second half of the second century an emerging custom of situating the turning of the year at a
pole other than Pascha. If that pole opposite Pascha were a more or
less definite time, it would be a custom of such late appearance
that one could not, without patent anachronism, ascribe it to the
risen Christ who addresses the apostles in that text. However, one
cannot argue to such a conclusion from the text alone. All that appears from chapter 17 of *Epistula Apostolorum* is that its second-
century author did not attach eschatological expectation to Passover or to the paschal Pentecost. That consummate coming (*adven-
tus* in the fifth/sixth-century Latin fragments of the text) would
fall between the day of Pentecost and the feast of Unleavened
Bread.

By the time of the writing of *Epistula Apostolorum*, of course, parousia had already the familiar double meaning that would prove so
important for homiletical and liturgical expression surrounding the
turning of the year: the coming of Christ at the consummation of
history, but also his first coming in the flesh at the incarnation.
Irenaeus repeatedly uses the term in the latter sense,[8] and Justin
Martyr wrote:

"For the prophets have proclaimed two advents [*parousias*] of His:
the one, that which is already past, when He came as a dishonoured and suffering Man; but the second, when, according to
prophecy, He shall come from heaven with glory, accompanied by
His angelic host. . . ."[9]

Justin refers neither of these, let alone both, to any particular point in the year, but at Rome both will continue to surround the Christian observance at the end of December as that emerges. By the fifth century, that festival is within the full light of history in the West and in much of the East, and, together with the feast of the Epiphany, constitutes the second pole of the liturgical year. Indeed, one or the other of these festivals was viewed as the beginning of that liturgical year that reached its central climax at Pascha.

3. THE EARLIEST EVIDENCE FOR CHRISTMAS

Our earliest documentary evidence for the observance of the nativity of Christ on December 25 shows it to be such a turning point of the liturgical year. This document is the Chronograph of 354, an almanac presenting (inter alia) lists of Roman holidays, consuls, city prefects, and two lists of burial dates, one of Roman bishops and another of martyrs, with the indication of the cemeteries in each case.[10] Both of these burial lists are in calendrical order, not historical order, and the first date given in the *Depositio Martyrum* is December 25, "VIII kal. Ian. natus Christus in Betleem Iudee." In the *Depositio Episcoporum* the first date is that for the burial of Dionysius in the cemetery of Callistus, "VI kal. Ianuarias," December 27. The list proceeds through two other depositions in late December and continues through the months of the year in normal calendrical order to the notice of the burial of Eutychianus on December 8.

That notice is followed, however, by those of the burials of two other bishops, not in calendrical order, the first in October and the second in April. The first of these notices is that of the burial of Marcus, who died in 336; the second is of Julius, who died in 352. Since these notices fall outside the calendrical order and are in historical order (although the years of the bishops' burials are not given), it may be safely concluded that the original calendar was prepared in 336, after the burial of Sylvester on December 31, 335, and that the notices for Marcus and Julius were subsequent additions to that original calendar. That calendar ran, as did the *Depositio Martyrum*, from December 25 to December 25, the date to which the martyrs' list assigns the nativity of Christ at Bethlehem. From 336, then, we may say that at Rome the nativity of Christ on December 25 marked the beginning of the liturgical year.

That is the earliest clear and certain datum for the festival of the nativity. Can we get behind it? Hippolytus, we noted in Part One, took March 25 to be the actual date of the passion. This datum, recorded in the tables carved on the statue discovered in the sixteenth century near Porta Tiburtina, is repeated in Hippolytus' *Commentary on Daniel* 4.23, where the text notes as well that the nativity occurred on Wednesday, December 25. One manuscript, the oldest (tenth century), includes as well the curious phrase *pro tessaron aprilion*, just preceding that date. If the reference to December 25 represents an emendation of the manuscripts, this added phrase in the oldest of them may well be fragmentary evidence of the original reading.

The commentary has been known in fragments since the seventeenth century, but the complete work became available only in the nineteenth century and received its critical edition from Bonwetsch in 1897.[11] In that same year, Hilgenfeld offered the opinion that the reference to December 25 was a subsequent interpolation.[12] Louis Duchesne admitted the text to be of doubtful authenticity,[13] and that assessment seems to have been shared by most patrologists. More recently, Jean Michel Hanssens has provided a slightly simplified but thoroughgoing analysis of the important manuscript data.[14] Hanssens, himself convinced of the inauthenticity of the text, finally left the question just barely open. However, there seems no basis at present on which we can depend on the fourth book of Hippolytus' *Commentary on Daniel* for help in establishing the origin of the feast of the nativity of Christ on December 25.

A rather more useful observation was made by Gottfried Brunner in 1936 and repeated by Hans Lietzmann in his *History of the Early Church*.[15] These noted that Augustine, in an Epiphany sermon (Sermon 202), says that the Donatists, having despised the unity of the Church, do not celebrate "with us" the feast of the Epiphany.

"With good reason have the heretical Donatists never wished to celebrate this day with us: they neither love unity, nor are they in communion with the Eastern Church where that star appeared. Let us, however, celebrate the Manifestation of our Lord and Savior Jesus Christ on which He harvested the first fruits of the Gentiles, in the unity of the Gentiles."[16]

This sermon makes it clear that the festival in question is the celebration of the visit of the Magi. Augustine makes no similar claim against the Donatists with regard to Christmas, however, neither in that sermon nor in any other, a peculiar circumstance given the greater importance of the nativity itself. Since in North Africa as at Rome it seems certain that Christmas was established before the Epiphany, one is left with the strong sense that the Donatists did celebrate Christmas. In such a case, that festival must antedate the Donatist schism, and the date of its establishment would thus be earlier than 311. Indeed, some have supposed that its observance could date from as early as 300 or even earlier and that the place of the origin of the festival could well have been North Africa, rather than Rome as has most commonly been presumed.[17]

4. CHRISTMAS AND THE HISTORY OF RELIGIONS

A date before 312 would place Christmas prior to the Church's enjoyment of the protection of Constantine, and that would set the most frequently encountered explanation of the origin of Christmas in a new and more problematic context. That most common explanation has been, and probably is today, the derivation of the feast of the nativity from a Roman pagan festival on the winter solstice, set on December 25 in the Julian calendar at its institution in 45 B.C.

It would be difficult to find in the ancient world a religious tradition that was not sensitive to the movements of the sun, and of other celestial bodies as well. That this was true of Judaism, for example, is shown by the well-known zodiac mosaic of the synagogue of Beth Alpha. While the spring equinox may have generated more religious symbolism (and perhaps more religious fervor) than the other quarter-tense days, it is by no means difficult to discern the religious response to the winter solstice in the literary and monumentary remains of the beginning of our era. The civic festivals, the rites of the various mysteries, Judaism, and Christianity all manifest in their several ways their sensitivity to the changing of the seasons. Behind this sensitivity surely lies a tradition that had its origins in agricultural concerns, but this sensitivity went beyond the concerns of the farmer. Humanity itself exists in a temporal frame of which the turning of the seasons is a particularly eloquent sign. We cannot oppose Christian belief in a transcendent deity to pagan veneration of nature itself in such a way as to imply that Christians were insensitive to natural phenomena such as the changing seasons. While it seems likely that the first generation of Christians invested relatively little energy in chronological computations, standing as they did in expectation of the imminent consummation of history, the break between Christians and the synagogues during the final decade of the first century entailed isolation from the necessary authoritative intercalation of the lunar calendar, now regulated by the Babylonian sages. Therefore, with that break came dependence on the Julian solar calendar, which would lead to the determination of solar equivalents of old lunar dates such as Passover, and also a heightened awareness of the turning of the seasons, as marked by the quarter-tense days, the solstices and equinoxes.

From the time of Paul Ernst Jablonski and the Bollandist Jean Hardouin, both in the eighteenth century, it has been common to account for the Christian celebration of the nativity of Christ on December 25 as a Christian adaptation of the Roman winter solstice festival, the *Natalis solis invicti*. That festival was established on December 25 by the emperor Aurelian in A.D. 274, and it seems likely that the same date was the occasion of Aurelian's dedication of a temple to the sun god in the Campus Martius.

The cult of the sun was not, of course, first introduced to Rome by Aurelian. In his study of *The Cult of Sol Invictus*, Gaston Halsberghe has traced earlier manifestations of sun worship at Rome.[18] Contending against Wissowa and others that there was at Rome an autochthonous sun cult, independent of Greek influence, he cites festivals marking the dedication of two temples. In *Fasti* of the first century B.C., there is the indication against the date of August 9: *Soli indigiti in colle Quirinali*. It was here on the Quirinal that the indigenous Roman sun cult was focused, maintained by the *gens Aurelia*. Again, following his conquest in Egypt, Augustus sent to Rome two obelisks, which were set up and dedicated to the sun. One of these was placed in the Circus Maximus, where the chariot races were under the protection of the sun (for the *quadrigae*, four-horse teams) and the moon (for the *bigae*). At Circus Maximus there was also a temple of the sun, the festival of its foundation on August 28. This indigenous sun cult at Rome does not seem to have been especially sensitive to the winter solstice or to any of the other quarter days. The second obelisk was set up in the Campus Martius, but there is no indication of the relation of that obelisk to the later temple built in the eastern part of that area by Aurelian.

That autochthonous cult of Sol fell into eclipse at Rome in the second Christian century, and eastern sun cults, Mithraism and the cult of *Sol Invictus Elagabal*, came to predominate. Neither of those cults has been shown to have supported a public festival on the day of the winter solstice, however, and the distinctive importance of that day must be assigned finally to the attempt of Aurelian to refound the cult of *Sol Invictus* as a genuinely Roman religion, by contrast to the bizarre (by Roman standards) orientalism of the Syrian *Sol Invictus Elagabal*, brought to Rome by the adolescent Heliogabalus as emperor. Indeed, Halsberghe, without suggesting that there was already a Christian festival on December 25, presents the probability that one item in Aurelian's religious agenda was the provision of an authentically Roman alternative to the increasingly successful Christian mission. What seems clear is that his cult of *Sol Invictus* was promulgated, in the words of Henry Chadwick, "as a comprehensive monotheism which could embrace all the cults of the empire,"[19] a religious component of the program for restoration of the unity of the empire that earned Aurelian the epithet "Restorer of the World." The syncretistic threat posed by Aurelian's solar monotheism was the single disruption of the peaceable circumstances in which the Church found herself between the extension of toleration by Gallienus (260–261) and the beginning of Diocletian's persecution in 303.

Given the well-documented devotion of Constantine to the cult of the sun, exemplified, inter alia, by his dedication of his life to Apollo while on the way to his encounter with Maxentius at Ponte Milvio, it is easy to believe that his reign would allow a blending of solar and Christian pieties. A devotee of *Sol Invictus* like his father before him, it is virtually certain that Constantine's restrictions upon certain occupations on Sunday had little to do with the Christian significance of that day, and was rather an expression of his own solar piety. That same influence surely enhanced the popularity of the festival of December 25, but if Sunday was observed by Christians prior to Constantine, we must allow the question of whether that was not true as well of the festival of December 25.

If we take the point of Brunner and Lietzmann and place the establishment of the nativity of Christ on December 25 prior to the Donatist schism, and therefore prior to Constantine's victory over Maxentius and the ensuing protection of the Church, it becomes much more difficult to understand the adoption by a still only tentatively tolerated Church of a relatively new pagan festival, a festival observed for only around a quarter century, and one that had had significant counter-Christian associations. The likelihood of such adoption of Aurelian's festival would surely become still more remote after the beginning of Diocletian's persecution in 303. Given the slight space between the end of that persecution and the troubles leading into the Donatist schism, we must, if we suppose that the Donatists continued to observe the nativity on December 25, view with a much more cautious eye the standard explanation that the nativity of Christ on December 25 is only a Christian adoption of the pagan Roman *Dies natalis solis invicti.* Even if adapted to be the *natalis solis iustitiae,* such a festival would nonetheless represent the Church's accommodation to less than friendly imperial religious sentiment, however successfully bent to the uses of the gospel.

That association of Christ with the "sun of righteousness" of Malachi 4.2 was by no means only a function of the establishment of the nativity of Christ on the winter solstice. The popularity of that text was assured both by its eschatological content and by the association of the resurrection with dawn. In fact, we have an important text that associates Malachi 4.2 with the birth of Jesus from the time before the establishment of Aurelian's festival. This is the opusculum *De pascha computus* spuriously ascribed to Cyprian. The work, which seeks to correct the paschal tables of Hippolytus, was issued in 243, probably in North Africa. As did Hippolytus, the author takes March 25 to be the historical date of the passion, a Friday that was also the fourteenth day of the moon. That date being Pascha (and also the spring equinox), the author takes it to be also the first day of creation. It was only on the fourth day, however, that the sun and moon were created; therefore, the incarnation, assigned to Wednesday, March 28, coincides with the creation of the sun.

"O how admirable and divine is the providence of the Lord, that on that day on which the sun was made on the same day was

Christ born, the fifth of the kalends of April, the fourth day of the week, and so rightly did the prophet Malachi say to the people: 'the sun of righteousness shall rise upon you, with healing in his wings.' "[20]

The author does not tell us the source of that March date for the nativity, but it is clear that he sees it already as *natalis solis iustitiae*, over three decades before the establishment at Rome of the *natalis solis invicti*. The appearance of *De pascha computus* in 243 probably establishes a *terminus post quem*, of course, for the observance of the nativity of Christ on December 25. If we suppose that that festival was kept by the Donatists, we may place its establishment between 243 and 311; otherwise, the *terminus ante quem* would be 336.

That association of Christ with the sun on the basis of the prophecy of Malachi, however, might be understood to encourage still further the Christian adoption of the festival of Aurelian once it was established. There can be no doubt that in time the association of the nativity of Christ with the day of *sol invictus* did occur, as we shall see. Whether it was that association that in the first instance suggested December 25 as the date of the nativity of Christ is another and more controverted question.

5. THE COMPUTATION OF THE NATIVITY FROM THE PASSION

An alternative explanation for the date of December 25 was presented by Louis Duchesne late in the last century. Noting that March 25 was taken as the historical date of the passion, he suggested that that same date's association with the annunciation was not based on computation backward from December 25 to the date of the conception, but was an aspect of the paschal date itself. We noted above in Part One, section 2, that the themes of Pascha included not only the passion and resurrection, but the incarnation itself, and quoted passages showing that theme in the *Peri Pascha* of Melito of Sardis. There, in all likelihood, the paschal date was April 6, and Duchesne suggested that such a paschal date (as noted for the Montanists by Sozomen) would put the nativity on January 6. As Duchesne put it, "fractions are imperfections which do not fall in with the demands of a symbolical system of numbers"; therefore the date of the death of Jesus would be taken as being that of his conception as well. To that hypothetical suggestion he added:

"This explanation would be the more readily received if we could find it fully stated in some author. Unfortunately we know of no text containing it, and we are therefore compelled to put it forward as an hypothesis, but it is an hypothesis which falls in with what we may call the recognized methods in such matters."[21]

He further wrote in the same place, "I would not venture to say, in regard to the twenty-fifth of December, that the coincidence of the *Sol novus* exercised no direct or indirect influence on the ecclesiastical decisions arrived at in regard to the matter."

Four years before Duchesne's death, André Wilmart published a study of the collection of thirty-eight Latin homilies spuriously ascribed to Chrysostom, one of which gives precise support to Duchesne's hypothesis, as Wilmart carefully noted.[22] That work is the tractate entitled *De solstitia et aequinoctia conceptionis et nativitatis domini nostri iesu christi et iohannis baptistae*, more briefly designated *De solstitiis et aequinoctiis* in the literature. Although it had been embedded in some of the very early printed editions of the works of Chrysostom, this tractate had remained relatively unknown and was clearly not known to Duchesne. Following that notice by Wilmart (which named an otherwise unknown Pontius Maximus as the author), the tractate received its standard edition by Bernard Botte, who included it as an appendix to his historical study of the origins of Christmas and Epiphany.[23]

Botte's study of the tractate showed that the Latin scripture citations in it contain variants peculiar to African authors, and he concluded that the work in its present form must have been produced there. In another instance, however, he recognized in the form of the angelic annunciation to Mary a clear semiticism, the substitution of *pax tecum* for the *chaire* of the Greek New Testament. *Pax tecum* is the Latin equivalent of *shlom lek* in the Peshitto.

Two decades after the appearance of Botte's edition, Hieronymus Engberding called attention to a further semiticism: in line 118 of Botte's edition we encounter the phrase, *metellitum sive scaenophegiam*, and in line 305, *scaenophegiae sive metellitidem*. These alternatives to *scaenophegia* (the Latinized form of the Greek term for "booths") are unknown in Latin; they are, on the contrary, rather clumsy transliterations of *metallē*, the Syriac term for the booths of the feast of Tabernacles. These semiticisms suggested to Engberding that the extant text is a North African Latin version of a work written in a Syriac-speaking region, most probably Palestine or Syria.[24]

That latter suggestion seems unlikely, however. The more probable explanation for those Syriac symptoms is simply that the Latin author had a Syrian (or at least Syriac) background. There is, in any case, good reason for doubting that the tractate was written in Syria. The document rests a good bit of its argument on Roman month names based on counting March as the first month, rather than April as was customary in Syria. March is here designated the first month because it is the month in which Pascha occurs, and Exodus 12.2 is cited; from this, therefore, *numeraremus et septimum septembrem et decimum decembrem.* (These month names, of course, are much older, dating from a time—perhaps the fifth century B.C.—when the Roman calendar had but ten months covering the agriculturally active part of the year and ignoring the rest.[25]) *Apostolic Constitutions* V.13.1, by contrast, orders the celebration of the nativity on the twenty-fifth day of the *ninth* month, revealing a tradition that associated the Pascha with April, making that the first month of Exodus 12.2. The paschal date in question here is surely that which we examined in Part One, April 6, adopted as the solar equivalent to 14 Nisan in the Asian calendar (Artemisios 14). It would be difficult indeed to fit the argument of *De solstitiis* into that Syrian environment, whatever its (probably African) author's semitic background.

A semitic background (however imprecise the author's treatment of Jewish liturgical times) could, perhaps, have contributed to a feature of *De solstitiis* and of Duchesne's "computation hypothesis" that has seemed to many to be contrived, namely, its setting the beginning and the end of Christ's earthly life on the same day. We have seen above that rabbinic thought had a tendency to set the births and deaths of the patriarchs on the same day, either Passover in Nisan or Tabernacles in Tishri. Still, *De solstitiis* represents a significant departure from that rabbinic habit of fixing the beginning and end on the same festival. Here all the four seasons are valorized in relation to the conceptions and births of the Forerunner and the Redeemer. The coincidence is not of Christ's birth and death, as with the patriarchs, but of his conception and death. The birth of Christ is nine months after that spring equinox, on the winter solstice.

The argument of *De solstitiis* begins, however, with the conception of the Baptist, identifying the time of the annunciation to Zechariah by reference to his priestly duties in connection with the festivals of Tishri. This sets the conception of the Baptist at the autumnal equinox, and that is the "historical" anchor of the entire scheme. That autumnal conception places the birth of John at the summer solstice. However, since Gabriel at the annunciation to Mary announced that Elizabeth was in the sixth month of her pregnancy (Luke 1.36), the conception of Jesus was six months from the Baptist's conception, that is, at the spring equinox. The birth of Jesus, therefore, was nine months later, at the winter solstice.

Of the occurrence of Christ's conception and death on the same day, the tractate expresses itself almost laconically, without labored argument:

"Therefore, our Lord was conceived on the eighth of the kalends of April in the month of March, which is the day of the passion of the Lord and of his conception. For on the day that he was conceived on the same he suffered."[26]

At that point, however, it quotes Exodus 34.25–26, which, in connection with Passover regulations, forbids boiling a kid in its mother's milk, since Christ, the Paschal Lamb, was immolated at the very time of his mother's lactation. It is interesting to find this text appealed to at this point, since the same image appears in a text of Augustine cited by Duchesne, *Quaestionum in Heptateuchum* II.90 (PL 34.629), as a late exemplification of the principle of his hypothesis.

The tractate has relatively little to say about the nativity of Jesus, apart from assigning that to the winter solstice, until toward the end of the work. Botte suggested that the purpose of the work was to aid in the promulgation of Christmas in Africa in the early years after its institution at Rome. That seems highly unlikely in view of the absence of reference to any Christian festival at any of the quarter days, and the modest attention given to the nativity itself.

The major discussion of the nativity of Jesus is in the following lines:

"But the Lord was born in winter, in the month of December, on the eighth of the kalends of January when the mature olives are pressed so that the ointment, that is *crisma*, is produced, to which yield other herbs are mixed; when the bleating lambs are born, the vine branches are cut back with the scythe so that the sweet vintage is brought forth from which the apostles were inebriated with the Holy Spirit: for he said, 'I am the vine and my Father the vinedresser; therefore every branch of mine that does not bear fruit is cut away and cast into the fire.' But also they call it the birthday of the unconquered. Who, surely, is so unconquered as our Lord who triumphed over conquered death? Assuredly, what they dedicate to be the birthday of the sun is himself the sun of righteousness of whom the prophet Malachi said: 'To you who fear his name the sun of righteousness shall rise and healing is in his wings.' "[27]

In contrast to the earlier appeal to that Malachi text in *De pascha computus*, here the *sol iustitiae* is identified with the *solis natalem* at the winter solstice, while Christ's victory over death identifies him as the *invictus* whose *natale* is this day. There is no explicit reference here to any public festival, but there is no reason to doubt that the text was written after the institution of Aurelian's *Dies natalis solis invicti*.

Given the equal or greater emphasis laid on the other quarter days, the summer solstice and the autumn and spring equinoxes, it is difficult to see this work as concerned solely or even primarily with the winter solstice. Further, if it does not take the starting point of its argument from the identification of the death date of the Lord with the day of his conception, nonetheless that notion is clearly and repeatedly stated and gives full substantiation to Duchesne's hypothesis. The computation of the day of Christ's nativity from that of his death and conception, and the historical validation of that conception date by computation from the annunciation of the conception of Elizabeth, all this is argued from biblical sources (however ill used) and without reference to pagan public celebrations.

At the same time, the solar theme already taken up in *De pascha computus* is here extended to reveal the four seasons of the annual

95

cycle as sacramental signs of the coming of the Messiah. It is no longer Pascha alone which gives significance to the year. The annual cycle, by the very turning of the seasons, speaks to the author of *De solstitiis* of the mysteries surrounding the incarnation: the conception of the Forerunner at the autumnal equinox and his birth at the summer solstice, the conception of the Redeemer at the spring equinox (the day of his passion) and his birth at the winter solstice. While there is no indication in the tractate that these times are observed as Christian festivals, all did come to be such and are such still, although the Conception of St. John is no longer observed in the West. That festival, normally observed on September 24, was celebrated at Constantinople on the previous day, September 23, the old beginning of the civil year at Constantinople and throughout Asia Minor. In the typikon of Hagia Sophia in the tenth century, the feast of the conception of the Baptist is still called "New Year," and marked the beginning of the course reading of the gospel of Luke, although the beginning of the civil year had been shifted to the beginning of September in the fifth century.

Augustine's awareness of this computation by identification of the day of Christ's death with that of his conception has already been noted above (*Quaest. in Heptateuchum* II.90), but he expresses it again in *De Trinitate* IV.5:

"Not without reason is the number six understood to be put for a year in the building up of the body of the Lord, as a figure of which he said that he would raise up in three days the temple destroyed by the Jews. For they said, 'Forty and six years was this temple in building.' And six times forty-six makes two hundred and seventy-six. And this number of days completes nine months and six days, which are reckoned, as it were, ten months for the travail of women; not because all come to the sixth day after the ninth month, but because the perfection itself of the body of the Lord is found to have been brought in so many days to the birth, as the authority of the church maintains upon the tradition of the elders. For he is believed to have been conceived on the 25th of March, upon which day also he suffered; so the womb of the Virgin, in which he was conceived, where no one of mortals was begotten, corresponds to the new grave in which he was buried, wherein was never man laid, neither before him nor since. But he was born, according to tradition, upon December the 25th. If, then, you reckon from that day to this you find two hundred and seventy-six days which is forty-six times six" (NPNF I.III, p. 74).

Both *De solstitiis* and these texts from Augustine take the date of the passion and conception to have been March 25. Other texts from the East, however, reveal vestiges of the similar association of these with April 6, the Quartodeciman paschal date reported by Sozomen for the Montanists. Chrysostom, in his sermon on the nativity (PG 49.351–362), a sermon preached on the December festival, reproduced the computation of the conception and birth dates of Christ from the conception of the Baptist, as we have seen it in *De solstitiis.* However, he does not refer to the solstices or equinoxes, and, significantly, presses the argument slightly (by twelve days?) to put the annunciation to Mary in April, the Antiochene Xanthikos (*Aprillios, hos esti Xanthikos*), which, we have noted on the basis of *Apostolic Constitutions* V.13, was remembered as the paschal "first" month in Syria. This slight variant in Chrysostom's presentation of the computation of Mary's conception from that of Elizabeth (PG 49.358) shows that Mary's conception was already associated with April, the paschal month, at the time when the nativity of Jesus was still assigned to January 6. Chrysostom's attempt to adopt the western computation of the nativity, rooted in the angelic announcement to Zechariah at the time of Tabernacles, should have brought Mary's conception to March. It is possible that his placing the conception in April rather than March reflects a distinct celebration of the annunciation on April 6. Chrysostom does not relate that month to the passion, however, beyond referring to it as the "first month." This bending of the computation to protect the association of the annunciation with April most probably reflects a vestige of the Asian fixed paschal date, April 6, although Chrysostom, of course, did not observe that Quartodeciman date.

Chrysostom, concerned primarily with the December nativity date, only alludes in passing to the conception in April. A text ascribed to Epiphanius, however, is more precise. This is a commentary on Luke preserved in an Armenian manuscript in the library of San Lazaro in Venice. Although the manuscript is late (1750),

Conybeare reported that the Armenian version is in the classical idiom of the fifth century, and, while allowing for interpolation by Armenian scribes, he supposed the ascription to Epiphanius to be genuine. Folio 74 builds the computation on the annunciation to Zechariah, as had Chrysostom and *De solstitiis*:

"Zachariah remained until the completion of the two feasts, twelve days, and it was on Tisri 22, on the fifth day of the week [that he fell dumb], and on the Friday (*urbath*) he went home and came in to his wife Elisabeth and she conceived at eventide of Urbath the lightgiving torch which was to precede the sun of righteousness. So that from that day until Nisan, the 6th of April there are 5 ½ months, a point set forth by the holy archangel when he said 'In the sixth month.' "

That text does not identify the day of Nisan according to the lunar cycle, but a preceding passage does associate the conception day with the Passover ritual, albeit with the *tenth* day of Nisan, the day for the selection and setting apart of the paschal lamb, according to Exodus 12.3:

"So then on the sixth of April according to calendarial art, and according to the lunar numbering of the Jews on the tenth of the moon, the day on which they shut up the lamb hidden with divine mystery, whence also by supernal command these two met on one and the same day, on the sixth of April, and the tenth of the moon, and the image of the day is Kyriakē, the lamb was shut up in the spotless womb of the holy virgin, he who took away and takes in perpetual sacrifice away the sins of the world."[28]

Epiphanius was a Palestinian, and his chronology of the passion, we may suppose, was rooted (as was that of Jerusalem) in the Matthean tradition, which placed the crucifixion on 15 Nisan, following the Passover eaten by Christ and the twelve in the night from Thursday to Friday. The identification of the tenth of Nisan with Sunday (*Kyriake*) in the above text would correspond to that pattern, putting 14 Nisan on Thursday. Such a synoptic passion chronology, of course, required a revision of the tradition rooted in the Quartodeciman Johannine chronology, which, Duchesne argued, had identified April 6 as the day of both the conception and the passion. Even where, as at Jerusalem, a different passion chronology was followed, that day continued to mark the annunciation, and the nativity was celebrated nine months later. In spite of that synoptic dating of the passion, Epiphanius in this text seeks to retain the relation of the annunciation to Passover. (Among the Armenians who preserve today much of the old Jerusalem calendar, the nativity of Christ is still celebrated on January 6, but the annunciation is now kept one day later than Epiphanius' date, on April 7.)

The argument for the western nativity date by computation from the annunciation to Zechariah at Yom Kippur was repeated again by Cosmas Indicopleustes in the sixth century (PG 88.196). While all of these testimonies are late, it is noteworthy that none of them refers to the coincidence of the conception days of the Forerunner and the Redeemer with the equinoxes. Indeed, those reflecting the oriental date for the conception of Christ (April 6) could hardly do so. Rather, taking Tabernacles (including Yom Kippur) as the time of the annunciation to Zechariah, they seek to establish the historical dates of the conception of the Forerunner and the conception and birth of Christ. While many of these texts relate Mary's conception date to Passover, the identification of that date with the crucifixion on 14 Nisan presumes the Johannine chronology, and we encounter variants in areas that follow the synoptic chronology.

In any case, the argument of these texts (apart from *De solstitiis*) is independent of solar symbolism. Nonetheless, given the traditional appeal to "the sun of righteousness" of Malachi 4.2 as we saw it already in *De Pascha Computus* and still in the commentary of Epiphanius just cited, it is not surprising that the western tradition of computation from the primitive paschal date, March 25, became suffused with solar symbolism.

6. SOLAR SYMBOLISM AT CHRISTMAS

If, however, this Christian solar symbolism is independent in its origins from Aurelian's cult of *Sol invictus*, and even if we suppose the festival of the nativity to have been established prior to the accession of Constantine, there is no doubt that the altered circumstances of the Church under his protection did bring about an interplay between Christian and pagan pieties such as has been taken to be the origin of Christmas by those who argue from the history of religions.

The tension between solar symbolism and the old solar worship is in full view in the preaching of Leo. On the one hand, he is sensitive to the astronomical significance of the solstice, and is appreciative of the natural change it marks. In the third of his sermons on the nativity (*Sermo XXIII*), he speaks of the delight afforded to unimpaired eyes by the light on this day as analogous to the joy given to sound hearts by the Savior's nativity (PL 54.199B). Again, in the sixth of those sermons (*Sermo XXVI*), he says:

"But this nativity which is to be adored in heaven and on earth is suggested to us by no day more than this, and by the new light, even now shining in its beginning, the splendor of this wonderful mystery (*sacramenti*) pours in upon our senses" (NPNF II.XII, p. 137).

On the other hand, Leo is uncompromising in his opposition to any confusion of the sun with its Creator. The second sermon on the nativity (*Sermo XXII*) attacks, "the pestilential notion of some to whom this our solemn feast day seems to derive its honour, not so much from the nativity of Christ as, according to them, from the rising of the new sun" (PL 54.198B). That this was not simply an attack on the absent faithless is indicated in the seventh nativity sermon (*Sermo XXVII*) where he rails against,

"the ungodly practice of certain foolish folk who worship the sun as it rises at the beginning of daylight from elevated positions: even some Christians think it is so proper to do this that, before entering the blessed Apostle Peter's basilica, which is dedicated to the One Living and true God, when they have mounted the steps which lead to the raised platform, they turn round and bow themselves towards the rising sun and with bent neck do homage to its brilliant orb. We are full of grief and vexation that this should happen, which is partly due to the fault of ignorance and partly to the spirit of heathenism: because although some of them do perhaps worship the Creator of that fair light rather than the light itself, which is his creature, yet we must abstain even from the appearance of this observance: for if one who has abandoned the worship of gods, finds it in our own worship, will he not hark back again to this fragment of his old superstition, as if it were allowable, when he sees it to be common both to Christians and to infidels?" (NPNF II.XII, p. 140).

In this, Leo shows no awareness of the considerable early Christian tradition for prayer toward the east. He, of course, presumably would be facing east during the liturgy at St. Peter's or the other major basilicas of Rome. The faithful, on the other hand, would not. While, therefore, the custom against which he vents his vexation may include an element from the old religion, it is entirely possible that among those who bowed toward the east before entering the basilica were Christians from other parts of the world who had mixed feelings about the Roman arrangement which put the altar at the west end of the nave. The old tradition of orientation in prayer is, of course, yet another example of solar symbolism in Christian spirituality, in this instance a tradition shared with the Essenes and rooted ultimately in the Old Testament, although abandoned by postexilic Judaism.[29] More to our point, however, is Leo's awareness of the pagan celebration of the sun on this day, and his opposition to whatever vestiges of that tradition that might yet live. He, at least, is witness against any suggestion that the festival of Christ's nativity is derived from that Roman festival.

Such derivation is first encountered in a Syriac gloss in the margin of a manuscript of Dionysius bar Salibi, a Syrian writer who died in 1171. That manuscript, first published by Assemani,[30] seems most likely to have been glossed after the original writer's death, therefore within the last three decades of the twelfth century. The unknown glossator is concerned to explain the reason for the transfer of the celebration of Christ's nativity from January 6 to December 25. He writes:

"The Lord was born in the month of January, on the day on which we celebrate the Epiphany; for the ancients observed the Nativity and the Epiphany on the same day, because he was born and baptized on the same day. Also still today the Armenians celebrate the two feasts on the same day. To these must be added the Doctors who speak at the same time of one and the other feast. The reason for which the Fathers transferred the said solemnity from the sixth of January to the twenty-fifth of December is, it is said, the following: it was the custom of the pagans to celebrate on this same day of the twenty-fifth of December the feast of the birth of the sun. To adorn the solemnity, they had the custom of lighting fires and they invited even the Christian people to take part in these rites. When, therefore, the Doctors noted that the Christians were won over to this custom, they decided to celebrate the feast of the true birth on this same day; the sixth of January they made to celebrate the Epiphany. They have kept this custom until today with the rite of lighted fire."

The text here has been translated from the French of Dom Botte,[31] one of the strong proponents of the derivation of Christmas from the *natalis invicti,* but he himself warns against drawing historical conclusions from such a late text and denies that it represents a genuine tradition going back to the origins of the feast. The fourth-century fathers who introduced the festival in the East, such as Chrysostom, were surely convinced that December 25 was, in fact, the historical date of Christ's birth, and they betray no awareness of any suggestion that the festival was derived from a pagan observance.[32]

As popular as that explanation of the origin of Christmas from a pagan festival has been in the scholarly literature of the past two centuries, we are still without any clear evidence that Leo's testimony is an attempt to alter the shape of a tradition or that there was a tradition which would be at variance with his testimony. There are many reasons why such a tradition might remain inaccessible to us, but it is important to remember that the more unqualified expressions of the derivation of the Christian feast from Aurelian's solstice festival are built finally on an unverified conjecture.

Although the derivation of Christmas from the *natalis solis invicti* rests upon conjecture, its popularity in the literature is neither surprising nor unaccountable. We must be impressed with the fact that there was a Roman public festival on December 25 by the time of our clear historical evidence for the Christian festival at the same place on that same date. That itself is a datum of no small significance, especially when we note the later evidence that associates the celebration of the nativity on December 25 specifically with the Roman church. The very precision of that attribution of the festival to the city where we also find the pagan festival's institution lends a degree of verisimilitude to the supposition of interplay between the two, which we cannot always accord to more generalized assertions regarding the derivation of other Christian festivals from much less well-defined pagan institutions.

If, for that reason, we should exercise caution in rejecting the "history of religions" hypothesis, we should not allow that caution to blind us to other data that are independent of the hypothesis. We have seen the fourth-century texts that identify the dates of the annunciation and the passion on March 25, that date assigned to the passion already in the early third century. We have seen also that the nativity date, nine months later, stands at the beginning of the liturgical year at Rome. Further, given the testimonies of *De solstitiis* and Augustine, both African sources, we should not allow the common association of the festival with Rome to exclude from further study the possibility that its first home was North Africa.[33]

7. SOLAR FESTIVALS IN EGYPT

The hypothesis that the festival of the nativity at Rome was derived from a local solar festival on the same date has been applied as well to the closely related festival of the Epiphany on January 6, the older festival of the nativity in the eastern churches. By contrast to the Roman and African testimonies for Christmas, the more frequently cited evidences for the Epiphany come from Egypt, and it has often been suggested that it was there that the festival originated. We shall leave to one side for the moment the earliest Egyptian testimony since it concerns a specifically Christian observance. To examine the relation of the Christian festival of January 6 to non-Christian festivities, we must look to the later fourth-century writings of Epiphanius, the Bishop of Salamis on Cyprus from 367 to his death in 403.

Prior to his election as metropolitan of Cyprus, Epiphanius had been for over thirty years the head of a monastery which he had himself founded at Eleutheropolis in Judea ca. 335. That village was Epiphanius' home, but prior to the founding of his monastery there (at about age 20), he had spent some time in Egyptian monasteries. He was a learned and scholarly man whose defense of orthodoxy was enthusiastic, if not always prudent. Jerome tells us that he knew Greek, Hebrew, Syriac, Coptic, and some Latin.

His major work, written 374–377, was *Panarion*, commonly

known and cited as "Refutation of all the Heresies."[34] It is in the fifty-first book of the *Panarion* that he gives the description of two rites that have suggested pagan backgrounds for the feast of the Epiphany: the "birth of Aion," the guardian of Alexandria from its founding, and a ceremony of *hydrevsis* in which water was drawn from the Nile. The latter of these will be discussed below. The first has to do with a festival held in the *Koreion*, the temple of Kore in Alexandria, a festival that Epiphanius takes to be copied from the Christian festival of the nativity of Christ. That Christian festival he places on January 6, thirteen days after the winter solstice.

"The Saviour was born in the 42nd year of Augustus, emperor of the Romans, in the consulate of the same Octavius Augustus for the 13th time and of Silanos as the consular fasti of the Romans show. For in those this is found: in the consulate of these, that is, of Octavius for the 13th time and of Silanos the Christ was born on 8 before the Ides of January, 13 days after the winter solstice and the increasing of the day and of the light. This day is celebrated by the Hellenes, i.e., by the idolaters, on 8 before the Kalends of January, called among the Romans 'Saturnalia,' among the Egyptians 'Kronia,' among the Alexandrians 'Kikellia.' This is the day on which the change takes place, i.e., the solstice, and the day begins to grow, the light receiving an increase. There are accomplished the number of 13 days until 8 before the Ides of January, until the day of the birth of Christ, the thirtieth of an hour being added to each day. As also the wise Ephrem testifed to the Syrians in his commentary, saying that 'thus was established the parousia of our Lord, his birth according to the flesh, that is his perfect incarnation which is called Epiphany, at 13 days interval from the augmentation of the light. That must be the type of the number of our Lord and his twelve disciples, which accomplishes the number of 13 days from the increasing of the light.' Many other things sustain and testify to this fact; I speak of the birth of Christ, that he has come and he comes" (*Panarion haer.* 51.22.3–8).

Epiphanius is mistaken, of course, in identifying the winter solstice on the eighth of the kalends of January with the Saturnalia, even in the extended sense in which that term was used to refer to the festival on December 17 (the Saturnalia in the strict sense) and the following week. Surely, this error stems from his knowledge of

104

the identification of Saturn with the Greek Cronos, although we may be surprised that the Alexandrian equivalent for Saturnalia is *Kikellia*, in his account, while the Egyptians outside that very Hellenic city designate the day by the more Greek term, *Kronia*. His error with regard to the date at least suggests that he was unaware of the *Dies natalis solis invicti*, just as he seems unaware of any other date being assigned to the nativity of Christ than that familiar to him, the eighth of the ides of January, i.e., January 6.

On the other hand, we may well wonder why Epiphanius is concerned to account for the interval between the festival of Christ's nativity and the winter solstice, a question which is the more poignant in view of his confusion about the pagan title of the festival of that day. It is interesting to note that Ephrem Syrus is just as clear about the relationship of the Christian celebration to the winter solstice. The particular commentary of Ephrem that is cited by Epiphanius cannot be identified, but a very similar passage is found in the fifth of his nativity hymns, including the rather odd symbolism of the number 13 for the interval between the solstice and the festival of Christ's nativity.[35] It is difficult not to wonder whether there is revealed here a disapproving awareness of the western nativity festival being celebrated on the solstice itself. Do we see, that is to say, in these texts of Ephrem and Epiphanius a later fourth-century tension related to attempts to introduce the December nativity festival in the orient? Why are these writers concerned to establish a symbolic significance for the thirteen-day interval between the winter solstice and the Epiphany, and why is Epiphanius concerned to discuss the pagan observance of the solstice? What were the solstice rites and how did they relate to the Aion festival in the night from January 5 to 6?

Whatever is to be said of those questions, it is on that latter day, Epiphanius tells us, that the "idolators" observed the rites through which their leaders sought to prevent the people's embrace of Christian truth.

"For also the leaders of the worship of idols are constrained to recognize a part of the truth, and being shrewd, to deceive the idolaters persuaded by them, they make in many places a very great feast in this same night of the Epiphany, so that those who believe in error may not seek the truth. First of all, at Alexandria, in the so-

called Koreion—it is a very large temple that is the sanctuary of
Kore. They watch all night, celebrating their idol with chants and
the sound of flutes and, the vigil ended, after cockcrow, they de-
scend, carrying torches, into a subterranean chapel and they bring
back a wooden statue, seated nude upon a litter, having a mark of
a cross in gold on the forehead, and on the hands two other such
marks and on the two knees two others, the five marks being similarly of gold. And they carry the statue seven times in a circle
around the temple with flute playing and kettledrums and hymns,
and having revelled they carry it back again to the underground
place. And asked what this mystery is, they answer and say: today, at this hour, Kore (that is, the virgin) has given birth to the
Aion. And this is done also in Petra, the metropolis of Arabia
which is written Edom in the scriptures, and they hymn the virgin
in the Arabic dialect, calling her in Arabic 'Chaamou,' that is Kore
or virgin, and the one born from her 'Dousares,' that is, only begotten of the Master. And this happens also in the city of Eleusis
throughout that night, as in Petra and in Alexandria" (*Panarion
haer.* 51.22.8–11).

   We know nothing of the source of Epiphanius' testimony regarding Petra and Eleusis but his account of the ceremony in Alexandria has the ring of eyewitness, and may well be based on his own
experience in Egypt in his youth. The five crosses borne by the image are regularly understood to be the *crux ansata*, the Egyptian
ankh, symbol of eternal life. It would be most unusual, however,
for five of these symbols to be marked on the body of the image,
the standard convention being the carrying of one such symbol in
the hand. Has the passage of time allowed Epiphanius' memory of
the clearly impressive rite to become elaborated? And, if so, how
precise is his testimony for Petra and Eleusis? Was he, indeed, correct about the date of the observance, or has his memory of its central meaning, the birth of a deity from a virgin, allowed him to
identify it with the Christian festivity he knows, the nativity of
Christ on January 6?
   Not all of those questions can have answers, but it would seem
that Epiphanius is generally correct about the date of the festival of
Aion. The sixth-century Byzantine antiquarian, Joannes Laurentius
Lydus, in his treatise on festivals, *Peri Mēnōn* (4.1), quotes the first-

century B.C. Roman writer, Messala, as noting the observance of the *heortēn Aiōnos* on January 5.[36] It is clear, then, that Epiphanius was close on the date of the festival of Aion. We are still left, however, with the question of the relationship between the feast of Aion on January 5 and that of the Kronia on December 25.

This question is particularly fascinating, since Macrobius describes a very similar Egyptian festival at the winter solstice itself. In his *Saturnalia,* having commented on various representations of gods at different stages of life, the fourth-century grammarian writes, "These differences in age have reference to the sun, for at the winter solstice the sun would seem to be a little child, like that which the Egyptians bring forth from a shrine on an appointed day, since the day is then at its shortest and the god is accordingly shown as a tiny infant."[37] This similarity to Epiphanius' description is heightened further by the scholion of Cosmas of Jerusalem on Gregory Nazianzen, which describes the Hellenes as celebrating a festival on the winter solstice with the festal shout, "the virgin has brought forth, the light grows," and the so-called Calendar of Antiochus, which places beside the entry for December 25 the remark, "birth of the sun, the light increases," although it notes the occurrence of the solstice itself on December 22.[38]

These later references do not specifically refer to Egypt as does that of Macrobius. They do, nonetheless, tend to reinforce the general impression that the Kronia referred to by Epiphanius is just such a festival as the one he described for the cult of Aion. While he was mistaken, as we noted, in placing the Saturnalia on December 25, that error reveals his familiarity with the generally accepted identity of Saturn with Cronos. Raffaele Pettazzoni has demonstrated further the identity of Aion with Cronos, and the interpretation of both as *Chronos,* time.[39]

A great many scholars have recognized this similarity between the festivals of December 25 and January 6 reported for Egypt by Epiphanius, and have puzzled over the difference in dates, given the considerable evidence that they are really the same festival. Pettazzoni concludes that they are two forms of the same original festival of the winter solstice. He does not attempt to account further for the difference in date between the two. Somewhat earlier than his own inquiry, however, Dom Bernard Botte adopted the explanation for the two dates devised in 1924 by the distinguished

German scholar, Eduard Norden. Pettazzoni does not cite Norden, but his suggestion seems likely to stem from Norden's work.

Norden had suggested that January 6 was an ancient solstice date in Egypt, assigning that date, in fact, to the winter solstice in 1996 B.C., during the reign of Amenemhet I, founder of the twelfth dynasty at the beginning of the Middle Kingdom.[40] However, Norden argued, because of a calendrical error of one day each 128 years, the actual solstice fell on December 25 by the time of the founding of Alexandria. Thus, for him, both January 6 and December 25 were winter solstice festivals in pre-Christian Egypt. The former of those represented only the traditional date on which the festival had been established in 1996 B.C. and was still observed. Norden's hypothetical explanation of the appearance of such similar festivals in Alexandria on December 25 and January 6 has been extremely popular in the literature, especially since the work of Botte, but it is nonetheless fatally flawed, as we must now seek to show.

8. THE JULIAN AND EGYPTIAN CALENDARS

Throughout his argument Norden was content to refer to those Julian calendar dates, but for the discussion of ancient festivals such Julian dates are meaningless, since the Julian calendar itself was devised and established only in 45 B.C. Further, the error of one day in each 128 years to which Norden appealed to explain the movement of the actual solstice to December 25 is the error in the Julian calendar itself, an error in accordance with which the solstices and equinoxes continued to fall one day earlier every 128 years until the correction of the calendar by Gregory XIII in 1582. If, after the manner of astronomers, we project the quarter-tense days backward by application of that Julian calendar error, we find that Norden was, in fact, reasonably correct in the data he gave. At the beginning of the second millennium B.C. the winter solstice fell near what Julian reckoning would designate as January 6, just as 128 years later it fell one day earlier. Such information, however, is of only astronomical interest, and says nothing of a date established then as an annual festival.

Norden, in fact, took his information on the calendrical error and the ancient Julian dates from Ginzel's standard handbook of chronology, with special reference to a table of spring equinox dates prepared on astronomical and chronological principles according to Greenwich Mean Time.[41] There, sure enough, the spring equinox fell on April 7 in 2000 B.C. and on April 6 in 1900 B.C. (with fractions of a day in each case). Such astronomical data, however, tell us nothing whatsoever about the dates of festivals in Egypt.

There, in the time of Amenemhet I and for a millenium and a half after him, the Egyptian calendar consisted of only 365 days per year, thus exhibiting an error not of one day every 128 years, but of one day every 4 years, and that error is in the opposite direction from that described by Norden.

To state the matter at its simplest, there was no January 6 in 1996 B.C. The calendrical system to which that date belongs was created in 45 B.C. for Julius Caesar, largely through the technical expertise of an Alexandrian astronomer, Sosigenes. Indeed, it seems entirely likely that in the time of Amenemhet I the Egyptian months had no names at all, being rather numbered only within the three seasons into which they were distributed.[42] That Egyptian year consisted of twelve months of thirty days each, divided into three seasons of four months each, to which were added five epagomenal days at the turning of the year. The first season was marked by and named for the inundation of the Nile, the time when the thawing snows from the mountains to the south caused the Nile to overflow its banks and irrigate the entire valley, that green strip through the desert that is the basis of Egyptian civilization. It was this critical phenomenon that prompted the remark of Herodotus, "Egypt is the gift of the Nile." That period of flooding was ideally signaled by the heliacal rising of Sothis, the appearance of the "dog star" just before dawn over the point where the sun would rise, and that day was reckoned to be the first day of the year. That first month of the season of inundation was eventually given the name *Thoth*, and the first of Thoth was and remains the beginning of the Egyptian year.

However, since that calendar was shorter than the solar year by approximately six hours, after four years that rising of the dog star would be observed on the second of Thoth, and after another four years on the third day of the month. That backward movement of the calendar against the solar year continued for 1,461 years, at which time the rising of Sothis would again fall on the first of

Thoth, the calendar having completed what was called a Sothic cycle. Censorinus informs us that the conjunction of the first of Thoth with the rising of the dog star (*apokatastasis*) occurred on July 21, A.D. 139,[43] and, in support of that, we know that coins commemorative of the event were issued at Alexandria by Antoninus Pius bearing the fabled phoenix with the legend, *Aiōn*.[44]

Macrobius stated that the Egyptians "are the only people who have always had an exact method of determining the measurement of the year. With other nations the methods varied; and, although the numbering might be different, all alike were in error."[45] Accustomed as we are to the high degree of accuracy attained by the Gregorian adjustment of the Julian calendar, it may seem odd that he would speak so of a calendar that wandered through the seasons as did the ancient Egyptian. However, an error of but a quarter of a day was a slight one by the standards of the ancient world. That error was recognized with some precision, and in the Decree of Canopus in 238 B.C., Ptolemy III Evergetes made the necessary reform, ordering a sixth epagomenal day to be observed every fourth year.[46] So sacrosanct was the ancient calendar, however, that Ptolemy's decree was voided by his successor, and following kings were required to swear that they would make no attempt to add to or subtract from the calendar so much as a single day.

Augustus, on the other hand, was not subject to that requirement and, after his victory over Mark Antony, decreed the addition of that sixth epagomenal day in every fourth year from the year 26 B.C. From that time forward at Alexandria the first of Thoth corresponded to the Roman (Julian) August 29. However, that Roman reform was no more popular in Egypt as a whole than had been the Decree of Canopus, and it was only the spread of Christianity outward from Alexandria that carried with it the Alexandrian calendar, adjusted to the length of the Julian. That saturation by the Alexandrian calendar was fairly complete by the later fourth century, but until that time it coexisted irregularly with the old *annus vagus*.

Only with that accommodation to the Julian calendar (ca. 26 B.C. in Alexandria, but much later in the countryside) did the Egyptian calendar come to manifest the error of one day every 128 years that Norden had sought to apply to the preceding milennia. Norden's sources made no reference to Amenemhet, nor did Norden himself ascribe a festal calendar to Amenemhet. Botte, however, did use that phrase, *le calendrier d'Amenemhet I*,[47] and since then writers dependent on him have referred to the calendar of Amenemhet I, as if to an item of documentary evidence. There is no such calendar, nor is there any meaningful basis for the association of the Julian date, January 6, with any festival connected with the winter solstice in the twentieth-century before Christ. Such winter solstice festivals may have existed in Egyptian antiquity, but they could not for long be associated with any fixed date in that wandering calendar.

Nor, in fact, were the dates assigned to the quarter-tense days in the Julian calendar astronomically correct. Sosigenes, the Alexandrian designer of the Julian calendar, set the solstices and equinoxes on the eighth days before the kalends of January, April, July, and October, dates that were themselves already inexact. Moreover, that calendar, a marvel of accuracy for its time, yet contained the error that would cause these quarter days to fall one day earlier every 128 years. By the late third century, therefore, the actual solstice was several days before December 25. While in the popular mind the winter solstice was identified with December 25, astronomers such as Ptolemaeus in the second century of the Common Era take note of the actual time of the solstice, and place it on December 22.[48] Therefore, we cannot always be sure that a festivity reported only as falling at the winter solstice would be on December 25. If the solstice date is ambiguous in the first centuries of our era, it was yet more so in Egyptian antiquity with its even less precise calendar.

Failing that solution to the problem of the apparent double celebration in Egypt of a single festival on dates separated by twelve or thirteen days, the data must simply be accepted as they stand. It is possible that the peculiar character of Aion as guardian of Alexandria demanded a separation of that festival from a more generally Egyptian celebration connected with the solstice, while the content of the older festival, the rebirth of time, was retained in the Aion feast, as was the distinctive procession with the image, albeit an image, judging from Epiphanius' description, of a somewhat more mature figure. Why the night of January 5–6 was chosen for this festival of Aion cannot be known. We can be sure that it was not

111

adopted in imitation of the Christian observance, as Epiphanius would have us believe, since we have the testimony of Messala that the Aion festival, whatever its character, was in place in the latter half of the first century before Christ.

Still, given other imprecisions in the testimony of Epiphanius (those we have seen and others to be noted shortly), we must leave open the possibility that the rites he associates with the festival of Aion really belonged to the solstice festival as described by Macrobius and that his own observance of the birth of the Redeemer on January 6 had contaminated his memory of an Egyptian celebration of a divine birth. As we shall see shortly, there is very good reason to doubt that Christ's nativity at Bethlehem was celebrated in Egypt on either of those dates at the time at which Epiphanius wrote.

9. THE DRAWING OF WATER ON JANUARY 6

That feast of the birth of Aion was, as we noted above, but one of two celebrations in Egypt assigned to January 6 by Epiphanius. The second, in which the water of the Nile is drawn and carried away in vessels by Egyptians, is described in *Panarion* 51.30 in the context of his assertion of the identity in date of Christ's nativity and his first miracle at the wedding feast in Cana. This is a rather singular position, since Epiphanius strongly resists the more common identification of the dates of Christ's nativity and baptism. He asserts that according to the Egyptians, the baptism occurred on 12 Athyr, the sixth of the ides of November (November 8), two months prior to the celebration of the Cana wedding feast (*Panarion* 51.16.1). We shall be concerned shortly to examine contemporary Egyptian evidence to the contrary. Indeed, Epiphanius stands quite alone in asserting this date for the baptism of Jesus. Nor, as we shall see, is there evidence that the Egyptians assigned both the nativity and the Cana miracle to January 6, as Epiphanius asserts.

It is, nonetheless, that miraculous conversion of water to wine that he sees reflected in similar wonders in many places where springs and rivers yield wine.

"Therefore, in many places up to our own day there is reproduced that divine prodigy which took place then in testimony to the unbelieving; thus they testify in many places to springs and rivers changed to wine. Thus the spring of Cibyra in the city of Caria, at the hour when the servants drew out and he said, 'give to the ruler of the feast.' And the spring in Gerasa of Arabia gives the same witness. We have drunk from the spring of Cibyra, and our brothers from the spring which is in the martyrium in Gerasa. And many in Egypt testify the same of the Nile. Therefore on the eleventh of Tybi according to the Egyptians all draw water and set it aside in Egypt itself and in many countries" (*Panarion* 51.30.1–3).

His reference to the hour at which the servants drew out the water become wine suggests that the phenomena he describes occur only on the day which commemorates that miracle, but it is the Egyptian custom of drawing water from the Nile that he assigns specifically to 11 Tybi (equivalent to January 6 in the stabilized calendar). In any case, it seems that the miraculous phenomena discussed by Epiphanius in this passage are, in his experience, phenomena that occur in Christian contexts as testimony to the unbelieving, one of his examples being associated with the reading of John 2 and another with the martyrium at Gerasa.

Although Epiphanius gives no further detail regarding the drawing of water, Antoninus, a pilgrim to Jerusalem from Plaisance, described around 570 the celebration of the Epiphany at the place of Jesus' baptism in the Jordan. In the course of his description of the conferral of baptism there, he speaks of Alexandrians in boats who pour aromatic substances into the water when it has been blessed, and then draw the blessed water and use it later to sprinkle their boats before setting out to sea.[49] We are probably justified in seeing here a later development of the custom as then observed on the Nile. Somewhat later, the continuing Nile ceremonies on this date, including bathing and feasts on illuminated boats, spread among the Moslem population to such an extent that the ceremony was eventually suppressed. At that point, the Christians continued their festive bathing in special pools (*mightas*), quite distinct from the baptismal fonts, in the churches themselves. That custom has passed away today, but it was continued at least until the seventeenth century, at which time it was described by the orientalist, Vansleben. The pool for the purpose (*mightas*), set into the floor, is still to be seen in the older Coptic churches.[50]

The popularity of this Christian water celebration, focused originally on the Nile, does not seem to represent the continuation of a discernible pre-Christian Nile festival on 11 Tybi, although many writers have assumed the contrary. The Nile certainly held a central place in Egyptian culture and religion, and several months, especially those of the season of inundation, had festivals whose themes related to one or another stage in the rising and falling of the Nile. None of these, however, is found on 11 Tybi in the composite calendar of known Egyptian festivals of the Ptolemaic and Roman periods compiled by Ginzel.[51] His note of a *hydreusis* on that date is based only on the testimony of Epiphanius as reported by Jablonski. Three of the calendars used by Ginzel note journeys by water during the last ten days of Tybi, but that is the only reference to the Nile (assuming that this was the "water" in question) in that month.

The rising and falling of the Nile still loom large in the intercessory concerns of the Coptic liturgy, where the river continues to define the agricultural seasons as it ever has. Egypt knows but three seasons, inundation, sowing, and harvest. In their current liturgy the intercessions appropriate to the harvest begin on the Epiphany, and Coquin considers this to be a transposition by two-and-a-half months from their place in the natural agricultural year.[52] In neither case, however, would 11 Tybi in the stabilized calendar occupy a significant moment in the phases of the river.

If there is no testimony to such an Egyptian ceremony prior to Epiphanius, nonetheless a ceremonial water-drawing is mentioned at Antioch by Chrysostom, and such a custom there may be one of the extra-Egyptian instances referred to by Epiphanius. The text of Chrysostom, however, comes from the decade after Epiphanius' writing; it is his homily on the baptism of Christ, preached in Antioch on the feast of the Epiphany in 387.

"For this is the day on which he was baptized and sanctified the nature of the waters. Therefore also on this solemnity in the middle of the night all who are gathered, having drawn the water, set the liquid aside in their houses and preserve it throughout the year, for today the waters are sanctified. And this evident marvel is produced, that this water is not corrupted by the long passage of time, but through an entire year or even two or three years the water drawn today remains pure and fresh, and after such a long time it rivals that just drawn from the spring" (PG 49.365–366).

The water-drawing referred to by Chrysostom has to do with the sanctification of water itself by Christ's baptism on Epiphany, and there is reason to believe that the same baptismal theme was central to the Epiphany in Egypt. Epiphanius' attempt to associate that not with the baptism of Christ but rather with the Cana miracle must be seen in the context of his peculiar dating of the baptism.

While Epiphanius may be understood to be describing only a Christian celebration associated with the miracle at Cana on January 6, a similar series of phenomena is reported by Pliny in his *Natural History*. Pliny is familiar with several instances in which water takes the flavor of wine, or wine is miraculously produced, but he does not, with one exception, associate these phenomena with any particular days of the year. That exception is his reference to the testimony of Mucianus, three times consul, "that the water flowing from a spring in the temple of Pater Liber on the island of Andros always has the flavour of wine on the nones of January."[53] That date, January 5, is not identified by Pliny as a particular festival, but the miraculous flow of wine is called *Dios Theodosia*, "the divine gift of Zeus." Both Botte and McArthur sought to bring that text into relation to a separate testimony of Pausanius a century later regarding an undated festival called "the Thyia," celebrated at Elea in honor of Dionysus.

"Of the gods the Eleans worship Dionysus with the greatest reverence, and they assert that the god attends their festival, the Thyia. The place where they hold the festival they name the Thyia is about eight stades from the city. Three pots are brought into the building by the priests and set down empty in the presence of the citizens and of any strangers who may chance to be in the country. The doors of the building are sealed by the priests themselves and by any others who may be so inclined. On the morrow they are allowed to examine the seals, and on going into the building they find the pots filled with wine. . . . The Andrians too assert that every other year at their feast of Dionysus wine flows of its own accord from the sanctuary."[54]

Here the Andrian phenomenon is identified as a festival of Dionysus, the Pater Liber to whom the temple of Pliny's description is dedicated. There is, however, no indication that the Thyia occurred on the same date as the Andrian feast of Dionysus. Therefore, we may wonder about McArthur's assurance that the discrepancy between the nones of January and the date of the Epiphany need not concern us. He urged that the difference constitutes no problem because what was involved at Andros was a nocturnal festival through the night from the fifth to the sixth,[55] a datum supplied by neither Pliny nor Pausanius. The festival at Elea was pernocturnal, but we are not told which night in the year that was. Indeed, it is impossible to establish even the season of the year in which the Thyia was celebrated, some asserting that it was in the spring, others in winter.[56] Its identification with the festival at Andros is by no means established and the descriptions of the two are quite different. We cannot postulate for the classical world but one single festival of Dionysus kept everywhere on the same date, as many writers have sought to do.[57] Indeed, at Athens, a principal seat of the cult of Dionysus, his festivals occurred in each of four months, beginning in December, with the major Dionysia in March.[58] The texts we have examined give us secure data only for a miraculous flow of wine in the temple of Pater Liber on Andros on a festival of Dionysus on January 5, Pausanias adding that the miracle occurred only every second year. This is hardly a secure basis in pagan religion for a festival of the birth or baptism of Christ on January 6.

The similarity between the phenomena cited by Epiphanius for Cibyra and Gerasa and several examples mentioned by Pliny and others of instances in which a source of water yields wine instead suggests that this was a far from uncommon phenomenon. Botte suggested that it may, in fact, have amounted simply to a generous and plainly human provision of wine for a festivity through a source normally associated with water, not unlike the fountains of sparkling wine that are frequently encountered at wedding festivities today.[59] That these reminded Epiphanius of Christ's miracle at the Cana wedding feast is a tribute to his piety. However, since the phenomena cited by Pliny and other classical authors are not encountered just on January 6 (or even January 5), there seems no reason to leap from such generous flowing of wine to the utterly unsupported hypothesis of a universally observed festival of Dionysus on January 6 as a pre-Christian foundation for the feast of the Epiphany.

When all is said and done, from all of the evidence we have considered for a pagan background to Epiphany, nothing points definitely to a widespread festival on January 6. Even if we accept Epiphanius' account of the Aion festival, we are left with severe problems. That festival seems to be distinguished from disquietingly similar observances on December 25 because the Aion feast is the distinctive local observance of the guardian of Alexandria, and thus not a widespread observance. If we do not accept Epiphanius' description of that rite as pernocturnal, then Messala's testimony to the Aïon festival is ambiguous, since he gives as the date of the feast not January 6 but January 5.

Egyptian data will show that the feast of the Epiphany at Alexandria was focused on Christ's baptism, the miracle at Cana being celebrated later in the same month at the time of Epiphanius' writing.[60] That first miracle in which Jesus manifested his glory is an important theme in the Epiphany festival, but the singular role assigned to it by Epiphanius must not be supposed to be general in the Church in his time. His unique dating for the baptism thrust the Cana miracle into peculiar prominence. The similarity of the water-drawing in the Nile to the testimonies of Chrysostom and Antoninus of Plaisance, which we have examined, should prepare us to understand that, like those, the Egyptian *hydrevsis* was grounded in Christ's sanctification of the waters at his baptism.

10. JANUARY 6 AS THE DATE OF JESUS' BIRTH

Both Epiphanius and Ephrem Syrus, we have seen, placed the birth of Jesus on the sixth of January. Ephrem expresses this in a number of his nativity hymns. In certain of the later collections of those hymns, a distinction is drawn between the nativity hymns and those for the Epiphany, but such a distinction belongs to a time when the December 25 festival had been adopted. The second of the Epiphany hymns, in fact, is identical with the eighteenth of the nativity hymns, being included in the Epiphany group only because of the occurence of the word "epiphany" (*denḥa*) in the first three strophes. It was not, for Ephrem himself, a hymn for any other festival than that of Christ's nativity, celebrated on January 6.

Our earliest evidence for the assignment of the nativity to that date is probably older than any liturgical phenomenon that we would normally describe as a festival. Indeed, that is the date assigned to the nativity by Clement of Alexandria around the turn of the second to the third century. Several writers have taken note of the interval given in *Stromateis* 1.21.145 between the death of the emperor Commodus in A.D. 192 and the birth of Jesus at Bethlehem.[61] Interpreting that interval in terms of the Julian calendar (or, in this case, the equivalent Alexandrian calendar), it has been shown that that interval would place the birth on November 18, a day that was, coincidentally, the first day of the civil year at Tyre.[62]

However, Professor Roland Bainton of Yale University noted (in the course of his doctoral research on Basilidian chronology) that the figures given in section 145 for the interval between the death of Commodus and the captivity under Vespasian are inconsistent with those given for the same interval in section 140 of chapter 21 of that first book of the *Stromateis*.[63] In section 140, Clement says that from the death of Commodus to the destruction of Jerusalem there were 121 years, 6 months, and 24 days. In section 145, he says that there were 121 years, 10 months, and 13 days. In the latter place he also states that Christ was born in the twenty-eighth year of Augustus (3/2 B.C.) and 194 years, 1 month, and 13 days before the death of Commodus on December 31, 192. This section, Bainton argued, is not only inconsistent with section 140, but is also inconsistent in itself, if it is to be read by the Julian calendar, since it would place the birth of Jesus in the twenty-seventh (4/3 B.C.) rather than the twenty-eighth year of Augustus.

Unwilling to dismiss one or the other set of figures as a lapse on the part of Clement, Bainton rather examined the two separate accounts against the Egyptian calendrical situation in the second and third centuries. He was brought to the conclusion that if both accounts were true, but came from different sources, then there was the very real likelihood that the longer interval in section 145 represented a statement of the period in terms of the shorter "old-style" Egyptian calendar of only 365 days, while the shorter interval in section 140 reflected the Alexandrian calendar, conformed in length to the Julian. The interval between the death of Commodus and the nativity, therefore, would have to be interpreted in terms of the earlier Egyptian *annus vagus*.

Bainton himself did that computation with the help of Schram's *Kalendariographische und chronologische Tafeln*,[64] and published the computations both with his original publication and in a later essay abstracted from that larger work.[65] Those who wish to do the computations for themselves would probably find it more convenient to use the table for the beginning of the years in that ancient Egyptian calendar published in Bickerman's *Chronology of the Ancient World*,[66] a more accessible volume today. In either case, however, the result yielded is that the interval between the death of Commodus and the birth of Christ reported in section 145 of the first book of Clement's *Stromateis*, computed in accordance with the ancient Egyptian calendar of but 365 days, gives January 6, 2 B.C. as the date of Jesus' birth at Bethlehem, the twenty-eighth year of Augustus, as Clement said.

That date coincides remarkably with another given by Clement in the immediately following passage (*Stromateis* 1.21.146): "The followers of Basilides celebrate the day of his baptism also, spending the night before in reading. They say that it was the fifteenth year of Tiberius Caesar, the fifteenth of the month Tybi, but some the eleventh of same month" (ANF II, p. 333). In the stabilized Alexandrian calendar, 15 Tybi = January 10 and 11 Tybi = January 6. Since we do not know when either date was set, it is impossible to determine whether the variation in the date of the Basilidian celebration again reflects the calendrical situation of ante-Nicene Egypt. If an Alexandrian Basilidian community observed the baptism on 11 Tybi, others outside the city who still followed the *annus vagus* but sought to synchronize their celebration with the Alexandrians would find that, after some sixteen years, their respective dates were as described by Clement. On the other hand, it is at least possible, since Clement gives the dates in inverse order, that he is contrasting the variant date (15 Tybi) to that which is more familiar to him.

For the Basilidians, of course, the content of the festival is not the birth but the baptism of Jesus, and many understood the two dates to be identical on the basis of Luke 3.23, taking that text to mean that Jesus was baptized on his thirtieth birthday. However, since that is far from explicit in the text, it is probably safe to conjecture that this interpretation represents an attempt to unify divergent traditions. Although Clement, as we have seen, was familiar with a tradition that set the nativity on January 6, there are many other evidences for the Epiphany in Egypt that suggest rather strongly that the theme of the festival there was, in the first instance, that of the baptism of Jesus and not the nativity at Bethlehem. Clement's early testimony to the practice of the Basilidians, therefore, seems to be significant for later Egyptian practice, whatever it meant to Clement himself.

It was the baptism, again, that constituted for Marcion the descent of Christ to which reference is made in Tertullian's *Adversus Marcionem* 1.19 (PL 2.267), Bainton believes. According to his analysis of that text, the descent referred to occurred in the first week of January, A.D. 29. While the text will yield no more precision than that, Bainton takes it to reflect, again, the association of the baptism of Jesus with January 6.

Bainton, following Arnold Meyer and others, supposed the date of the Epiphany, January 6, to be that of an "Epiphany of Dionysus" widely observed in the East, and took the Christian festival on that date to be derived from the pagan observance. He is aware, however, of the tradition that computes the date of the nativity from that of the conception and passion. He suggests, therefore, that that computation was employed in reverse to produce the Montanist date for the passion, April 6, reported by Sozomen.[67] The reason he gives for this reverse computation is that April 6 is not a significant solar date.[68]

In Part One, on the contrary, we argued that April 6 constituted the solar equivalent to 14 Nisan in Asia Minor, where each month began nine days before its Roman counterpart, putting the beginning of the first month of spring, Artemisios, on the Roman March 24, and the fourteenth day of that month on April 6. That understanding of the significance of that solar date would surely suffice to establish its originality, and that would disallow Bainton's argument for a Montanist familiarity with any assignment of Jesus' birth or baptism to January 6 (although such familiarity is probable). That, however, would hardly diminish the force of his argument, viz., that to find such an agreement on that January date among warring factions demands our assigning its recognition in the Church to the very early second century, prior to the theological struggles that separated the various groups from one another. That argument might lend some strength to the very bold hypothesis of Allan McArthur regarding the fourth gospel's opening:

"Tradition attributes this Gospel to Ephesus. It may be dated in the closing years of the first or the opening years of the second century. We may therefore put forward the wholly tentative hypothesis that by the end of the first century the Epiphany, the transformation of a pagan celebration into a Christian festival, was in existence at Ephesus, the capital of the province of Asia, the region which at that period constituted the most vigorous area of the Church's expansion. It was against the liturgical background of this festival that John 1.1–2.11 was written."[69]

Having discussed above the difficulties surrounding attempts to identify a widely observed pagan festival on January 6, the likelihood of a Christian transformation of a pagan festival at the opening of the second century does not immediately commend itself. Leaving those problems (if, as I believe, they are problems) to one side, we shall, nonetheless, have occasion to return to McArthur's suggestion that the reading of the fourth gospel began on January 6 at Ephesus at a very early date. That would entail the treatment of January 6 as such an initial point for the liturgical year as was noted above for December 25 in the Chronograph of 354.

11. THE BAPTISM OF JESUS ON JANUARY 6

The Basilidian celebration of the baptism of Jesus on January 6, reported by Clement of Alexandria, was not to remain a peculiarity of that sect. That the baptism of Jesus was the primary theme of the Epiphany in Egypt in the fourth century is stated explicitly in the sixteenth of the *Canons of Athanasius*, edited by Riedel and Crum.[70] Perhaps because of the diffidence of Renaudot regarding the authenticity of that document, Botte and other writers on the history of the Epiphany prior to Coquin have failed to take note of that datum.[71]

The document is preserved entire in an Arabic translation, divided into 107 sections. That division, as noted already by Abu 'l-Barakat in the fourteenth century, occurred within the Arabic manuscript tradition, and those divisions are not found in the more fragmentary Coptic text, preserved in a sixth-seventh century papyrus of the British Museum.[72] Riedel, after careful consideration of the external and internal evidences, suggested believably enough that the Greek original behind that Coptic version may be the otherwise lost tract on the "Commandments of Christ" produced by Athanasius (according to the Chronicle of John of Nikiou)[73] in connection with a synod assembled in 364 upon his return from his fourth exile.

Even if that identification is rejected, the Greek original, he argued, must be the work of an Egyptian, and probably Alexandrian, bishop of the second half of the fourth century. It is that authority and dating that concern us, rather than authorship itself. The sixteenth canon (to accept, as did Riedel and Crum, the Arabic numbering) is one of several having to do with the bishop's responsibility to the poor.

"A bishop shall not be any Sunday without almsgiving. And the poor and orphans shall he know as doth a father, and shall gather them together at the great festival of the Lord, vowing and distributing much alms and giving unto each whereof he hath need. And at the feast of Pentecost he shall refresh all the people, because that on that day the Holy Ghost came down upon the church. And at the feast of the Lord's Epiphany, which was in (the month) Tûbah, that is the (feast of) Baptism, they shall rejoice with them. The bishop shall gather all the widows and orphans and shall rejoice with them, with prayers and hymns, and shall give unto each according to his needs; for it is a day of blessing; in it was the Lord baptised of John. The poor shall rejoice with thee, O bishop, at all the feasts of the Lord and shall celebrate with thee these three seasons, each year: the Paschal feast shall be kept unto the Lord our God and a feast at the end of the fifty days and the new-year's feast, which is (that of) the gathering in of the harvest and the fruits. The last of all fruits is the olive, which is gathered in that day; wherefore by the Egyptians this is called the feast of the beginning of the year. As with the Hebrews New Year's Day was at the Pascha, which is the first of Barmûdah. So again in the month Tûbah did our Saviour appear as God, when, by a wondrous miracle, He made the water wine."[74]

122

Here, although it is the baptism of Jesus that is the primary content of the Epiphany, the miracle at Cana is celebrated in the same month, as it is remembered still on 13 Tybi in the Coptic rite.[75] Two other significant points are to be made about this text. First, there is no reference at all to any feast of the nativity. We have already noted the assertion of Epiphanius that in Egypt the *ensarkos genesis* of the Lord was observed on 11 Tybi (*Panarion* 51.29.7), thirty years before the miracle at Cana. A generation after Epiphanius we will encounter the testimony of John Cassian for the celebration of both the nativity and the baptism on this day, but our canon makes no mention at all of the nativity. The silence of this canon regarding the nativity may best be understood, perhaps, as a function of the determinative role played by the gospel of Mark in the early organization of the Alexandrian liturgy.

Second, a considerable point is made of Epiphany being the beginning of the year. Such a marking of the liturgical year from the Epiphany, we have noted, is paralleled at Rome by the organization of the Philocalian lists from December 25 in the Chronograph of 354. There, of course, the event celebrated at the head of the year was the nativity, not the baptism as in this text. Those need not, however, be contradictory. Although Clement had known January 6 as the nativity date, evidently, that date, taken as the beginning of the liturgical year, would have been observed with the beginning of the reading of the gospel of Mark, i.e., the baptism of Jesus. It would be possible to view the festival, therefore, as celebration of both the birth and the baptism even though the evangelical content of its liturgy was only the baptism.

While it is easy to understand how gnostics might prefer a christology that would identify Jesus' baptism as the point of his identification as Son of God, it is less than clear that such a focus on the baptism was characteristic only of "heterodox" circles, the historical point of the incarnation being ambiguous in the earliest literature. The two closing chapters of the *Epistle to Diognetus* have often been considered (on the basis of 11.3–5) to be a separately composed homily for the Epiphany:

"3. And for his sake he sent the Word to appear to the world, who was dishonoured by the chosen people, was preached by apostles, was believed by the heathen. 4. He was from the beginning, and appeared new, and was proved to be old, and is ever young, as he is born in the hearts of the saints. 5. *He is the eternal one, who today is accounted a Son*, through whom the Church is enriched, and grace is unfolded and multiplied among the saints, who confers understanding, manifests mysteries, announces seasons, rejoices in the faithful, is given to them that seek, that is, to those by whom the pledges of faith are not broken, nor the decrees of the Fathers transgressed" (emphasis added).[76]

The temptation to set this passage in a heortological context is not diminished by 12.7–9:

"7. Let your heart be knowledge, and your life the true and comprehended word. 8. And if you bear the tree of this and pluck its fruit you will ever enjoy that which is desired by God, which the serpent does not touch, and deceit does not infect, and Eve is not corrupted but a virgin is trusted, 9. and salvation is set forth, and apostles are given understanding, and *the Passover of the Lord advances, and the seasons are brought together, and are harmonised with the world*, and the Word teaches the saints and rejoices, and through it the Father is glorified; to whom be glory for ever, Amen" (emphasis added).[77]

The phrase in 11.5, "who today is accounted a Son," clearly has incarnational reference, but it is difficult to know whether that reference is to the conception (as 12.8 might suggest, especially if that was identified with the Pascha of the following verse), or to the nativity in Bethlehem, or to the baptism in Jordan. The last possibility is rendered stronger if we recall the quotation of Psalm 2.7 in the reading of Luke 3.22 in *Codex Bezae:* "Thou art my beloved Son, this day have I begotten thee."

Such an understanding of the baptism of Jesus as the historical focus of the incarnation became problematic with even early christological development, but it was not so from the beginning. Indeed, the text that western tradition has associated most closely with the nativity, the prologue of the fourth gospel, tells us that "the Word was made flesh and dwelt among us" only after we have been introduced to John the Baptist. It is very difficult to suppose that that hymn has Jesus' nativity at Bethlehem in view, even though its christology is higher than that of the synoptics, insisting as it does on the eternal existence of the Word who became incarnate.

Even as late as Chrysostom's sermon on the baptism of Christ, it was clear to him that Jesus was not revealed to the world at his nativity, important as he considered that to be. The revelation of Christ to all came only at and following his baptism, for which reason he continued to call that feast the Epiphany, by contrast to the Cappadocian transfer of that title to the separate festival of the nativity on December 25 when that was adopted.[78]

Prior to the adoption of the festival of December 25 (a process that we shall trace shortly), it seems clear that from Constantinople, through Cappadocia, to Syria, the Epiphany celebrated both the nativity and the baptism of Jesus. Among the eastern churches in the fourth century, only Palestine (and Cyprus, if the view of the Palestinian Epiphanius prevailed there) omitted the theme of the baptism in the Jordan from the festival of January 6.

It was that theme of the festival, we have observed, that prompted the drawing of water and its reservation by the faithful, because on this day Christ, by his baptism, had sanctified all the waters of the earth. In Egypt, that water was drawn from the Nile, the river whose lifegiving role in that land now took on a specifically Christian significance. The source of the water referred to by Chrysostom at Antioch is not specified, but it is likely that this, too, was a natural source of flowing water, a spring or stream. There the people gathered at midnight and filled the vessels they had brought for the purpose, "for today," Chrysostom says, "the waters are sanctified," *hagiasthētōn tōn hydatōn* (PG 49.366).

It is not clear whether that text refers to a liturgical hallowing of the water or merely to its association with the baptism of Christ, who by that act (Chrysostom has said but a few lines earlier) sanctified the nature of the waters. An actual liturgical blessing of the water, however, is ascribed to Peter the Fuller at Antioch in the fifth century. This rite, transferred by his authority from midnight to the evening, was spoken of as an invocation (*epiklēsis*) on the waters.[79] The principal prayer for this blessing of water on the Epiphany today, that which begins, "Great art Thou, O Lord, and wonderful are Thy works," is encountered in all the oriental rites. Armenian tradition assigns its composition to Basil of Caesarea, but Syrian sources more accurately, it would seem, assign it to

Proclus, the fifth-century archbishop of Constantinople.[80] While the prayer is clearly related to the baptism of Jesus in the Jordan and the sanctification that he conferred upon the water then, it has nothing to do with Christian initiation, with the conferral of the sacrament of baptism.

On the other hand, the account of the Epiphany celebration given by the sixth-century pilgrim, Antoninus of Plaisance, at the place of Jesus' baptism in the Jordan, makes it clear that baptism was being conferred at that celebration, and notes that the Alexandrians draw the water only after it is blessed.[81] That does not mean, however, that the old Epiphany water blessing had been subsumed to the baptismal liturgy everywhere. As for the Alexandrians, de Puniet, on the authority of James of Edessa, says that the Copts still did not have a blessing of water on the Epiphany at the close of the seventh century.[82] In such a case it is likely that their adoption of the rite came only with the proscription of their old celebrations in the Nile itself and the substitution of pools built in the churches. Elsewhere as well the older flowing water sources gave way to more controllable liturgical environments, the fountains in the atria of churches and eventually vessels small enough to be carried in procession or placed on the altar for the blessing. This latter development led in Syria to a likening of the blessing of the water to the consecration of the eucharist. Popular piety often regarded (and sometimes regards still) the water blessed on Epiphany as a sacramental medium of the Holy Spirit analogous to the presence of Christ in the eucharistic species, some fourteen centuries of theological criticism to the contrary notwithstanding.[83]

It is clear that by the later fourth century, the association of the Epiphany with the baptism of Jesus did lead to the conferral of baptism on that day in some churches. Yet the history of that development and its relation to the other baptismal days (Pascha and Pentecost) is rather more obscure than some have thought.[84] Several of the hymns of Ephrem Syrus, designated for the Epiphany and distinguished from those of the nativity in the liturgical manuscripts of the ninth to the eleventh centuries, are concerned with the baptism of catechumens.[85] While these hymns seem to be his compositions, it is less than certain that they were employed on that festival in the time of Ephrem. Other of his texts make it clear that he took January 6 to be the date of the nativity and that he took Pascha to be the time for baptism of catechumens. It is not clear just when the festival of December 25 was adopted at Edessa. Yet Beck believes that, due to that adoption, the content of the January 6 festival was limited to the baptism of Jesus and that the celebration of baptism on the Epiphany was a function of that thematic focus.[86]

At Constantinople also, Botte and Mossay have suggested, Epiphany became a baptismal day only when the unified celebration of the birth and baptism was divided through the adoption of the feast of December 25, leaving the Epiphany devoted to the baptism alone.[87] Others may find the evidence somewhat more complex. *Oratio XL* of Gregory Nazianzen reveals Epiphany, Easter, and Pentecost to be significant occasions for baptism, although the same evidence also suggests that the association of baptism with only certain festivals was breaking down. A major concern of Gregory in this oration is to persuade his hearers not to wait for a certain time or place to be baptized, but to proceed to the sacrament as soon as possible.[88] If he succeeded with some, then they may have presented themselves on the Epiphany on which the oration was delivered, but that would have been a decision made ad hoc and without further process of candidacy. If, as it seems, Gregory is urging baptism without regard to festal seasons, neither Epiphany nor Easter nor Pentecost, then the roots of that triad of baptismal days may be much older in Cappadocia than we think. Of that, however, we find no positive evidence at present.

In the West a letter of Himerius, bishop of Tarragona in Spain, to Damasus, bishop of Rome, evidently mentioned the custom of conferring baptism on both Christmas and Epiphany, as well as on festivals of many martyrs and apostles. The response to that letter, however, came only from Damasus' successor, Siricius. He is strongly critical of that practice, and reasserts the importance of long preparation for baptism, forty days or more.[89] Similar Roman opposition to Epiphany baptism was addressed to the bishops of Sicily by Gelasius a century later. Both that fourth-century Spanish practice and Gregory Nazianzen's Constantinopolitan oration give the impression of a decay in the classic initiatory process, which was still being maintained at Rome, Milan, and Jerusalem.

Later Byzantine documents present a full baptismal liturgy only on the Epiphany, the Saturday of Lazarus, the Paschal Vigil, and

Pentecost.[90] Apart from the Saturday of Lazarus (a special case to be discussed in Part Three), these are the great festivals observed and honored throughout the eastern church and frequently paralleled to the pilgrim festivals of the Old Testament. On each of these baptismal days at Constantinople, when the baptized and chrismated neophytes have been led into the basilica, the usual entrance chant of the eucharist, Trisagion, is replaced by the baptismal troparion, "As many as have been baptized into Christ have put on Christ." That substitution is still made on those occasions today, although there is no baptism.

An unexplained anomaly is that the same substitution was (and is) made on Christmas Day, December 25, although no record exists of baptism on that day at Constantinople. Nor can we believe that that troparion was substituted for Trisagion already when the festival of December 25 was adopted in the fourth century. That entrance chant entered the Byzantine liturgy only in the fifth century. A curious series of notes by Byzantine historians of the seventh century report a riot in the city while the emperor was making the procession on the feast of the Presentation (*Hypapantē*). These historians date that incident forty days after the celebration of the birth of Jesus and a few days after the marriage of Theodosius, the emperor's son. Martin Higgins has collected these materials and shows that the wedding was celebrated from February 9 to 15, A.D. 602.[91] If that date (from the *Chronicon Paschale*) is correct, then the accounts of the riot put the festival on February 14, the date of that festival still in the Armenian rite. That would mean that in 602, the nativity of Jesus was celebrated at Constantinople on January 6, not December 25. We know nothing more of such a return of the nativity festival to January 6, but if such was the case for a time, the subsequent settlement of the nativity festival once again on December 25 could very well carry with it the custom of substituting the baptismal troparion for Trisagion.

Such an explanation of a minor detail would raise questions far more significant than the one it answers, and one hesitates to press those questions. But, however that baptismal text on Christmas is to be explained, it does recall the original unitive character of the Epiphany, and with that (however confused in the folds of history) a lingering witness to the primitive understanding of the baptism of Jesus as in some way a dimension of the mystery of the incarnation.

In addition to the description of the baptismal liturgy on the day of the Epiphany, the *typika* of the ninth and tenth centuries also describe the blessing of water on the eve of the feast.[92] The patriarch blessed the water in the sanctuary of Hagia Sophia and afterward processed to the baptistry for the distinct blessing of the baptismal font, although baptism was not conferred until the following morning. This is an exception to the practice on other baptismal days, which placed the blessing of the water in the context of the baptismal rite itself. It is difficult to doubt that this exception was due to the significance attached to the blessing of the Epiphany water for distribution to the faithful, a rite still maintained in all the oriental liturgies today, even though conferral of baptism is now seldom associated with the Epiphany.

12. THE BEGINNING OF THE GOSPEL AT THE BEGINNING OF THE YEAR

While a great many writers have espoused a pagan origin for the date of the festival of January 6, it is important to note that the parallel between this date and December 25, when the two are viewed in relation to April 6 and March 25 as paschal dates, suggests that the latter dates (December 25 and March 25) are related to the winter solstice and the spring equinox only accidentally, since the same relationship is visible between April 6 and January 6 without any reference (pace Norden!) to the quarter days. Rather, these winter dates can both be derived, as Duchesne argued, from the spring dates for the Pascha discussed in Part One: March 25 as the supposed actual equivalent to 14 Nisan in the year of our Lord's passion (since Hippolytus) and April 6 as the annual equivalent to 14 Nisan in the Asian recension of the Julian solar calendar. Following established Jewish thought forms, these dates assigned to the death of the Lord were assigned as well to the incarnation, a regular theme (together with the passion and resurrection) of the central festival of our redemption in Christ. The inclusion of the incarnation in the paschal themes would, indeed, be virtually unavoidable when Pascha was the sole annual festival.

At one point, nonetheless, this Christian tradition differs from its Jewish background. While the themes of the primitive Pascha include the incarnation, the early texts suggest that this was celebrated as a theological concept, with no historical distinction between the conception of Jesus and his birth. Such general reference to the incarnation can still be seen around 165 in a passage from Melito of Sardis, already quoted.

"He came on earth from heaven for suffering man, becoming incarnate in a virgin's womb from which he came forth as man; he took on himself the sufferings of suffering man through a body capable of suffering, and put an end to the sufferings of the flesh, and through his spirit incapable of death he became the death of death which is destructive of man."[93]

Jewish tradition regarding the patriarchs would in most instances, as we noted above, identify the days of their births and deaths. The identification of the date of Jesus' death with the date of his conception, and the consequent projection of the date of his birth to a point nine months later, seems to be a Christian development. The reasons for this are less than clear. Nonetheless, what once seemed contrived in Duchesne's computation hypothesis, the identification of the Lord's death date with that of the incarnation, can seem so no longer when we consider the appearance of that identification in the literature and against the background of Jewish tradition. It is more difficult to know what prompted the understanding of the incarnation as the conception, rather than the birth, and the projection of the nativity to a point nine months later. If that development is to be assigned to the second or even the third century, we may at least be sure that docetic opposition to the enfleshment of the Logos provided the theological context for that development.

As those winter dates become more visible in the data of the fourth century, we see that the feast associated with the nativity of Jesus marks a turning of the year at a point outside the paschal Pentecost. Further, his coming in the flesh is referred to as his *parousia* in that fourth-century literature, as it was already, evidently, when Irenaeus grew up in Asia Minor. Can we see the seeds of the appearance of a new turning of the year already in chapter 17 of *Epistula Apostolorum*, where the parousia, contrary to what one would expect, is situated by the risen Christ between the Pentecost and the following Passover? Nothing in that text, of course, suggests a festival of the nativity as such, nor does the text point to any specific date.

We may suppose, nonetheless, that within that major portion of the year there was a point at which the reading of the gospel of John was begun, a course reading that would bring the liturgical community to the passion narrative at the following Passover. That reading might at the outset have begun in the autumn, influenced by *Simḥat Torah*, which began the reading of the Law in the synagogues following the feast of Tabernacles; indeed, some have suggested that the gospels were shaped in relation to the course reading in the synagogues.[94] Nonetheless, whenever the reading of the gospel of John began, it began with the proclamation that, "In the beginning was the Word . . . and the Word was made flesh and dwelt among us." It would speak of the baptism of Jesus and of his first miracle at the wedding feast in Cana, that "beginning of the signs" in which he "manifested his glory" (*ephanerosen tēn doxan autou*).

Then, given the association of his birth and baptism with January 6 by "orthodox" and heretics alike, it seems more than possible that the beginning of the course reading of the gospel fell on that date in the second century, first in Asia but quickly adopted as the beginning of the year in neighboring churches also, in Syria, Palestine, and Egypt. In some other places as well it would be the point from which the reading of the gospel began, although not that of John. Jerusalem's tenacious commitment, in the fourth century and later (and still among the Armenians), to the celebration of the nativity on the Epiphany is probably rooted in the antiquity of the local tradition, for which the beginning of the reading of Matthew made the nativity alone the theme associated with January 6.

Such was still the case at Jerusalem in the time of Egeria's visit there (383) and in the Armenian lectionaries of the first half of the fifth century.[95] As with Pascha, these sources provide a detailed picture of the Epiphany liturgy at Jerusalem, but also give a glimpse into its development. The eight-day festival was initiated at Bethlehem with a vigil through the night begun in "the place of the shepherds." No account of this vigil is given in what remains of Egeria's pilgrimage narrative, which takes up, after a lacuna, with the procession back to Jerusalem in the early morning of the sixth. In the Armenian lectionaries, however, the place of the first gathering in Bethlehem is specified, and it is not the basilica over the cave of the nativity, but the "shepherds' field," rendered *Poimnion* or *Poimaneion* in the Greek literary sources.[96] This synaxis, held at four o'clock in the afternoon, the hour to which the fifth-century lectionaries usually assigned such extraliturgical assemblies, gives expression to Luke 2.8, "there were shepherds out in the field, keeping watch over their flock by night," the gospel reading that provides the only lesson at that gathering.

At that point, the surviving Armenian manuscript suffers a lacuna, but later texts show the vigil proper assembled first in the cave of the nativity, and then in the basilica. The gospel at the vigil is Matthew's account of the visit of the Magi, a chronological anomaly that we shall discuss presently.

Egeria describes a procession back to Jerusalem very early on the sixth, with the dismissal at the Anastasis just before dawn. The liturgies on the days of the octave were celebrated in several churches around the city and on the Mount of Olives. In Egeria's time, the liturgies of the first three days were celebrated in the Martyrium, the liturgy of the fourth at Eleona, the fifth at the Lazarium in Bethany, the sixth at Sion, the seventh in the Anastasis, and the eighth at the Cross (i.e., in the courtyard).[97] By the time of the Armenian lectionaries, the second day of the octave is at the Martyrium of Stephen, and the fourth at Sion, moving the stations at Eleona and the Lazarium to the fifth and sixth days.[98]

The gospel of the first day at the Martyrium is Matthew 1.18–25 and that of the third day is Matthew 2.13–23, skipping over the story of the visit of the Magi, Matthew 2.1–12. Between those falls the station at the martyrium of Stephen where the gospel is appropriate to his martyrdom, John 12.23–26, as that at the Lazarium on the sixth day is the account of the raising of Lazarus (Jn 11.1–46). The station at the martyrium of Stephen had been established only after the discovery of his relics in 415. Its gospel is the same as that appointed for the feast of Stephen on December 27 (26 in one manuscript). The reason for this station so shortly after that feast is less than clear, but it does seem likely that, prior to the new memorial of Stephen, the gospel of the second day at the Martyrium, mentioned by Egeria, was Matthew 2.1–12, the visit of the Magi. The lectionaries, we have seen, report that pericope at the vigil in Bethlehem, but it is unlikely that this was the case in Egeria's day. It is tempting to wonder whether an earlier vigil pericope had been the genealogy, Matthew 1.1–17, which does not appear in the fifth-century lectionaries.

While the answer to that question remains uncertain, our reconstruction would show a course reading of the Matthean narratives over the first three days of the octave at the Martyrium, readings that may well antedate the building of the Martyrium. Such a reconstruction would also suggest that while the relocation of the second of those pericopes (Mt 2.1–12) was possible, its suppression was unthinkable. This points to the fundamental importance attached to the Matthean gospel at Jerusalem, and also reveals the secondary character of those functions designed for the accommodation of pilgrims, such as the assembly in the shepherds' field and, at a different level, perhaps even the observance of the vigil in Bethlehem. These functions constitute a secondary stratum in the Jerusalem liturgy that often confuses but does not finally obscure the more sober tradition of the city as it was prior to the Constantinian building program. At the Epiphany, as in the Great Week examined in Part One, that primitive cursus seems to be built on the course reading of Matthew.

In Egypt, on the other hand, the baptism seems to be the original theme, "the beginning of the Gospel of Jesus Christ" according to Mark, the evangelist who gave his name to the see of Alexandria and to its liturgy. Regarding the feast of the baptism on January 6, the *Canons of Athanasius* (can. 16) say: "by the Egyptians this is called the feast of the beginning of the year."

Such an understanding of the beginning of the year as the beginning of the course reading of a gospel is admittedly hypothetical; nonetheless, we shall be concerned to develop that idea further with particular reference to Mark in Part Three. It is interesting that we are unable to assign the gospel of Luke to any particular church, and it is the only gospel that presents itself as addressed to an individual, a sort of "first epistle to Theophilus," by contrast to the more liturgically appropriate proclamatory openings of the other gospels. Nonetheless, the Byzantine tradition, which now begins its course reading of Luke from Holy Cross Day (September 14), earlier began that cursus at the beginning of the civil year, September 23. The tenth-century typikon of Hagia Sophia, we noted above, still indicates that date as the "New Year" and begins its reading of Luke on that day, even though the Roman calendar was adopted in the second half of the fifth century and the beginning of the liturgical year was at that time moved back to September 1. This suggests a *terminus ante quem* of ca. 465 for the liturgical disposition that begins the reading of Luke at the New Year, dated from the birthday of Augustus, September 23 (the first day of Kaisarios in the Asian recension of the Julian calendar). By contrast to some other churches that celebrated the conception of the Forerunner on the traditional autumnal equinox, September 24, at Constantinople that festival was transferred one day earlier to coincide with New Year's Day. It is not possible to see a more primitive course reading of Luke, but this beginning of the course reading at the beginning of the year does conform to our hypothesis, if it does not support it. Of course, Luke's is not the only gospel read in course at Constantinople, and we shall be concerned in Part Three to argue that we find in the Constantinopolitan Lent the ancient beginning of Alexandria's Marcan cursus.

13. THE ADOPTION OF CHRISTMAS IN THE EASTERN CHURCHES

As with most other questions surrounding the festivals of Christmas and Epiphany, the dissemination of the December festival in the East (and, as we shall see, the reverse process in the West) has been surrounded by controversy that will not soon, it seems, yield to perfect agreement. In Syria a festal list in *Apostolic Constitutions* V.13 gives first place to a feast of the nativity (*genethlion*) on the twenty-fifth day of the ninth month,[99] that month number representing the Syrian acceptance of April as the paschal first month. That festival of the nativity is followed, on the sixth day of the next month, by the feast called *epiphanios*, on which, the text says, "the Lord made to you a manifestation of his own deity." That description would fit either the baptism or the miracle at Cana, and may have reference to both. Here, in any case, the December festival is known as the Nativity and that in January retains the title of Epiphany. The presence of both festivals here is a critical item in the

134

difficult question of the date of *Apostolic Constitutions*. Funk, largely on that basis, assigned the collection to the turn of the century, ca. 400. Others (Altaner, Quasten) have favored a date some twenty years earlier.

Botte argued that at Antioch itself the festival of December 25 was introduced in the first year of Chrysostom's preaching, 386. This argument is based upon a careful analysis of several of his sermons. The first of these is the first sermon on Pentecost. In the course of situating that festival within the general scheme of the year, Chrysostom enumerates three festivals, Theophany, Pascha, and Pentecost, and says specifically that the Theophany is the first, on which, "God has appeared on the earth and lived with men [Bar 3.38], and thereafter God the only begotten Son (*pais*) of God was with us, and is so still, for he said, 'Behold I am with you all the days until the consummation of the age' [Mt 28.20]" (PG 50.454). Two points urged by Botte with regard to that sermon are that it makes Theophany the first festival of the year and that it makes it the festival of the incarnation.

In another sermon, on December 20, 386, a feast of St. Philogonios, Chrysostom announced the coming celebration of the nativity of Christ and urged all the people to prepare themselves for this feast. It is of great importance, he urges, because all the other festivals, Theophany, Pascha, Ascension, and Pentecost, take their origin from it, since if Christ had not been born in the flesh, he could not have been baptized, and it is that baptism that is celebrated at Theophany (PG 48.752).

A third sermon was preached by Chrysostom on the feast of the Nativity itself, December 25, 386. There he declared that he had long wished to see that day. He added that this date of Christ's birth had been known for less than ten years. Does that mean that the festival had been celebrated at Antioch for some years already? That is the point at which scholarly opinion divides. Botte, and others following him, have urged that Chrysostom's first Pentecost sermon was preached prior to the introduction of Christmas and so makes no reference to it, placing the Theophany as the first of the festivals of the year. For Botte, indeed, that Pentecost sermon associates the incarnation with Theophany so strongly that the distinction made in the (subsequent?) sermon on the feast of St. Philogonios can only be understood as a change of orientation.

However, a fourth sermon, preached on the Epiphany following December 25, 386, makes the point that Christ was not revealed to the majority at his nativity; that revelation of his divine identity to all the people came only at his baptism. So understood, what is said of Christ in that first Pentecost sermon (viz., that at Theophany God appeared on the earth and lived among men) could still be said after the adoption of the December nativity feast. As for the indication there that Theophany is the first of the festivals of the year, the question must be posed whether Chrysostom is naming all the festivals or only that older triad of Epiphany, Pascha, and Pentecost as analogous to the pilgrim festivals of the Old Testament: Tabernacles, Passover, and Weeks. That analogy is frequently encountered in patristic literature and, indeed, Chrysostom himself relates the festivals of the New Testament to the Old in that very Pentecost sermon, citing Exodus 23.17 (PG 50.453). If a distinct festival of the nativity is not included in that triad, neither is the Ascension, another festival on which Chrysostom preached and to which he refers in this same Pentecost sermon (PG 50.456).

It remains uncertain, then, whether the first sermon on Pentecost was preached prior to those on Blessed Philogonios and on the nativity. With that uncertainty arises the further uncertainty regarding Chrysostom's statement that the date of the birth of Christ had been known for fewer than ten years. If the first sermon on Pentecost does not limit the introduction of the feast of December 25 to the year 386, then that expression might well mean that the festival had been celebrated at Antioch for some years.

More interesting, perhaps, than the disputed historical question of the year that the December festival was introduced at Antioch is Chrysostom's conviction of the historicity of the nativity date and his argument for that. In his sermon *Eis tēn genethlion*, Chrystostom says, as mentioned, "it is not yet the tenth year since this day has become clearly known to us," adding that like a noble sapling planted in the earth, "this, which has been known from of old to the inhabitants of the West and has now been brought to us, not many years ago, has developed so quickly and has manifestly proved so fruitful" (PG 49.351). That provides the point of the first of Chrysostom's three demonstrations of the historicity of the nativity date, viz., the very speed with which the feast has blossomed (*anthēsai tēn heortēn*), appealing to the argument of Gamaliel in Acts 5.38f. to show that it is of God and not of men. His second demonstration is based on the census mentioned in Luke 2, and the assurance he has received from those in Rome that records of such a census exist. His third demonstration (of which notice was taken in Section 5 above) replicates the argument of the tractate *De solstitiis*, making Zechariah the high priest in the Holy of Holies on the Day of Atonement when he received the announcement that Elizabeth would conceive. After six months came the annunciation to Mary, and nine months from that, this day of the nativity, although, as noted above, his setting of the annunciation in April reveals a vestige of the older oriental paschal conception date. Chrysostom's presentation of these computations, devoid of reference to the quarter-tense days, is further interesting in that the reasoning employed in *De soltitiis* was not treated merely as fanciful solar symbolism, but as historical computation.

To whatever year we assign the introduction of Christmas at Antioch, the feast was observed at Constantinople from around the beginning of the reign of Theodosius I. In the imperial city, the accession of Theodosius in 379 marked the end of that church's Arianism and brought a new theological and political climate. One symptom of the resurgence of orthodoxy was the invitation issued to Gregory Nazianzen to come to Constantinople, where he was made archbishop in 381 and reigned for a brief period. From his time there, we have sermons on the nativity (which he calls "Theophany") and on the feast of Christ's baptism (which he calls "The Feast of Lights") preached, respectively, on December 25, 380, and on January 6, 381. In the latter of those sermons, Gregory refers back to the festival of December 25, and says, "At his nativity we duly kept festival, both I, the *exarchos* of the feast, and you and all that is in the world and above the world" (PG 36.340). Dom Botte takes that term, *exarchos*, to mean that Gregory was the founder of that festival in Constantinople and personally responsible for its institution there. A number of commentators, however, have made the point that this is not necessarily the meaning of the term at all. It need mean nothing more than that he presided over the liturgical celebration. We cannot, on the basis of the occurrence of that term alone, date the appearance of the December festival in Constantinople.

What can be said with reasonable assurance is that it seems highly unlikely that the festival would have been adopted from Rome under an Arian emperor. Therefore, if not adopted since the death of Valens, it would have had to be a very early feature of the Byzantine liturgy, given the brevity of the episodes of orthodoxy in the imperial city between Constantine and Theodosius. If the institution of Christmas at Rome had as much to do with Constantine's solar piety as has been urged by some, one would expect him to have pressed for the festival in his new capital, but of that we have no evidence whatsoever. If, on the contrary, we are to look for the introduction of the festival of December 25 after the fall of Valens, then the interpretation of *exarchos* becomes somewhat academic. If Gregory Nazianzen did not preside at the first celebration of Christmas in Constantinople in 380, that occasion was no more than the second such celebration of the feast.

In Cappadocia the situation is similar to that in Constantinople, the nativity festival on December 25 is called "Theophany" (but sometimes *Genethlia*) and the festival of January 6 celebrates Christ's baptism and is called "The Feast of Lights." This was the case with Gregory of Nyssa and Basil, as well as others in Cappadocia.[100] Amphilochius of Iconium, in a Christmas sermon (PG 39.3644), uses only *ta genethlia* to designate the festival. The Byzantine tradition finally settled on that title for the December feast, using both *Theophania* and *ta phōta* of that in January in the typika of Hagia Sophia in the ninth and tenth centuries.[101]

From the time of the restoration of orthodoxy with the accession of Theodosius, then, the observance of the nativity festival on December 25 extended smoothly and swiftly from Constantinople, across Cappadocia to Antioch. The older festival of January 6 continued to be observed with the theme of the baptism of Jesus. If between Constantinople and Antioch there continued some confusion as to which of these was the Theophany of Christ, we can suppose that this was an ambiguity already in the earlier unitive celebration of the birth and baptism on that day. The reference of the incarnation to a precise point in the life of Jesus is ambiguous, indeed, in the prologue of the fourth gospel.

It was otherwise, however, in Jerusalem and Alexandria. At Jerusalem the old festival of January 6 celebrated the nativity alone, without reference to the baptism. This was also true for Epiphanius, a native of Palestine (although he set the Cana miracle on the same day). As did Chrysostom, Jerome argued in his commentary on Ezekiel that at his nativity, Christ was not manifested, but hidden, contrary to this Palestinian tradition (PL 25.18C–19A). Still, that tradition continued firm at Jerusalem throughout the fourth century and beyond.

There are signs that the December festival was adopted at Jerusalem at some point in the fifth century, and the episcopate of Juvenal (424–458) is indicated. We have two sermons for the feast by Hesychius, preacher in the Holy City from 412 to his death in 451 (PG 93.1449). Nonetheless, that institution of the feast proved to be only temporary, since around the middle of the following century Cosmas Indicopleustes (PG 88.197) comments that the church of Jerusalem is unique in celebrating the birth of the Savior on the Epiphany, commemorating David and St. James on December 25. That was also the situation earlier, in the lectionaries from between 417 and 439 preserved in Armenian, where December 25 is the feast of David and James. However, a principal manuscript of that Jerusalem ordo (Jerusalem, arm. 121) adds to the title of that feast the rubrical note, "in other cities the birth of Christ is celebrated." The editor shows conclusively that this note belonged to the Jerusalem ordo itself prior to the introduction of the festival by Juvenal.[102]

Just when the December nativity feast was introduced in Jerusalem and just when it was given up cannot be more closely specified. That it was no longer observed in the sixth century is testified to not only by Cosmas Indicopleustes but also Abraham of Ephesus (530–553) who, in a sermon on the Annunciation,[103] indicated (as did Cosmas) that the Palestinians were alone in rejecting the feast of the birth of the Savior on December 25. The celebration of the feast throughout the empire was ordered by the emperor Justin II (565–578), according to the historian Nicephorus Callistus (PG 147.292), and a letter of Justinian a few years earlier (561) had called upon Jerusalem authorities specifically to keep the Annunciation (previously not observed at Jerusalem) on March 25 and Hypapante on February 2, forty days after December 25, rather than February 14. That letter also makes it clear that by then the Epiphany at Jerusalem celebrated both Christ's nativity and baptism, an arrangement jealously defended by Monophysite forces against the separate celebration of the bodily nativity on December 25. Nonetheless, shortly after the death of the patriarch Macarius II (567/568), Jerusalem finally adopted the December festival, and the itinerary of Antoninus of Plaisance in 570 reports the observance of the Epiphany not at Bethlehem but at the place of Jesus' baptism on the Jordan.[104]

In Egypt, also, the feast of December 25 was resisted for some long while. From the end of the fourth century we have the testimony of John Cassian that the content of the Epiphany in Egypt was both the nativity and the baptism, celebrated together. His testimony is the first secure notice we have of a liturgical observance of the nativity of Christ in Egypt. Cassian, writing at Marseilles between 418 and 427, says in the tenth of his *Conferences* (chap. 2) that the themes of birth and baptism are united in the one festival.

"In the country of Egypt this custom is by ancient tradition observed that—when Epiphany is past, which the priests of that province regard as the time, both of our Lord's baptism and also of his birth in the flesh, and so celebrate the commemoration of either mystery not separately as in the Western provinces but on the single festival of this day—letters are sent from the Bishop of Alexandria through all the churches of Egypt, by which the beginning of Lent, and the day of Easter are pointed out not only in all the cities but also in all the monasteries" (NPNF II.XI, p. 401).

Since the writer's purpose here is to describe the issuance of the festal letters by the bishop of Alexandria, it is unlikely that he is describing a variation in the festal theme in different parts of Egypt, although it is certain that there were variant customs within that country. Cassian, nonetheless, evidently indicates a double theme in Alexandria itself. It is impossible to know how long that double theme had attached to the festival. We can only say that the identification of the date as that of the nativity reaches back as far as Clement, as does its association with the baptism, but that earlier in the fourth century the feast was focused on the baptism to such an extent that the *Canons of Athanasius* make no reference at all to any festival of the nativity. It may well be that while the strong Marcan tradition at Alexandria made the baptism (with which Mark's gospel opens) stand out as the content of the celebration on January 6, the memory persisted that the gospel was begun on that day because it was the day of the Lord's nativity.

It was only in the fifth century, in any case, that the festival of December 25 was adopted at Alexandria. There, following the Council of Ephesus, Paul of Emessa preached before St. Cyril on December 25, 432, and again on the following January 1 (PG 77.1432). This marks the first celebration of the nativity on December 25 at Alexandria of which we have record. In view of its relation to the Council of Ephesus, it seems likely that the December festival's adoption in Alexandria was motivated by christological concerns, as was the case earlier at Constantinople and through Asia Minor to Antioch following the death of the Arian emperor, Valens. The adoption of Christmas at Alexandria, again, may have contributed to the unsuccessful and temporary establishment of the feast a bit later in Jerusalem.

14. EPIPHANY IN THE WEST

The earliest mention of the festival of January 6 in the West is the notice of its observance in Gaul by the emperor Julian, still (but only) publicly Christian, recorded by the pagan writer, Ammianus Marcellinus.[105] The year was 361, and the account refers specifically to the title of the festival, *Epiphania,* and to the time of its observance, *mense Januario.* Nothing is said about the content of the festival, but Botte has noted that this same story about Julian is recounted in the twelfth century by the historian Zonaras. In his account, the festival in question is referred to as *tēs genethliou tou sōtēros hēmeras,* the nativity of the savior. Since there is no reason to believe that Zonaras was unfaithful to his sources in such a minor detail, it seems likely that no contradiction exists between those sources and Ammianus. The content of *Epiphania* in Gaul in 361 was the nativity, and the feast was well established there. Botte admits that such a construction is fragile and can be taken only as hypothetical,[106] but it would be consistent with the general picture we have of the oriental influences operating in transalpine Gaul. It is there alone in the West that we lack evidence for the observance of December 25 in the fourth century.

The account of Zonaras makes no mention of any other theme than that of the nativity, but if our understanding of the unity of nativity and baptism themes in the Anatolian and Syrian traditions is correct, a more complex content would be expected. By the first half of the fifth century, such was surely the case in Gaul, as a poem of Paulinus of Nola[107] and the Fasti of Polemius Sylvius[108] testify. By that time, the festival of December 25 had been adopted for the nativity, while the Epiphany celebrated the visit of the Magi, the baptism in the Jordan, and the miracle at Cana, the *tria miracula* that would long remain the content of the Epiphany festival in Gaul.

The situation was different in the fourth century, and notably in northern Italy, at Brescia, ca. 385–391. There the *Hereseon Liber* of Filastrius takes note of three themes in connection with the Epiphany, but these are the visit of the Magi, the baptism, and the transfiguration, *transformationis in monte*. Only the first of these is the theme in his own church.[109] He refers to "some" who celebrate the baptism of Jesus on that day, and "others" who observe the transfiguration. He betrays no familiarity with the celebration of the Cana miracle in connection with the Epiphany. Further, the Epiphany for him is secondary to Christmas, the festival of the nativity. That December festival is accorded a heightened solemnity, being preceded by a fast, a dignity not accorded the Epiphany. We know that the festal climate following Christmas would not necessarily preclude a fast before the Epiphany, since Filastrius mentions fasts both before and following the Ascension, as we noted in Part One.[110]

At that same time the situation seems to have been more conservative at nearby Milan. We noted in Part One that in the time of Ambrose, the Pentecost remained unbroken there for fifty days. There also the Epiphany was celebrated primarily as the baptism of Christ in the Jordan, as at Alexandria in the earlier fourth century. Again as at Alexandria, it was the occasion for the announcement of the date of Easter. The Epiphany was the occasion for the enrollment of *competentes* for Easter baptism, as was the case as well with Ambrose's contemporary, Maximus, in nearby Turin.[111] We shall argue in Part Three that this, too, may reflect an Alexandrian connection.

The baptism was not the only theme associated with the festival, however. Of the four extant Epiphany sermons of Maximus, two are concerned only with the baptism in the Jordan, one with both

142

the baptism and the wedding at Cana, and one with the wedding at Cana alone. Mutzenbecher considers this to reflect an uncertainty regarding the content of the festival, a conflict of traditions, rather than a complex themeology.[112]

For Milan itself, Hieronymus Frank has argued persuasively that the baptism of Christ was the original content of the Epiphany, although Ambrose later reflects other themes, including the miracle at Cana and the visit of the Magi.[113] That, for Frank, does not mean that Ambrose himself instituted the festival of December 25 at Milan, as some have argued, although he leaves that possibility open. It is more probable, he believes, that Christmas was already established there when Ambrose became the bishop of the city, and that it is to that festival that the phrase *natalis salvatoris* refers in the sermon (at the veiling of his sister, Marcellina), which he ascribes to Liberius of Rome in the third book of his *De virginibus* in 377.[114] The other scriptural themes mentioned in that sermon, such as the Cana wedding feast, are chosen for their appropriateness to the occasion of Marcellina's religious profession and should not be taken for themes of the liturgical festival that was the occasion of that profession.

Such an understanding of that frequently discussed "Liberius" sermon is much more satisfying than the attempts of Usener, Lietzmann, Holl and others to identify the date of Marcellina's profession in Rome as January 6, 353, and to establish on such a basis that Rome observed that festival as the celebration of the nativity before the adoption of Christmas, a liturgical change that they can only assign to 354.[115] As we have seen, the list of *Depositiones Episcoporum* in the Chronograph of 354 arranges those dates within a year that began with the nativity on December 25, although the festival on that date is given only in the *Depositiones Martyrum*. The list of bishops' burials was originally drawn up in 336, well before the episcopate of Liberius.

The evidences available in northern Italy, nonetheless, do suggest a considerable variety in the themes associated with the Epiphany. We have noted the vacillation between the themes of the baptism and the Cana miracle at Turin. Something of the same variety can be seen in Ambrose's hymn, *Inluminans Altissimus*, even if we agree with Frank that the original theme in Milan was the baptism. Still the successive verses of that hymn introduce each new theme with the conjunction *seu* or *vel*, suggesting that these were seen as various themes known to Ambrose, not the *tria miracula* celebrated together at the single festival. It is similarly clear that at Brescia, the Epiphany celebrated the visit of the Magi, although Filastrius takes note that "some" observe the baptism of Jesus on that day. His testimony to the celebration of the transfiguration by still "others" is unique, and his silence regarding the wedding at Cana, in view of other northern Italian sources of the time, is difficult to explain.

In general, we encounter the visit of the Magi, distinct from the nativity itself, as a theme of the Epiphany only where and when the festival of the nativity is celebrated on the alternative date, December 25. The adoration of the Magi, that is to say, represents a division of the content of the nativity story to supply the themes of two distinct festivals, both associated with the nativity of Christ in Bethlehem. It seems most likely that the division of the nativity narrative is the result of the adoption of the January festival in Rome and Africa at some time after the Donatist schism. Augustine's *Sermo* 202 details that their contempt for the unity of the Church had led them to ignore this festival of great antiquity in the East, now observed in the West as well. Is more precision possible?

Botte placed considerable emphasis on a Christmas sermon of Optatus of Milevis that celebrated the entire nativity story, including the visit of the Magi and the slaughter of the innocents.[116] That sermon, preserved under the name of Augustine, was edited in 1917 by Germain Morin.[117] The ascription to Optatus, which would place the single observance of nativity and the adoration of the Magi together on December 25 well within the second half of the fourth century, was made by André Wilmart in 1922[118] and, if supported, would yield a later and more useful *terminus post quem* for the introduction of the Epiphany in Africa. While it has been argued that the author of the sermon is himself a Donatist,[119] and while that opinion may weaken the value of this testimony, the Donatist ascription is rejected by E. Dekkers,[120] and it seems likely that he speaks for the broader stream of scholarly opinion. The sermon is undated, and we can say little of Optatus' dates save that he flourished between 365 and 385. Such a *terminus post quem* for the African and Roman adoption of the Epiphany would accord with its absence from the calendar of festivals in the Chronograph of 354. There, as we have seen, the nativity on December 25 marks the beginning of the year for the martyrs' list. The presence in that list of the *Natale Petri de catedra* on January 22, however, suggests that all festivals of fixed date are included, and the Epiphany is not among them.

If the adoration of the Magi stems from a Roman duplication of the nativity, we have for a *terminus ante quem* the evidence of Filastrius, ca. 385–391, probably some ten years earlier than Augustine's sermon. At about that same time, Himerius was conferring baptism at Tarragona in Spain on both Christmas and the Epiphany (*apparitio*). We do not know the theme of the latter observance, but the decretal of Siricius to Himerius in 385, while critical of that baptismal practice, reflects no unfamiliarity with such a festival. It is difficult to avoid the impression that the feast was already observed in Rome.[121] Massey Shepherd included the Epiphany (as *Theophania*, its designation in the Gelasian Sacramentary) in his reconstruction of the ferial calendar of Damasus, Siricius' immediate predecessor.[122] In the context of Shepherd's erudite assessment of the role of Damasus in the establishment of the Latin liturgy of Rome, one could conjecture (not done by Shepherd himself) that the adoption of the festival of the Epiphany at Rome took place during the pontificate of Damasus, 366–384, leaving open the possibility that this, as much else in Latin liturgical tradition, was under an African influence.

The close similarity of the January 6 festival to that already established at Rome on December 25 is reflected in three formulae for the Epiphany in the Gregorian Sacramentary—the preface, proper *Communicantes*, and a collect—all of which could be appropriate to the nativity itself.[123] These formulae seemed especially significant to some who argued that Rome had shifted its nativity festival from January 6 to December 25 in the time of Liberius. It has been pointed out, however, that one of them, the *Communicantes*, contains specific reference to the Magi in its earlier form in the Gelasian Sacramentary.[124] In all three cases, the central verb is *apparuit*, recalling the *apparitio*, which was the Latin equivalent of *epiphania* already in the letter of Siricius to Himerius in 385. Even so, it seems clear that the western Church did not simply seize upon the visit of the Magi as a significant event in the gospels that cried out for liturgical commemoration. Rather, just as the Roman nativity festival was adopted in the East, so the eastern nativity festival was adopted in the West. In the latter case, however, it is significant that the January festival was taken over not as celebration of Christ's baptism in the Jordan, as it remained in the eastern solution, but as an alternative date for the nativity, its probable theme, we have seen, in Gaul in 361. As such a doublet for the nativity festival in December, the Epiphany required a distinction, which led to the division of the nativity story and the assignment of the adoration of the Magi to the January date.

That assignment quickly yielded its own reinterpretation of the meaning of *ta epiphania*. In the preaching of both Augustine and Leo that rich classical concept has been narrowed to the "manifestation of Christ to the Gentiles," the theme that has continued to supply the principal content of the festival in the West to our own day.[125] For the Cappadocians, albeit on December 25, that *Theophania* was the nativity itself, while for Chrysostom it was Christ's baptism. Cassian tells us that for the Alexandrians it was both of these, kept on the same day, not separately as in the West. His testimony shows that in his experience, the content of the Epiphany in the West is the baptism. We have reason to believe such was the case in Milan and Turin, a tradition known to Filastrius of Brescia, even though he followed the evidently Roman custom of celebrating the adoration of the Magi on that day. That, together with the baptism and the first miracle at Cana, would emerge shortly as the *tria miracula* in Gaul, all celebrated on the same day, which would eventually affect the gospel assignments for the Sundays after the Epiphany. This multiple theme and the liturgical poetry it inspired carried forward much of the tradition regarding the close interplay between the incarnation, the baptism, and the first miracle, represented already by the first two chapters of the fourth gospel. Yet for the mainstream of western Church life, the theme that prevailed for the festival itself was the adoration of the Magi, and the classical notion of *epiphania* as the manifestation of a god in human flesh, the meaning of the term already in Homer,[126] became in the West a further vehicle for anti-Jewish sentiments, the celebration of the passage of the covenant to the Gentiles, with its attendant elaboration of the "historical" details regarding the Magi, their royalty, their names, and their physical appearance.

In the light of the theological struggles prior to and just following the victory over Arianism in 381, the exclusion at Rome and in Africa of the baptism of Jesus from the themes of what had been the oriental *epiphania*, the celebration of the incarnation, is not difficult to understand. In Cappadocia, similar considerations led to the transfer of that title for the celebration to the new December nativity date, while at Alexandria we find that the old celebration of the baptism on January 6 now came to celebrate the nativity as well. In the closing decades of the fourth century, theological development engendered a measure of embarrassment with the baptism of Jesus as the beginning of the gospel, although that theme seems to have been significant in liturgical patterns from the time of the composition of the gospel of Mark. Indeed, what seems to have been the oldest gospel assignment for the celebration of the nativity at Rome, the prologue of the fourth gospel, may also have been read at Ephesus in the beginnings of what would become the feast of the Epiphany. There we encounter the *Grundtext* of orthodox teaching on the incarnation, *kai ho logos sarx egeneto*, but the context of that declaration is the witness of a man sent from God, whose name was John.

15. THE PREPARATORY FAST

In all the major traditions today the feast of the nativity is preceded by a more or less extended season of fasting. We noted above that Filastrius, ca. 385, reported a fast before Christmas, but none preceding the Epiphany, a sign of the higher dignity accorded to the December festival. He gives no indication of the duration of the pre-Christmas fast, one of four fasts in the year discussed by him at that point.[127] The second fast is described first as *in pascha*, and the following sentence defines that further as *quadragensimae*. The third fast, discussed in Part One, is preparatory for the feast of the Ascension, the fortieth day after Pascha. The fourth fast seems to reflect two different practices, the first (for which apostolic precedent is claimed) is a fast from the Ascension to Pentecost; the other, alternative practice is a fast after Pentecost (*aut postea*). The latter of these, as we have seen, represents the primitive resumption of fasting after the full fifty days of paschal rejoicing. Such a resumption is noted for Jerusalem by Egeria at about that same time, "From the day after the Fiftieth Day they fast in the way which is usual during the rest of the year."[128] Somewhat closer to hand, the same seems to have been the custom of Milan.[129] Given Filastrius' treatment of the alternative forms of the Pentecost fast, it seems more likely that the former, the fast from Ascension to Pentecost, was the custom of Brescia. For him, each of these four fasts leads into a festival and is preparatory for it. Such is the case with the fast *in natale*. In other places, the simple identification of fasting with preparation for a festival is less clear, the fast after Pentecost being a case in point.

While Filastrius presents the four fasts as announcing the mysteries of Christianity, he is aware of other reasons given for fasting at four times in the year. He says that some hold, for example, that there should be fasts at the four seasons (*alii autem putant secundum quattuor tempora anni*).[130] That immediately suggests the *quatuuor tempora* at Rome, the fasts known to us in English as the "Ember Days," via the German *Quatember*. The precise dates associated with those fasts have varied, but the oldest tradition associates two of them with times dependent on the date of Easter, viz., the first week of Lent (which many believe to be of more recent origin than the other three) and the week following the day of Pentecost, solemnizing such a resumption of fasting as noted above. The other two fasts have most commonly been set in the weeks following the Ides of September and December, more closely specified since medieval times as the Wednesday, Friday, and Saturday following Holy Cross Day, September 14, and the feast of St. Lucy, December 13. For a time in the Carolingian period, Gallican canonists placed the fasts in the first week of the first month, the second week of the fourth month, the third week of the seventh month, and the fourth week of the tenth month. The last of those appointments, however, was always hedged about with warnings that the fast should not impede the observance of the vigil of the nativity.[131]

Jose Janini has sought to assign the institution of these seasonal fasts to the pontificate of Siricius, who succeeded Damasus as bishop of Rome in December of 384.[132] If, however, Filastrius referred to this Roman fast practice when he mentioned "others" who associate the fasts with the four seasons, and if we accept 385 as the date of his writing, then we might better follow Karl Holl's suggestion that the institution can best be assigned to the episco-

148

pate of Damasus.[133] In either case, that institution would most probably have been only a process of regularization and of liturgical appointment. Certain of the fasts, such as that following Pentecost, are surely much older.

The explanation of the origin of the Ember Days offered by Germain Morin toward the end of the last century,[134] a still frequently reiterated theory that sought to relate the Ember Days to three pagan agricultural *feriae conceptivae,* fails to take account of the state of classical studies, even of those studies appealed to by Morin himself.[135] The theory must be abandoned. Of the three *feriae* presented by Morin, only one can be identified with any precision, the *feriae Sementivae.* That festival is clearly situated in January, however, according to the sources cited by Morin himself,[136] and cannot, as he wished, be appealed to as background for the December Embertide.

Nonetheless, the second half of December had been a time of celebration at the conclusion of the agricultural year, a series of festivals stretching from December 15 (*Consualia*) to December 23 (*Laurentalia*). The atmosphere of thanksgiving that runs through the nine sermons we have from Leo I for the December fast, our earliest detailed evidence for the fast, is consistent with the celebration of agricultural bounty. Those sermons reflect a spirituality in continuity with the best in pre-Christian Roman piety, but there is also evident an eschatological nuance that will be reflected also in the Advent liturgy. In sermon 19, for example, he says:

"When the Saviour would instruct His disciples about the Advent of God's Kingdom and the end of the world's times, and teach His whole Church, in the person of the Apostles, He said, 'Take heed lest haply your hearts be overcharged with surfeiting and drunkenness, and care of this life.' And assuredly, dearly beloved, we acknowledge that this precept applies more especially to us, to whom undoubtedly the day denounced is near, even though hidden, for the advent of which it behoves every man to prepare himself lest it find him given over to gluttony, or entangled in cares of this life."[137]

That Advent theme is all the more remarkable in that at no point in the sermons for the December fast does Leo refer to the coming festival of the nativity of Christ. However appropriate to the end of the agricultural season or even the civil year, the Roman December fast in the time of Leo I is not a preparation for Christmas such as the fast mentioned in the previous century by Filastrius. It does, nonetheless, focus on the end time, the consummation of the year, and is, thus, a liturgical sign of the consummation of history. An important element in the spirituality of Advent is already present in the Roman December fast before the adoption of that preparatory season, which originated elsewhere.

While we may be sure that the Advent season developed first outside of Rome, to say more than that is not as easy as one might wish. Usener suggested, as have many others, that we see the beginnings of Advent in the fourth canon of a Council of Saragossa in 380.[138] That canon urges the constant presence of the faithful in the church, calling on them not to stay at home or run off to the country or the mountains during a period of twenty-one continuous days, beginning from December 17 and reaching to the Epiphany.[139] From that Usener concluded that the nativity was celebrated on January 6 and that Christmas was still not known in Spain in 380. Some have also suggested, although without supporting data, that this was a period of preparation for baptism at the Epiphany. Those suggestions were examined closely and rejected by Dom Botte,[140] but his argument does not finally make this text irrelevant to the Advent question. Within that Spanish jurisdiction, baptism was conferred on the Epiphany by 384, but it was also conferred on Christmas, December 25, as we have seen in the letter of Siricius to Himerius of Tarragona. It is altogether likely, Botte argued, that both festivals were already being observed at the time of the synod at Tarragona in 380, and thus the three-week period mentioned there was not simply oriented toward the Epiphany, but included Christmas. In any case, the canon in question says nothing about preparation for baptism, nor does it mention fasting.

The canon need not be read as setting a period of preparation for either festival or for both. Rather, it can be seen as a Christian counterobservance to the Saturnalia and other festivals of the end of the year, a holiday season that afforded a period of leisure that the fathers of Saragossa seem to fear could be misused. The first day of the three-week period is, in fact, the Saturnalia. That popular festival still appears in the Christian *Fasti* of Polemius Sylvius in fifth-century Gaul as *Feriae servorum*. In spite of many shifts and changes, that date is still the most common for the beginning of the "Great O" antiphons that have characterized vespers (and perhaps lauds originally) during the latter days of Advent from perhaps as early as the seventh century.[141] Those antiphons, like the Saturnalia, run from December 17 to 23. Even if that fourth canon of Saragossa was not in the first instance concerned to establish a preparatory period for Epiphany or Christmas, we can see there (as we did in the eschatological themes in Leo's Sermon 19) seeds that would later come to fruition in the Advent liturgy.

More secure data for Advent as a preparatory fast come from the sixth century. A synod at Tours in 567 laid out in its canon 17 the fast practice expected of monastics.[142] Suspended entirely in the seasons of high festivity, fasting was otherwise enjoined on Mondays, Wednesdays, and Fridays as normal practice. The specific seasons of intensified daily fasting were three in number: Lent, the entire week following Pentecost, and the month of December up to Christmas. Those regulations had to do only with monastic discipline, but fourteen years later, in 581, a council at Mâcon ordered an Advent fast for the laity.[143] From the feast of St. Martin (November 11) to Christmas, fasting was enjoined on Mondays, Wednesdays, and Fridays. (Here, as with the normal fasting of monks, it is significant that Monday is added to the older weekly station days, and that there is no sign of fasting on the Sabbath, as was customary at Rome.) We cannot know how widely these regulations were observed, but they represent a point in the progressive dissemination of what came to be called "St. Martin's Lent." Late in the previous century, St. Gregory of Tours, in his *Historia Francorum*, had attributed such a fast practice to his predecessor, Perpetuus.[144]

The accommodation of the duration of Advent to that of Lent seems obvious, but to conclude from such accommodation that Advent, as Lent, had its origins in a program of final preparation for baptismal candidates is less likely. The evidence for baptism at Christmas and Epiphany that we have noted in the decretal of Siricius to Himerius shows that the practice of Tarragona failed to provide for such an initiatory process. Other early evidence for baptism on those days is lacking. As our sixth-century Gallican sources suggest, the Advent fast is a matter of ascetical discipline

151

rather than a liturgical process, either baptismal or penitential, however much the *quadragesima* served as a penitential tariff. In Irish monasticism, the fast after Pentecost also took a quadragesimal form, along with the forty-day fasts before Christmas and Easter, and penitentials frequently suggest for particular sins the special observance of the three *quadragesimae*. The martyrology of Oengus the Culdee,[145] composed most probably at Tallaght around 800, shows three quadragesimal fasts, the fast of Jesus before Easter (begun on January 7!), the fast of Moses after Pentecost, and the fast of Elijah before Christmas. Although, as we shall discuss at greater length in Part Three, many today believe this to represent Coptic influence on Celtic monasticism, K. Holl believed that such a threefold fasting pattern was characteristic of Irish and British Christianity as early as the middle of the sixth century.[146] The fast of *eli* (Elijah) in the calendar of Oengus begins on the ides of November, November 13, a close approximation to the fifth- and sixth-century evidences that we have seen for "St. Martin's Lent" in Gaul.

"St. Martin's Lent" comprises forty-two days. It is not surprising, therefore, that many of the lectionaries of the seventh and eighth centuries provide for six Sundays of Advent, although there are others that provide only five.[147] At Milan from the seventh century there have been six Sundays of Advent. The last of these has for centuries been celebrated as the feast of the Annunciation, that day and those of the week following up to Christmas being titled *De exceptato*, a term that seems to be the Milanese equivalent of Annunciation.[148] This, of course, is the gospel assignment for the Fourth Sunday of Advent in the present Roman lectionary's four-Sunday scheme, although it does not replace the festival of March 25.

This celebration of the annunciation in Advent is already evident in the action of a council meeting at Toledo in 656.[149] The fathers of that council take note of the difficulty of celebrating the Annunciation on March 25, establishing thereby that such was already the case. The problem with the established date is that it occurs during Lent, and not infrequently in Holy Week! That, of course, is not surprising at this point in our study, having examined the evidences for identification of the day of our Lord's passion with that of his conception. That identification was lost on the fathers at Toledo, however, and they decreed that the Annunciation would thenceforth be celebrated one week before the nativity, on December 18, a decree that reveals with great clarity the difference in their own minds between Lent and Advent. The festival of the Annunciation, while inappropriate in Lent, was regarded as utterly proper in Advent.

It was otherwise with the Council in Trullo some decades later. There (in 692) canon 52 provides that in view of the probability that the Annunciation would fall during Lent, it would be accorded the same dignity as Sabbath and Sunday on whatever day March 25 fell, and would be celebrated with the eucharist, which was not allowed on fast days in Byzantine tradition. That solution to the problem of a feast of such dignity falling in Lent resolved the problem that must have been encountered at Constantinople many times since the feast was established on March 25 in the time of Justinian or even earlier in the sixth century. That they did not take the same course as the Spanish fathers at Toledo is probably due to the fact that the feast of the Annunciation had been established on the first or second Sunday before Christmas in the first half of the fifth century. The Council in Trullo was not prepared to return to the already discarded date, but instead assigned to March 25 the liturgical privilege appropriate to its dignity.[150]

Not all in the East attached such significance to that date, however. Armenians associated the conception of Christ with April 6, the paschal date reported for the Montanists by Sozomen, nine months before January 6 as nativity date. Such is the case, e.g., with Ananias of Shirak in the seventh century.[151] The Nestorians observe four "Sundays of the Annunciation" before Christmas, but it seems impossible to fix with significant precision the age of that institution.

Such association of the Annunciation with the nativity, on the one hand, and its continued association with established dates for the passion, on the other, sums up the problems associated with the celebration of the time of Christ's Advent. As we noted at the outset of this part of our study, there was a broad tradition in first-century Judaism that associated the expected parousia of Messiah with the Passover, the festival of liberation at which Christ died, and that tradition set the births and deaths of the patriarchs on that same day. Another stream of the tradition looked to Tishri, the month of the feast of Tabernacles, for the coming of Messiah, and associated the births and deaths of the patriarchs with that month. Christianity, it would seem, very early included the incarnation among the themes of the total mystery of Christ celebrated at Pascha, following the Passover tradition. That incarnation theme was more theological than historical, however, and before long the tolerable ambiguity of the time of the incarnation was drawn to a sharper focus by early christological controversy. The emerging understanding of the incarnation as the taking of flesh by the preexistent Logos directed attention from the baptism of Jesus, at which he was acclaimed to be the divine Son, to the beginning of Jesus' life as the beginning of the messianic mission, which would reach its climax at Pascha. With that, then, the incarnation as it was included in the themes of Pascha came to be understood as the conception of the Lord, the annunciation, and that itself defined the date of the nativity. It is not entirely clear why that nativity date was regarded as the beginning of the lived liturgical year, but that it was so is suggested by the practice of some local churches of beginning the reading of their local gospel on that occasion. The status of the nativity festival as head of the year is overt as our evidence becomes visible in the fourth century.

The liturgical year was not yet a succession of festivals, each with its own roots and history. Indeed, for much of the Church in the early second century there was no liturgical year, but only the liturgical week. Yet, one suspects, out of the community nurtured in the tradition of the fourth gospel the computed date of the birth of the Lord, nine months after the Asian solar equivalent to the date of Passover, became the time for the beginning of the reading of that gospel, the beginning in which was the Word and the Word made flesh. That community had already suffered a schism related to christological development, and those gnostics who claimed the fourth gospel surely saw that text as situating the incarnation at the baptism. To begin the reading of the gospel at nine months' remove from Pascha would identify the original incarnation theme as the conception of the Lord, and set that prologue in the context of his birth.

The two preceding paragraphs are, of course, highly speculative and can be offered only as a hypothesis, and an incomplete hypothesis at that. They do seek to take account of the data presently available to me. Still, however hypothetical, in some such process the date of the nativity, rather than Pascha, came to be seen as the day of his coming, the epiphany of the parousia that is and is to come. With that, however complex its later development, the second pole of the liturgical year was in place.

NOTES

1. B. Botte, "Maranatha," *Noël, Épiphanie: retour du Christ. Lex Orandi* 40 (Paris 1967) pp. 25–42.

2. H. Usener, *Das Weihnachtsfest* (Bonn 1911); B. Botte, *Les origines de la Noël et de l'Épiphanie* (Louvain 1932).

3. Tal. bab., *Rosh Hashanah* 10b–11a.

4. Ibid. The standard English translation of the Talmud published by Soncino Press, London, contains an error in 10b where R. Eliezer is made to say, "In Nisan they will be redeemed in the time to come." Our own text depends on the older German version of Goldschmidt. Prof. Lawrence Hoffman of Hebrew Union College has been good enough to examine this disagreement in the versions and give assurance that the reading in the Soncino edition is not supported by the manuscripts or the tradition.

5. See R. de Vaux, *Ancient Israel: Its Life and Institutions* (London 1961) p. 185.

6. B. Lohse, *Das Passafest der Quartadecimaner* (Gütersloh 1953).

7. Carl Schmidt, *Gespräche Jesu mit seinen Jüngern nach der Auferstehung. Uebersetzung des äthiopischen Textes von Dr. Isaak Wajnberg.* TU 3.13 (1919) p. 338. Wajnberg's translation of the relevant text (p. 58, lines 1–2) places the parousia *in den Tagen des Passah- und Pfingstfestes*, a reading that disagrees with the Coptic, and with the earlier reading of the Ethiopic by L. Guerrier (PO IX.3 [Paris 1913]). To the ms. evidence used by Guerrier, Wajnberg adds only a Stuttgart ms. and his apparatus gives its reading as: "wenn die Tage des Passah- und Pfingstfestes vorbei sind." He acknowledges two other Paris mss. which read, "zwischen dem Pfingst- und dem Passahfeste." His translation, contrary to these readings, is not specifically defended.

8. Irenaeus, *Adv. haer.* 1.7.1, 4.26.1, 4.38.

9. Justin, *I Apol.* 52.3.

10. *Monumenta Germaniae Historica. Auctores Antiquissimi,* IX (part 1; 1892) pp. 13–196.

11. G. N. Bonwetsch, *Hippolyts Werke,* I. GCS (Berlin 1897).

12. A. Hilgenfeld, *Berliner philologische Wochenschrift XVII* (1897) 1323–1326, cited from H. Leclerq, DACL 12[1], col. 909.

13. L. Duchesne, *Christian Worship, Its Origin and Evolution* (London 1949) p. 258.

14. J.-M. Hanssens, *La liturgie d'Hippolyte.* OCA 155 (Rome 1959) pp. 270–282.

15. G. Brunner, "Arnobius ein Zeuge gegen das Weihnachtsfest?" JLW 13 (1936) pp. 178–181; H. Lietzmann, *A History of the Early Church*. III: *From Constantine to Julian* (Cleveland and New York 1953) p. 317. K. Holl (*Gesammelte Aufsätze zur Kirchengeschichte*, II. p. 141, n. 1) assigns this observation to a 1916 review by Jülicher not available to this study.

16. Thomas Comerford Lawler, trans., *St. Augustine: Sermons for Christmas and Epiphany*. Ancient Christian Writers, no. 15. (Westminster, Md. 1952), p. 170.

17. So, e.g., Leonhard Fendt, "Der heutige Stand der Forschung über das Geburtsfest Jesu am 25.XII und über Epiphanias," TL 78.1 (January 1953) cols. 1–10; also, M. H. Shepherd, Jr., "The Liturgical Reform of Damasus I," *Kyriakon. Festschrift Johannes Quasten*, II, p. 854.

18. Gaston Halsberghe, *The Cult of Sol Invictus* (Leiden 1972).

19. Henry Chadwick, *The Early Church* (Harmondsworth 1967) p. 120.

20. *De pascha computus* 19. Hartel, ed., CSEL 3.3, 266: "O quam praeclara et divina Domini providentia, ut in illo die quo factus est sol in ipso die nasceretur Christus V kl. Apr. feria IIII. et ideo de ipso merito ad plebem dicebat Malachias propheta: *orietur vobis sol iustitiae, et curatio est in pennis eius.*"

21. Louis Duchesne, *Origines du culte chrétien* (Paris 1889) pp. 250f. The quotation here is in the translation of the fifth edition by M. L. McClure, *Christian Worship: Its Origin and Evolution* (London 1949), pp. 263f.

22. A. Wilmart, "La collection des 38 homélies latines de Saint Jean Chrysostome," JTS xix (1917–1918) pp. 305–327, esp. 316f.

23. Botte, pp. 88–105.

24. H. Engberding, "Der 25. Dezember als Tag der Feier der Geburt des Herrn," ALW II (1952) 25–43, esp. p. 36. Cf. the review of this essay by Botte, *Bulletin de Théologie ancienne et médiévale* VII (1954–1957), no. 918, p. 198.

25. Lines 78–84 in the edition of Botte cited above. For the Roman numbering of the months from March, see E.J. Bickerman, *Chronology of the Ancient World* (London 1968) pp. 44f.

26. Translated from Botte's edition, lines 230–233.

27. Lines 426–439: "Sed et dominus nascitur mense decembri hiemis tempore octavo kalendas ianuarias quando oleae maturae premuntur ut unctio, id est crisma nascatur, quo seges ab herbis extraneis seritur, cum agni balantes nascuntur, vineae falcibus sarmenta amputantur ut mustum suavitudinis adferant ex quo inebriati sunt apostoli sancto spiritu: *Quia ego sum inquit vitis et pater meus agricola: omne igitur sarmentum in me non adferens fructus excidetur et in ignem mittetur.* Sed et invicti natalem appellant. Quis utique tam invictus nisi dominus noster qui mortem subactam devicit? Vel quod dicant solis esse natalem ipse est sol iustitiae de quo malachias propheta dixit: *Orietur vobis timentibus nomen ipsius sol iustitiae et sanitas est in pennis eius.*"

28. F. C. Conybeare, "The Gospel Commentary of Epiphanius," *Zeit-*

schrift für die neutestamentliche Wissenschaft 7 (1906) pp. 318–332. The latter of the passages quoted is on p. 324; the former from folio 74 is on p. 325. On p. 325 the writer acknowledges that some take the day of the week on which the annunciation occurred to have been Wednesday, but reasserts his contention that it was Sunday.

29. On orientation in prayer, see C. E. Pocknee, *The Christian Altar* (London 1963) pp. 88–100. Also H. Leclercq in DACL 12² 2665–2669.

30. *Bibliotheca Orientalis* II (Rome 1721).

31. Botte, p. 66.

32. Botte (ibid.) acknowledges this, but adds: "Néanmoins, cette glose est intéressante parce qu'elle montre que l'explication est naturelle. Duchesne disait que son explication serait plus vraisemblable si on la trouvait toute faite; mais on ne la trouve pas." That statement seems inexplicable coming from the editor of *De solstitiis* in the volume to which he appended that document which Wilmart had earlier recognized as a definitive demonstration of Duchesne's hypothesis.

33. See n. 17 above. O. Cullmann, "The Origin of Christmas," *The Early Church* (Philadelphia 1956), p. 22, n. 5, seems to report the computation from March 25 to the nativity on December 25 in the third-century *Chronography* of Julius Africanus, but the note is imprecise. I have been unable to confirm his suggestion from the extant fragments of the African writer (PG 10.63–94).

34. The standard edition is that of Karl Holl, GCS 31 (Leipzig 1922).

35. Edmund Beck, *Hymnen de Nativitate* 5.13 (CSCO 186, p. 48; German trans., CSCO 187, p. 41).

36. Karl Holl, *Gesammelte Aufsätze zur Kirchengeschichte, II. Der Osten* (Tübingen 1927) p. 150.

37. *Saturnalia* I.18.10. Percival Vaughan Davis, trans., *Macrobius: The Saturnalia* (New York 1969) p. 129.

38. Holl, *Gesammelte Aufsätze*, II, p. 145.

39. Raffaele Pettazzoni, "Aion—(Kronos)Chronos in Egypt," *Essays on the History of Religions. Studies in the History of Religions (Supplements to Numen)* I (Leiden 1954) pp. 171–179.

40. Eduard Norden, *Die Geburt des Kindes: Geschichte eine religiösen Idee. Studien der Bibliothek Warburg,* III (Berlin 1924) pp. 38f.

41. F. K. Ginzel, *Handbuch der mathematischen und technischen Chronologie,* Band I (Leipzig 1906) p. 101.

42. See the pictographic designations in Ginzel, op. cit., pp. 156–157.

43. Ibid., pp. 181–195.

44. R. van den Broek, *The Myth of the Phoenix according to Classical and Early Christian Traditions* (Leiden 1972) p. 70 and Plate VI, fig. 8.

45. *Saturnalia* I.12.2. P. V. Davies ed., p. 84.

46. Ginzel, op. cit., pp. 196–200.

47. Botte, p. 71. A typographical error on that page gives 1196 for 1996 as the date to which Norden (p. 38) assigns Amenemhet.

48. Ginzel, op. cit., p. 206.

49. P. Geyer, ed., *Antonini Placentini Itinerarivm.* 11. CC Lat. CLXXV (Turnhout 1965) p. 135.

50. Johann Michael Vansleben, *The Present State of Egypt; or, A New Relation of a Late Voyage into that Kingdom* (London 1678, reprinted 1972) pp. 205–207. See also Gérard Viaud, *Les Coptes d'Égypte* (Paris 1978) p. 41. Viaud identifies the *mightas* as surrogate for the Nile. A description of these tanks is given in O.H.E. KHS-Burmester, *A Guide to the Ancient Coptic Churches of Cairo* (Cairo n.d.) p. 11: "In the narthex of some of the ancient churches there is a deep oblong tank about 2 metres deep × 2.75 metres long × 2.25 metres wide, sunk in the floor, and now covered over with boards. This tank was formerly used for the Service of the Blessing of the Water on the Feast of the Epiphany; now, however, a portable basin is used for this service." This tank is to be distinguished from the smaller and shallow but similarly disused "Mandatum Tank" formerly employed for the pedilavium on Great Thursday.

51. F. K. Ginzel, *Handbuch der mathematischen und technischen Chronologie*, Band I. (Leipzig 1906) pp. 205–207.

52. R.-G. Coquin, "Les origines de l'Épiphanie en Égypte," Botte, Mélia, etc., eds., *Noël, Épiphanie, retour du Christ. Lex Orandi* 40 (Paris 1967) p. 157. While Coquin is perhaps correct with regard to present reckoning of the natural harvest, it is worth noting that Ginzel (loc. cit.) notes from the calendar of Edfu a harvest festival of the goddess Renenutet on 7 Tybi, although the Theban list for the Augustan period puts that festival on 1 Pharmuthi (Julian March 27).

53. C. Plinii Secundi, *Naturalis Historiae*, II.106 (103): "In Andro insula templo Liberi patris fontem Nonis Januariis semper vini sapore fluere Mucianus ter cos. credit: *Dios Theodosia* vocatur."

54. Pausanias, *Description of Greece*, VI.26. The translated text here is taken from A. McArthur, *The Evolution of the Christian Year* (London 1953) pp. 66–67.

55. A. McArthur, *The Evolution of the Christian Year*, p. 66.

56. Pauly-Wissowa, *Real-encyclopädie der classischen Altertumswissenschaft.* II: Reihe, 11. Halbband (Stuttgart 1936) col. 684, lines 31–42.

57. E.g., Arnold Meyer, *Das Weinachtsfest, seine Entstehung und Entwicklung* (Tübingen 1912).

58. Pauly-Wissowa, *Real-encyclopädie der classischen Altertumswissenschaft*, 9. Halbband (Stuttgart 1903) col. 1021.

59. Botte, p. 73.

60. Wilhelm Riedel and W. E. Crum, *The Canons of Athanasius of Alexandria* (London 1904) pp. 26–27.

61. A. Strobel, *Ursprung und Geschichte des frühchristlichen Osterkalenders.* TU 121 (Berlin 1977) p. 150.

62. E. J. Bickerman, *Chronology of the Ancient World* (London 1968) p. 50.

63. R. Bainton, "Basilidian Chronology and New Testament Interpretation," *Journal of Biblical Literature*, XLII, parts I and II (1923).

64. Robert Gustav Schram, *Kalendariographische und chronologische Tafeln* (Leipzig 1908).

65. R. Bainton, "The Origins of Epiphany," *Early and Medieval Christianity. The Collected Papers in Church History*, Series One (Boston 1962) pp. 22–38.

66. E. J. Bickerman, *Chronology of the Ancient World* (London 1968) Table IV (pp. 146ff., but esp. pp. 151–152) shows the relation of the beginning of the Egyptian *annus vagus* to the relevant Julian years.

67. HE VII.18. Sozomen is probably in error in reporting that the Montanists observed equal months of thirty days, an Egyptian peculiarity not followed in Asia, but otherwise his description is consistent with this Asian recension of the Julian calendar.

68. Bainton, "The Origins of the Epiphany," *Early and Medieval Christianity*, p. 34.

69. A. McArthur, *The Evolution of the Christian Year*, p. 69.

70. Wilhelm Riedel and W. E. Crum, *The Canons of Athanasius of Alexandria* (London 1904).

71. R.-G. Coquin, "Les origines de l'Épiphanie en Égypte," Botte, etc., *Noël, Epiphanie: retour du Christ. Lex Orandi* 40 (Paris 1967) pp. 140–154.

72. Br. Mus. Coptic papyrus XXXVI.

73. Riedel and Crum, op. cit., p. xxv.

74. Ibid., pp. 26–27.

75. That date for the celebration of the Cana miracle was established at least as early as the Alexandrian synaxary, given its present form by Michael of Malig in the first half of the thirteenth century. I. Forget, *Synaxarium Alexandrinum*. CSCO Arab. III.18 (Rome 1921) p. 338.

76. Trans. by Kirsopp Lake, *The Apostolic Fathers*, II. Loeb *Classical Library* (Cambridge, Mass. 1959) pp. 375–377.

77. Ibid., p. 379.

78. PG 49.365.

79. According to Theodore the Lector, *Hist. Eccles.*, II, fragm. 48 (PG 86.209).

80. DACL 2¹, 704–707.

81. P. Geyer, ed., *Antonini Placentini Itinerarivm*, 11. CC Lat. CLXXV, p. 135.

82. DACL 2¹, 707. The place in James of Edessa is not given.

83. For the opposition of James of Edessa to such an interpretation, see G. Khouri-Sarkis and A. du Boullay, "La bénédiction de l'eau la nuit de l'Épiphanie, dans le rite syrien d'Antioche," *L'Orient Syrien* 4 (1959) pp. 224–229.

84. There is, e.g., no evidence at all to support the assertion of W. Ledwich—"Baptism, Sacrament of the Cross," *The Sacrifice of Praise* (Rome

1981) p. 209—that the Epiphany was the primary baptismal day at any time in the eastern church.

85. E. Beck, trans., *Des heiligen Ephraem des Syrers Hymnen de Nativitate (Epiphania)*. CSCO 187 (Louvain 1959) pp. 134–155, inter alia.

86. Ibid., p. vi. See also Beck, "Le baptême chez Saint Ephrem," *L'Orient Syrien* 1 (1956) pp. 111–130.

87. Botte, p. 28; J. Mossay, *Les fêtes de Noël et d'Épiphanie d'après les sources littéraires cappadociennes du IVe siècle* (Louvain 1965) pp. 9–10.

88. Greg. Naz., *Orat. XL*, PG 36.

89. Mansi, III.656B.

90. Juan Mateos, *Le Typikon de la Grande Église*. OCA 165, 166 (Rome 1962, 1963).

91. Martin Higgins, "Note on the Purification (and Date of Nativity) in Constantinople in 602," ALW 2 (1952) pp. 81–83.

92. Mateos, *Le Typikon*, I, pp. 182–183.

93. Melito of Sardis, *Peri Pascha* 66. The translation is that of Thomas Halton from the French of A. Hamman, ed., *The Paschal Mystery. Alba Patristic Library* 3 (Staten Island, N.Y. 1969), p. 33.

94. So, e.g., M.D. Goulder, *The Evangelists' Calendar: A Lectionary Explanation of the Development of Scripture* (London 1978).

95. A. Renoux, *Le codex*, II. pp. 210–225.

96. Ibid., pp. 202–203.

97. Egeria, 25.10–12.

98. On the martyrium of Stephen, see Renoux, op. cit., pp. 197–202.

99. Funk, p. 269.

100. Botte, p. 29.

101. Mateos, *Le Typikon*, I, pp. 174, 184.

102. Renoux, *Le codex*, I. pp. 75–78.

103. PO 16.443.

104. See Michel van Esbroeck, "La Lettre de l'empereur Justinien sur l'Annonciation et la Noël en 561," *Analecta Bollandiana* 86 (1968) pp. 351–371.

105. Ammianus Marcellinus, *Rerum Gestarum Libri qui Supersunt*, XXI.2.4–5. *Loeb Classical Library II*, pp. 98–101.

106. Botte, p. 46.

107. PL 61.649.

108. *Corpus Inscriptionum Latinarum*, I (Berlin 1893) p. 257.

109. F. Heylen, ed., *Filastrius Episcopi Brixiensis Diversarum Hereseon Liber*. CC Lat. IX (Turnhout 1957) p. 304. CXL [112].1: ". . . nasceretur VIII Kal. Ian. et appareret, ut apparuit magis post duodecim dies. . . . et sic a magis adoraretur." CXL.4: "Quidam autem die Epiphaniorum baptismi, alii transformationis in monte quae facta est esse opinantur".

110. Ibid., CXLIX [121].3, p. 312.

111. Almut Mutzenbecher, "Der Festinhalt von Weihnachten und Epiphanie in den echten *Sermones* des Maximus Tauriensis," *Studia Patristica* 5. part III. TU 80 (Berlin 1962) pp. 109–116; Hieronymus Frank, "Die Vor-

rangstellung der Taufe Jesu in der altmailändischen Epiphanieliturgie und die Frage nach dem Dichter des Epiphaniehymnus Inluminans Altissimus," ALW 13 (1971) 115–132.

112. A. Mutzenbecher, op. cit., pp. 110–111.

113. Hieronymus Frank, "Zur Geschichte von Weihnachten und Epiphanie," JLW 13 (1936) pp. 19–20.

114. PL 16.231ff.

115. Usener, *Das Weihnachtsfest* (Bonn 1911) p. 281; Lietzmann, *Petrus und Paulus in Rom* (1915) p. 79; Holl, *Gesammelte Aufsätze zur Kirchengeschichte*, II (Tübingen 1927) p. 133.

116. B. Botte, *Les origines*, p. 39.

117. G. Morin, *S. Augustini tract. sive sermones inediti* (1917) pp. 170–177. PL Suppl. I.288.

118. A. Wilmart, in *Revue des sciences religieuses* 2 (1922) 271–302.

119. A. Pincherle, in *Ricerche Religiose* 18 (1947) 161–164, cited by Dekkers (see note following).

120. Eligius Dekkers, *Clavis Patrum Latinorum*, editio altera. *Sacris Erudiri* 3 (1961) 65.

121. Mansi, III.656B.

122. Massey H. Shepherd, "The Liturgical Reform of Damasus I," *Kyriakon: Festschrift Johannes Quasten*, II (Münster Westfallen 1970) p. 854.

123. These are formulae nos. 89, 90, and 93 in Jean Deshusses, *Le Sacramentaire Grégorien*, Tome Ie. *Spicilegium Friburgense* 16 (Fribourg Suisse 1971) pp. 114–115.

124. C. Mohlberg, *Liber Sacramentorum Romanae Aeclesiae Ordinis Anni Circuli. Rerum Ecclesiasticarum Documenta. Series maior: Fontes IV* (Rome 1960) p. 15 (formula no. 66).

125. E.g., *Sermones XXXII, XXXIII* (PL 54.237–244).

126. C. Mohrmann, *Études sur le latin des chrétiens* (Rome 1958) p. 247.

127. F. Heylen, ed., *Filastrii Episcopi Brixiensis Diversarum Hereseon Liber*. CXLIX [121].3. CC Lat., vol. IX, p. 312.

128. Egeria, 44.1.

129. Ambrose, *In Luc.* 8.25 (CSEL 32.4.403). So Josef Schmitz, *Gottesdienst im altchristlichen Mailand. Theophaneia* 25 (Köln/Bonn 1975) p. 236, n. 22.

130. *Diversarum Hereseon Liber*, CXLIX [121]. 6.

131. So, e.g., canon 34 of the Council of Mainz in 813. *Monumenta Germaniae Historica. Legum, Sec. III: Concilia.* Tom. II, pars I (Hanover 1906) p. 269.

132. Jose Janini, *S. Siricio y las cuatro temporas* (Valencia 1958).

133. K. Holl, "Die Entstehung der vier Fastenzeiten in die griechischen Kirche," *Gesammelte Aufsätze zur Kirchengeschichte*, II, p. 189.

134. G. Morin, "L'origine des quatre-temps," *Revue bénédictine* 14 (1897) 337–346.

135. E.g., see the study of C. Jullian, s.v. "Feriae," in Daremberg et Saglio, *Dictionnaire des antiquités grecques et romaines*, II², pp. 1051–1052.

136. Ovid, *Fasti*, I.657. Here Ovid deals with the *Feriae Sementivae* under the dates January 24–26, although the day in January was set by the pontiffs.

137. NPNF II.XII, p. 127.

138. H. Usener, *Das Weihnachtsfest*, p. 220.

139. PL 85.66.

140. Botte, pp. 49–53.

141. *Corpus Inscriptionum Latinarum*, I¹, p. 279. C. Callewaert, "De groote Adventsantifonen O," *Sacris Erudiri* (1940) pp. 405–418.

142. Cited in K. Holl, *Gesammelte Aufsätze zur Kirchengeschichte*, II. p. 191, n. 3.

143. Ibid., n. 4.

144. *Historia Francorum*, X.31. *Monumenta Germaniae Historica, Scriptores rerum Merov*. I.1.444, 29ff.

145. Whitley Stokes, ed., *The Martyrology of Oengus the Culdee*. Henry Bradshaw Society, vol. xxix (London 1905) pp. 34, 43, 234. The beginning of the prepaschal Lent, "Jesu's Lent," on January 7 is to be seen in relation to the mention on the previous day of no Epiphany theme save the baptism. The beginning of Lent on the day following the celebration of the baptism of the Lord will be discussed in Part Three. The translation of the note on January 7 (p. 43) renders *Cargus eli* as "Another Lent," but K. Holl (*Gesammelte Aufsätze zur Kirchengeschichte* II, p. 192, note 5) gives the improved reading by Kuno Meyer, on the basis of a Berlin manuscript, as "Elijah's Lent."

146. Op. cit. (see previous note), pp. 192–197.

147. The plans of the lectionaries are presented schematically in A. McArthur, *The Evolution of the Christian Year*, p. 75.

148. Cabrol, DACL I², 2249.

149. Mansi XI.33–34.

150. Ibid., XI.968. On the earlier history of the Annunciation at Constantinople, see P.-M. Gy, "La Question du système des lectures de la liturgie byzantine," *Miscellanea Liturgica in onore di sua eminenza il cardinale Giacomo Lercaro*, II (Rome 1967) p. 258 and n. 26. Gy cites a work unfortunately unavailable to this study, D. M. Montagna, "La liturgia mariana primitiva," *Marianum* 24 (1962) pp. 84–128.

151. F. C. Conybeare, "Ananias of Shirak upon Christmas," *The Expositor. Fifth Series* IV (1896) p. 334.

Part Three

The Process of Conversion

The advent of the messianic kingdom is, and has ever been, a radical challenge to established cultural presuppositions, so that the announcement of that advent is, and has ever been, a call to transformation, conversion, repentance, *metanoia*. From before the preaching of John the Baptist, but still in that preaching and since, the demand for conversion has been the starting point of the process of incorporation into the redeemed community. Studies in the phenomenology of religion repeatedly demonstrate a rhythm of death and rebirth in rites of passage, a kenotic stripping away of status incumbencies as an integral part of the process of coming to a new identity. Such a process of conversion can be seen also in the ritual of proselyte baptism in the Talmud,[1] and it is the motive of the entire catechetical tradition in Christianity. Baptism, the radical conferral of new life in the risen Lord, includes, as integral to that new life, the renunciation of the old. Of that transition, the paschal mystery of Christ's death and resurrection is the fundamental paradigm, and the realization of that paradigm has played a large role in the liturgical organization of time.

1. EARLY CATECHESIS

Acts 2 records Peter's sermon on Pentecost, his eschatological announcement of the fulfillment of the prophecy of Joel and his identification of the risen Christ as the Lord on whose name one must call to be saved in "the great and manifest day," concluding, "Let all the house of Israel therefore know assuredly that God has made him both Lord and Christ, this Jesus whom you crucified." And to the questioning response of his hearers, "brethren, what shall we do?" he answers, "Repent, and be baptized every one of you in the name of Jesus Christ for the forgiveness of your sins; and you shall receive the gift of the Holy Spirit."

Later accounts of baptism in the New Testament do not add to that account any further details of the length of the catechetical process, but it is clear that this process became more extended in the course of the second century, and perhaps earlier. The first six chapters of *Didache* are generally recognized to be a catechetical manual, and that appears as well in the *Epistle of Barnabas.* If, as seems most likely, the manual in *Didache* is based upon a Jewish catechetical method, then we must suppose that some such extended catechesis was already being practiced when *Didache* was produced. The date of that crucial document is still uncertain, but recent studies, we have seen, have shown a clear tendency toward an earlier rather than a later date. J.-P. Audet placed its earliest stratum well within the first century.[2] More recently, Joan Hazelden Walker has tentatively suggested that *Didache* was produced at Antioch to serve as a manual for the apostles sent out from there in the early mission of the Church.[3]

However early it may have been, *Didache* itself tells us little about the length of prebaptismal catechesis. Nor, indeed, does the account of baptism in the *First Apology* of Justin Martyr. There again, it is clear that some time was given to the formation of candidates, but Justin's account gives no detail regarding that.

The classic account of the ante-Nicene catechetical regimen is surely that of the *Apostolic Tradition.* There, admission to the catechumenate itself was controlled by rigorous examination of the applicant's profession, marital status, legal status, and so on. Once admitted, the normal duration of the catechumenate was three years, although that might be shortened for those whose formation was perceived to have proceeded more swiftly. At a given point in the year, those perceived to be ready for baptism were selected from the larger body of catechumens, if their sponsors could testify that they had been diligent in visiting the sick and caring for the widows and the indigent. This suggests that an important dimension of catechetical formation was the development of patterns of responsibility within the Church. While those years of catechetical formation surely had a didactic element, it is surprising to find that only after selection for baptismal candidacy was the gospel heard.

164

That final period of candidacy was marked by daily exorcism, conducted by the bishop himself as the time for baptism came near.

Although Cantalamessa has questioned whether the vigil that immediately preceded baptism was exclusively paschal, there is no reason to doubt that the final catechetical period described in the *Apostolic Tradition* fell prior to Pascha, even if a similar immediate preparation occurred also at other times for those who could not be baptized at Pascha itself.[4] (Pentecost became the standard alternative baptismal day for Rome.) We are probably safe, therefore, in seeing in this final immediate preparation of candidates for baptism the seeds of that season we know as Lent.

While *The Apostolic Tradition* is very clear about the normal length of the total catechetical program, it is indefinite regarding the duration of this period of more immediate preparation of candidates. The following two centuries yield two testimonies to the duration of Lent at Rome, and the later of those, while obviously inaccurate for the time at which it was written, may afford a clue to the duration of the immediate preparation of candidates for baptism in the *Apostolic Tradition*. This is a passage in the *Ecclesiastical History* of Socrates, a fifth-century Byzantine historian. The form in which his history has come down to us is a revision of the original work, undertaken in consequence of his recognition of the unreliability of Rufinus of Aquileia, one of his principal sources. The text itself reflects a measure of confusion, but it may be that it points to an outdated truth. It is at least useful in demonstrating the complexity of the question of the duration of Lent.

"The fasts before Easter will be found to be differently observed among different people. *Those at Rome fast three successive weeks before Easter*, excepting Saturdays and Sundays. Those in Illyrica and all over Greece and Alexandria observe a fast of six weeks, which they term 'the forty days' fast' (*tesserakostē*). Others commencing their fast from the seventh week before Easter, and fasting three five days only, and that at intervals, yet call that time 'the forty days' fast.' It is indeed surprising to me that thus differing in the number of days, they should both give it one common appellation; but some assign one reason for it, and others another, according to their several fancies" (HE V.22. [NPNF II.II, p. 131], emphasis added).

165

Socrates is clearly wrong in asserting that the Romans do not fast on Saturdays, and indeed reverses himself on that point later in the same chapter. Two sources in the later fourth century, Jerome's letter to Marcella in 384 and the previously cited decretal of Siricius to Himerius of Tarragona in the following year, show a fully established fast of forty days or longer,[5] so we may be sure that Socrates is mistaken concerning the Roman practice of his own day. His testimony to three successive weeks, however, is curiously echoed in later Roman evidence. The Gelasian Sacramentary provides on the third, fourth, and fifth Sundays of Lent masses *pro scrutiniis*, which probably reflect what were earlier the occasions of the public scrutinies of baptismal candidates.[6] It is in these masses that the sacramentary reveals for the first time the baptismal concern of Lent, there being no baptismal reference in the first two weeks. The scrutinies themselves, falling in the sacramentary following the fifth Sunday, are placed on indeterminate days within the third, fourth, and fifth weeks of Lent, the announcement of them falling on Monday of the third week. A. Chavasse has argued that these originally fell on the fourth, fifth, and sixth Sundays, the three successive weeks mentioned by Socrates, and were moved back a week and shifted to weekdays after Rome adopted the Lent of six weeks.[7]

Michel Andrieu has argued convincingly that the scrutinies themselves in the Gelasian Sacramentary (Gel. I.xxix-xxxvi) are an interpolation into that document and represent an abbreviation and contraction of the rites in *Ordo XI*. By the time of the composition of that ordo (end of the 6th cent.), the catechumenate was in decline and the "scrutinies" were only vestigial ritual observances, seven in number, including functions other than the classical scrutinies. That broader use of the term in *Ordo XI* encourages us to believe that we see an earlier, if less explicit, pattern in the Sunday masses *pro scrutiniis* of the Gelasian, masses built around the scrutiny of the baptismal candidates on the last three Sundays. It is on the Friday following the third Sunday that the Roman liturgy began a course reading of the gospel of John that continued to the passion of John on Good Friday, and Chavasse takes that *cursus* to have begun originally on the fourth Sunday.

This supposition is supported by the documents that assign to weekdays of the fourth week of Lent the title *in Mediana*. This *Hebdomada in Mediana* is concluded with the fifth Sunday, called *Dominica in Mediana*. That designation of the fifth Sunday is perfectly understandable if the fast consisted of but the three weeks preceding Easter. Camillus Callewaert, by contrast, supposed that Socrates erred in believing the three weeks to be continuous, and that the week styled *in Mediana* is to be contrasted with the Embertide of the first week and the final Holy Week as the three separated weeks given to intensified fasting. As we shall see, Maximus of Turin in the fifth century did speak against such occasional fasting. Callewaert's understanding, however, still would not explain the first appearance of baptismal reference in the third week and the focusing of baptismal scrutinies over but the final three weeks.

In the third century, Pascha was appearing as the preferred time for baptism in many parts of the Church, and the final preparation of candidates is a concern of the period just preceding the great festival. This has encouraged the general view that preparation for baptism is antecedent to any extended period of ascetical preparation for the festival itself. However, M. F. Lages, in a meticulous analysis of the Armenian lectionary for Jerusalem, found evidence that there, too, the original preparation for Pascha was of but three weeks, and suggested that this was the model for the Roman Lent. Further, Lawrence Hoffman has recently offered a fascinating and important examination of connections between such a seminal three-week Lent and the preparation for Passover in Judaism. This could well suggest that the three-week preparation for Pascha antedates its employment as the framework for baptismal preparation.[8]

However that may be, we can say that the masses *pro scrutiniis* point to the older core of preparation for paschal baptism. Around that grew the more extended Lent of "forty days or more" of which Siricius spoke in 385. While the context (his opposition to more immediate conferral of baptism on Christmas, Epiphany, and feasts of apostles and martyrs) would limit Siricius' language, he nonetheless speaks of even that longer period exclusively in terms of preparation for baptism.

2. THE PREPASCHAL QUARANTINE IN THE FOURTH CENTURY

As we noted in Part One, it was long common to consider the reference to *tesserakostē* in Canon 5 of Nicea as our earliest reference to the Lent of forty days. Increasingly, however, that is taken to be a reference to the fortieth day of paschaltide, that which would become the feast of the Ascension. It remains true, however, that the Council of Nicea is something of a watershed for the fast of forty days. Prior to Nicea, no record exists of such a forty-day fast before Easter. Only a few years after the council, however, we encounter it in most of the Church as either a well-established custom or one that has become so nearly universal as to impinge on those churches that have not yet adopted it.

The earliest direct evidence is the second festal letter of Athanasius, issued in 330. Those letters, we have seen from John Cassian (*Conferences* 10.2), were issued on the Epiphany each year by the patriarch of Alexandria, announcing the date of Easter and the beginning of the Paschal Fast. Such determination of the date of Easter was necessary once the fixed date gave way to the observance on Sunday. The custom of issuing these letters probably goes back to the correspondence exchanged with Alexandria mentioned by the bishops of Palestine in the late second century. As for Alexandria itself, such letters can be seen from the time of Dionysius in the middle of the third century (Euseb., HE 7.20), and one of his festal letters is extant.[9] The Paschal Fast there, of course, is the fast of six days discussed in Part One. This is also the only fast before Pascha mentioned in the first of Athanasius' festal letters in 329. The letter of the following year, however, announces the beginning of the forty-day fast, the beginning of the six-day Paschal Fast, the date of Easter, and it enjoins seven weeks of feasting during the Pentecost.

While it is now generally agreed that this letter belongs to 330, it has not always seemed so. An alternative arrangement of the letters by Eduard Schwartz in 1904 made that of 337 the first to announce the fast of forty days. Since that letter was written from exile in Trier, it was argued that the practice of Lent was of western origin and was introduced to Egypt through Athanasius' experience in the West. However, more recent studies of the letters by

Th. Lefort, and his edition of those that remain in Coptic, have shown clearly that the letter that gives our earliest explicit description of the fast belongs to the year 330.[10] The letter, like all the festal letters, concludes with the formal announcement.

"We begin the fast of forty days on the 13th of the month Phamenoth [March 9]. After we have given ourselves to fasting in continued succession, let us begin the week of the holy Easter (*Pascha*) on the 18th of the month Pharmuthi [April 13]. Then ceasing on the 23rd of the same month Pharmuthi [April 18], and keeping the feast afterwards on the first of the week, on the 24th [April 19], let us add to these the seven weeks of the great Pentecost, altogether rejoicing and exulting in Christ Jesus our Lord, through Whom to the Father be glory and dominion by the Holy Ghost, for ever and ever. Amen."[11]

Not all of Athanasius' letters, in fact, give the beginning of the fast of forty days. His many exiles meant that these letters were often sent from other parts and in many cases were sent, no doubt, after Lent had begun. From the letters that do give the beginning of that fast, however, a number of facts can be ascertained.

First, the older paschal fast of six days comprises the final week of the fast of forty days. The total fast before Easter is of six weeks, but the date for the beginning of the last of those weeks, the ancient paschal fast observed since at least the time of Dionysius, is separately indicated in the letters.

Second, there seems to have been no concern about the number of actual fast days. Letter VI for 334, for example, makes it clear that Sundays are not fasted, nor, following general oriental usage, are Sabbaths, except that of the Pascha itself. There are, then, but thirty-one days of actual fasting, five days in each of six weeks plus the paschal Sabbath.

Third, while Athanasius makes frequent reference to scriptural models of a quadragesimal fast, he never refers this fast of forty days to the fast of Jesus. In one or another letter he refers to the figures of Moses, of David, and of Daniel, but the fast is presented purely as an ascetical preparation for Pascha.

Fourth, there is no indication that the fast of forty days before Pascha has any relation to baptism. The rites of Christian initiation do not figure in these letters at all.

Fifth, it appears that the fast of forty days is something of an innovation, and an unpopular one at that. The first letter to announce the fast was, as noted, in 330. Still, a full decade later, in 340, Athanasius is concerned that this fast is not being observed in Egypt. The festal letter for that year is missing from the series, but we do have a covering letter to his friend, Serapion, to whom, around April 340, he sent the letter for the following year for promulgation, being himself in exile at Rome at the time.[12] He writes to Serapion:

"But I have further deemed it highly necessary and very urgent, to make known to your modesty—for I have written this to each one—that thou shouldest proclaim the fast of forty days to the brethren, and persuade them to fast; to the end that, while all the world is fasting, we who are in Egypt should not become a laughing-stock, as the only people who do not fast, but take our pleasure in these days. For if we do not fast, because the Letter is [only] then read, it is right that we should take away this pretext also, and that it be read before the fast of forty days, so that they may not make this an excuse for neglect of fasting. Also, when it is read, they may be able to learn respecting the fast. But, O, our beloved, whether in this way or any other, exhort and teach them to fast forty days. For it is even a disgrace that when all the world does this, those alone who are in Egypt, instead of fasting, should find their pleasure."[13]

From that it is clear that Lent was being observed in Rome, and evidently with some care, in 340. There, however, it would entail thirty-six days of fasting since the Sabbaths were fasted. There is, however, no indication in the earlier documents that this was considered a problem. The fast was an unbroken period of ascetical exercises whose integrity, evidently, was not considered to be compromised by the long-standing prohibition against fasting on Sunday (and, in the East, the Sabbath). The number of forty days is to be reckoned, for this early period, from Monday of the first week through Friday of the sixth. Such was the case, evidently at Alexandria and Milan. (For Rome, C. Callewaert argues that the period was reckoned from Sunday through Thursday.[14])

Also, unless we have seriously misinterpreted the *Apostolic Tradition,* it seems virtually certain that at Rome that season of fasting (or a part of it, at least) would have focused upon the final preparation of candidates for baptism. Indeed, it is quite possible that Lent was also being employed for the performance of public penance at Rome during Athanasius' stay there, even though our earliest direct evidence is somewhat later.[15]

In the north of Italy in the time of Ambrose the situation is similar to that of both Rome and Alexandria, appearing as something of a blend of those two traditions. At Milan, as at Alexandria, there is on the Epiphany an announcement of the date of Pascha. As at Alexandria, neither Sunday nor the Sabbath can be a fast day. As at Rome, on the other hand, the period is focused on preparation for baptism, and the period serves for the public penance of those seeking reconciliation. As with both of those cities, the fast is observed for six weeks, the last of which is Holy Week.[16]

At about that same time, the penultimate decade of the fourth century, *Apostolic Constitutions* V.13 points to a similar fast running for six weeks from Monday of the first week through Friday of the sixth. At that point, however, it orders the suspension of fasting for two days, and the Paschal Fast of six days begins on the following Monday. That insistence on the suspension of the fast for those two days, the Sabbath and Sunday at the end of the sixth week, is instructive. As we have seen, those two days were never fasted during Lent, and their explicit exclusion from the fast here can only mean that the fast of forty days has been completed and the paschal fast has not yet begun. Those days fall between the two fasts as a festal interlude. This is the pattern of fourth-century Antioch and will be the pattern of the prepaschal fasts at Constantinople, at Jerusalem in the fifth century, at Alexandria in the seventh, and eventually throughout the oriental churches. In this system, Lent and Holy Week are totally distinct. Indeed, they are not even continuous, but are separated by two festal days, the otherwise undesignated Sabbath and Sunday in *Apostolic Constitutions* V.13, but known already in some churches as the Saturday of Lazarus and Palm Sunday, days which, we shall be concerned to argue, mark the festal conclusion of Lent itself.

In fact, approximately contemporary with *Apostolic Constitutions*, Egeria reports at Jerusalem both a visit to the tomb of Lazarus on that Saturday preceding the Great Week and a procession with palms down the Mount of Olives on the following day. The uncommon richness of our sources for the liturgy of Jerusalem in the later fourth and early fifth centuries has long accustomed us to thinking of many of the rites described there as having originated in the Holy City, tied as they are to the holy places peculiar to the actual scene of so much of the gospel. On the basis of such a habit of thought, indeed, Dom Gregory Dix virtually ascribed the creation of the liturgical year to the work of Cyril of Jerusalem. It would, in fact, be difficult to overemphasize the importance of Jerusalem for the early history of the liturgy, but, however difficult, such overemphasis is possible. Having placed some emphasis in Part One on the importance of the Jerusalem paschal vigil lessons for later history, we must take some time to argue that the same determinative role does not seem to belong to the hagiopolitan tradition in the matter of the organization of Lent.

Egeria (27.1) informs us that Lent at Jerusalem lasts for eight weeks since there are but five days fasted in the week, so that eight weeks are required to make the number of forty days. That is the first evidence we have seen for a concern for the number of actual days of fasting. It would be bold, perhaps, to suggest that such an eight-week fast was unknown elsewhere, and much too bold to suggest that Egeria is simply mistaken. Somewhat less perilous would be the suggestion that she is discussing the private fast practice of ascetics rather than the liturgical season, or at least failing to distinguish between the two. However, that, too, would be difficult to defend in light of her careful description of lenten liturgical observances. It may well be that the same eight-week fast was observed at Antioch at this time, but no text from there is as clear as this before Severus of Antioch in the sixth century.[17] The concern to bring to forty the number of actual days of fasting later became a general preoccupation, East and West, but this clear testimony of Egeria seems to be unique for the fourth century.

Egeria's testimony to that definition of Lent would constitute no problem at all but for the contrary evidence of the Armenian lectionaries for Jerusalem in the early decades of the following century. These manuscripts, on which we depend so heavily for our more precise knowledge of the Jerusalem liturgy, show just such an organization of the prepaschal fasts as we noted in *Apostolic Constitutions* V.13, a six-week Lent followed by the six days of Great Week, a total of only seven weeks. It is still more surprising that the lectionaries provide for no eucharistic liturgies at all during Lent except for the Saturday and Sunday between the six-week fast and the six-day paschal fast. Indeed, even the provisions for the liturgy of the hours are limited to Wednesdays and Fridays save for two weeks, the *second* week of Lent and Great Week; for these two weeks there are liturgical appointments for every day. This has suggested to many scholars that the second week was once the first week, and that behind the scheme in those fifth-century lectionaries lies such a pattern as we have noted for Alexandria, Rome, and Milan, a total of six weeks, the last of which was Holy Week.[18]

Such an understanding of the data would be consistent with the report of Sozomen, who adds some further precision to that of Socrates noted above. In particular, Sozomen shows the two patterns we have noted in the Armenian lectionaries in relatively close geographical proximity, Palestine and Phoenicia.

"In some churches the interval called Quadragesima, which occurs before this festival [Pascha], and is devoted by the people to fasting, is made to consist of six weeks; and this is the case in Illyria and the Western regions, in Libya, throughout Egypt, and in Palestine; whereas it is made to comprise seven weeks at Constantinople, and in the neighboring provinces as far as Phoenicia. In some churches the people fast three alternate weeks, during the space of six or seven weeks, whereas in others they fast continuously during the three weeks immediately preceding the festival."[19]

If Sozomen's information is correct (even if slightly out of date), we may suppose that the separation of the six weeks of Lent from the Great Week as we perceive it in the Armenian lectionaries was a relatively recent development.

Nonetheless, confronted between 417 and 435 with liturgical documents suggesting that a six-week fast has become a seven-week fast, we encounter as well Egeria's testimony, which tells us that in 383 there were eight weeks of fasting. This is not an incidental assertion by Egeria, but a conviction that she repeats more than once. Given the improbability of so many shifts in such a short time, it could seem likely that one or another of the lenten patterns reflected in the Armenian lectionaries was the form of the liturgical season at Jerusalem in the later fourth century, and that the religious with whom Egeria associated, concerned to imitate more perfectly the fast of Jesus, added the extra one or two weeks to fulfill the forty days of actual fasting. Such a supposition might encourage us to believe that the liturgical Lent in Egeria's day was as Sozomen describes it for Palestine, a total of six weeks including the paschal fast, as at Rome, Milan, Alexandria, and (to follow Sozomen) Illyria and Libya. That, however, would be an unwarranted conjecture. However complex it may seem, the more likely history of the development is that a six-week Lent before Egeria had become eight weeks by her time, and in the early fifth century that more extended period gave way in turn to a six-week Lent followed by the six days of Great Week, the total of seven weeks presented in the Armenian lectionary and practiced, according to Sozomen, from Phoenicia to Constantinople.

3. LENTEN CATECHESIS AT JERUSALEM

Whatever the length of the liturgical Lent, it is nonetheless clear that at Jerusalem, as at Rome and Milan (but not in the festal letters of Athanasius), Lent was the time for the final formation of those to be baptized at Easter. Egeria (45.1–4) gives a detailed picture of the procedure, repeating her assertion of its eight-week duration.

"Names must be given in before the first day of Lent, which means that a presbyter takes down all the names before the start of the eight weeks for which Lent lasts here, as I have told you. Once the priest has all the names, on the second day of Lent at the start of the eight weeks, the bishop's chair is placed in the middle of the Great Church, the Martyrium, the presbyters sit in chairs on either side of him, and all the clergy stand. Then one by one those seeking baptism are brought up, men coming with their fathers and women with their mothers. As they come in one by one, the bishop asks their neighbours questions about them: 'Is this person leading a good life? Does he respect his parents? Is he a drunkard or a boaster?' He asks about all the serious human vices. And if his inquiries show him that someone has not committed any of these misdeeds, he himself puts down his name; but if someone is guilty he is told to go away, and the bishop tells him that he is to amend his ways before he may come to the font."

The catechesis itself, she continues, is given by the bishop daily from six to nine every morning. It is an exposition of the sacred scriptures from Genesis forward. After five weeks of scriptural teaching, the catechesis turns to the exposition of the creed. That, evidently, occupies the sixth and seventh weeks, since Egeria is quite clear that the catechesis is completed prior to the beginning of Great Week. At the end of the seventh week (the day is not specified) the bishop sits in his place in the apse of the Martyrium. The candidates one by one, accompanied by a sponsor, come to the bishop and recite the creed to him. At the conclusion of that *redditio*, the bishop addresses the candidates:

"During these seven weeks you have received instruction in the whole biblical Law. You have also learned all you can as catechumens of the content of the Creed. But the teaching about baptism itself is a deeper mystery, and you have not the right to hear it while you remain catechumens. Do not think it will never be explained; you will hear it all during the eight days of Easter after you have been baptized. But so long as you are catechumens you cannot be told God's deep mysteries" (Egeria 46.6).

Those further instructions during Easter Week are, of course, the *Mystagogia*, of which we possess so many examples from many parts of the Church in the late fourth century. Those for Jerusalem have been discussed in Part One. Our concern here is rather with the catecheses delivered to the *photizomenoi* during Lent. We possess a significant set of these by Cyril of Jerusalem, their authorship less questioned than that of the *Mystagogia* transmitted in his name. They are probably to be assigned to the end of the first half of the century, ca. 347–350.[20] Although these are called "Catecheses," normal catechumens were excluded from hearing them, and the candidates were forbidden to discuss them with catechumens. Cyril explains this in the *Procatechesis*, delivered, evidently, just after the inscription of the names of the candidates at the beginning of Lent. There emphasis is laid not only on the importance of the instructions, but also on the exorcisms by which the evil influences that the candidates brought with them were expunged. These seem to have been exercises of considerable emotional rigor, during which the candidates wore veils covering their faces, "lest a roving eye cause a roving heart." The exorcists are likened to smiths at the forge, who, "infusing fear by the Holy Ghost, and setting the soul on fire in the crucible of the body, make the evil spirit flee, who is our enemy, and salvation and the hope of eternal life abide; and henceforth the soul, cleansed from its sins, hath salvation."[21]

The first five of the catecheses of Cyril are of a general doctrinal nature and we see nothing of the systematic exposition of the scriptures mentioned by Egeria. The last thirteen of the series are given to the exposition of the Jerusalem creed. It is not asserted that we have in this series of eighteen lectures the entire lenten series, but given the connections between them, it does seem probable that those from Lecture 14 to the end occupied the last week before Great Week. Lecture 14, on the resurrection and ascension, was surely delivered on a Monday, as the text itself establishes. The previous lecture, on the crucifixion and burial, would have been on the previous Friday, ostensibly. It is not clear whether Lectures 6 through 13 could have been delivered in that penultimate week, but it seems more likely that the exposition of the creed took in this year more than the two weeks given to it in Egeria's account. In any case, the less closely connected five lectures before those on the creed were clearly not the only lectures for the initial weeks, and we may assume that the exposition of the scriptures occupied the catecheses of that period. If the exposition of the creed was completed, as seems the case, on the Friday before Great Week, the further assembly described by Egeria for the individual recitation of the symbol by each candidate would have taken place on Saturday or Sunday.

4. LAZARUS SATURDAY AND PALM SUNDAY AT JERUSALEM

The fast of a total of seven weeks effected the separation between the six weeks of Lent and the Great Week by observing two festal days between them, the memorial of the resurrection of Lazarus on the Saturday and Palm Sunday on the following day. We cannot be certain of the stage of their development in any particular church when Egeria was in Jerusalem in 383, but there is good reason to believe that they were sufficiently defined to have an impact on the liturgy of Jerusalem.

176

That last statement, however, needs explanation, if not defense. One of the permanent influences of the Jerusalem liturgy of the fourth century on the rest of Christian liturgical history, it is commonly observed, is the introduction of a procession with palms on the Sunday before the Paschal Fast. Egeria says that that Sunday is the opening of Great Week. Similarly, the less universally observed Saturday of Lazarus is taken to have had its beginning in a visit to the tomb of Lazarus on Saturday afternoon, described by Egeria. However, these two days, if they are the festal interlude between Lent and Great Week mentioned in *Apostolic Constitutions* V.13, would seem to be a characteristic of the seven-week pattern of pre-paschal exercises, and we have seen reason to doubt that such a pattern had been adopted in Jerusalem at the time of Egeria's visit. In fact, neither the visit to the tomb of Lazarus on Saturday nor the procession with palms down the Mount of Olives on Sunday bears the marks of belonging to the traditional Jerusalem liturgy.[22]

We have noted in Parts One and Two the growth in Jerusalem of a secondary stratum of rites whose whole purpose was to employ the sacred sites in such a way as to enrich the experience of pilgrims. These rites, therefore, do not belong to the original hagiopolitan liturgical tradition, but are innovations occasioned by the Constantinian building program and the vast number of pilgrims drawn to the Holy City in consequence of that program. These came from all over the world, and came bringing their own liturgical traditions, which shaped their expectations of their visits to the holy places.

Egeria, we have noted repeatedly, marvels again and again that, "everything is appropriate to the day and to the place." In some instances, however, we need to ask what that might mean. Why, to be specific, is it considered appropriate to visit the tomb of Lazarus on the day before Palm Sunday? Or, surprising as the question may seem, why is it considered appropriate to process down the Mount of Olives bearing branches on the day before Monday of Great Week? None of the synoptic gospels suggests any chronological connection between Christ's entrance into Jerusalem and his passion, and the Great Week readings at Jerusalem, we saw in Part One, follow Matthew. But even if the Jerusalem community had adopted at this point the chronology of the fourth gospel, why does that dramatic celebration of Christ's triumphal entry have no relationship to the Sunday morning liturgy? In Egeria's account, the celebration is organized on the Mount of Olives at one o'clock in the afternoon, the same hour as the visit to the Lazarium at Bethany on the previous day, an hour that places those observances outside the normal cursus of Jerusalem services.

On the Saturday afternoon all gather at Bethany, stopping first about a half-mile from the Lazarium, "the spot where Lazarus' sister Mary met the Lord" (Egeria, 29.4). There the monks meet the bishop, and all go into the chapel on that spot where there is one hymn, an antiphon, and the gospel reading about the meeting between Jesus and Lazarus' sister. No further precision regarding that reading is given, but it must have been the beginning of John 11, perhaps as far as verse 27, perhaps through verse 37. Then, the procession goes on to the Lazarium itself.

This visit to the Lazarium is particularly problematic since that was also the station for the liturgy of the fifth day of the Epiphany octave in Egeria's day, while the introduction of the commemoration of Stephen after 415 makes the Lazarium the station for the sixth day of Epiphany in the Armenian lectionaries. Since the miracle at Bethany is recorded only in the fourth gospel, that station in the Epiphany octave interrupts what seems to have been a Matthean cursus and suggests a liturgical employment of the Lazarium independent of and prior to the introduction of the visit on the Saturday before Great Week. The Saturday visit to the Lazarium should have some other source than the accessibility of the tomb itself, if the Lazarium was already the station for the fifth (later sixth) day of the Epiphany octave. For that Epiphany station, the gospel reading in the Armenian lectionary is the account from the gospel of John (11.1–46) of the raising of Lazarus, while on the Saturday before Great Week, that which will come to be known as the "Saturday of Lazarus," the gospel in the lectionaries is not that of the raising of Lazarus, but rather of a subsequent visit of Jesus to Bethany, "six days before the Passover," the occasion on which Jesus was anointed by Mary (John 11.55–12.11).

Nonetheless, as we have seen, the preliminary station at Bethany has to do with the meeting of Jesus by Mary before the raising of Lazarus. Egeria, having observed that the first part of the account in John 11 had been read at the first station, says nothing more of the readings at the Lazarium itself, save that they, as the antiphons and the rest, are "suitable to the day and the place." At that point (29.5), however, she adds a note that explains the reading in the Armenian lectionaries:

"Then at the dismissal a presbyter announces Easter. He mounts a platform, and reads the Gospel passage which begins 'When Jesus came to Bethany six days before the Passover.' After this reading, with its announcement of Easter, comes the dismissal. They do it on this day because the Gospel describes what took place in Bethany 'six days before the Passover,' and it is six days from this Saturday to the Thursday night on which the Lord was arrested after the Supper. Thus they all return to the Anastasis and have Lucernare in the usual way."

Had there been an earlier gospel reading at the Lazarium, including the raising of Lazarus? It is impossible to say from the account of Egeria. This "announcement of Easter," which she places at the dismissal from the Lazarium, nonetheless has become in the Armenian lectionary the only gospel passage read at Bethany. In that fifth-century text, the first station at the place of Jesus' encounter with Lazarus' sister, with its reading of the opening of John 11, has been abandoned. At the Lazarium itself, the assembly now at four o'clock, the psalms and epistle are the same as those for the sixth day of the Epiphany octave: Psalm 29 [30] with verse 4 [3] as antiphon ("O Lord, thou hast brought up my soul from Sheol, restored me to life from among those gone down to the Pit"); 1 Thessalonians 4.13–18 ("But we would not have you ignorant, brethren, concerning those who are asleep"); Alleluia verse from Psalm 39 [40] ("I waited patiently for the Lord; he inclined to me and heard my cry"). All these, of course, are appropriate to the celebration of the raising of Lazarus assigned to that sixth day of Epiphany, but the gospel that recounts the miraculous event is not read on the Saturday before Great Week, being replaced by that which Egeria described as the "announcement of Easter," John 11.55–12.11.

The reading of this Johannine passage to announce the coming Passover is peculiar since the Passover it announces is determined on the basis of the gospel of Matthew, Thursday of Great Week, called, "the Thursday of the Old Passover," in the Armenian lectionaries. For John, of course, the preparation of the Passover was on Friday of Great Week. The adoption of the Johannine gospel on the preceding Saturday had, we have noted, a deleterious effect on the old Matthean course reading, the original pattern for Jerusalem that was in many ways becoming disordered in the fifth century. On Wednesday of Great Week the gospel appointed in *Jerusalem 121* is Matthew 26.3–16, Matthew's account of that same anointing of Jesus at Bethany, although Matthew makes it but two days before the Passover. Another manuscript of the Armenian lectionary, *Paris arm. 44*, reflecting a somewhat later stage in the development of the Jerusalem liturgy, shows itself at many points to be concerned to remove redundancies. Since Jesus' anointing at Bethany was now read in its Johannine version on the preceding Saturday, *Paris 44* reduces the reading on Wednesday to but three verses, Matthew 26.14–16, omitting the duplication.[23]

Further development of the liturgy of Jerusalem from the second half of the fifth to the eighth centuries is detailed in the lectionaries preserved in Georgian. There on the Saturday before Great Week the epistle, which had also accompanied the gospel of the raising of Lazarus in the Epiphany octave, has been changed to Ephesians 5.13–17. This continues the resurrection theme, but it points as well, as does the following gospel (still John 11.55–12.11), to the week to come. The title given to the function in Bethany is: *DIEI PALMARUM SABBATO. Synaxis in Bethania. Commemoratio Lazari.*[24] There is no longer a station at Bethany in the Epiphany octave. The gospel account of the raising of Lazarus (John 11.1–46) is read only at another *Commemoratio Lazari* on September 7, the appointments other than the gospel taken from *Palmarum Sabbato*. If we did not know of the Saturday of Lazarus from other traditions, it is unlikely that we would see any connection between this fifth-century Jerusalem synaxis and the raising of Lazarus, save the location itself. As Michel Aubineau, the editor of the sermons of Hesychius, has observed, "it seems indeed that the liturgical feast of the Saturday was oriented rather toward the proximate 'Great Week,' toward Pascha and the Passion of the Lord."[25]

Were it not such a commonplace to trace the origins of the Saturday of Lazarus and Palm Sunday to Jerusalem, that long development would be of only antiquarian interest. It does, however, encourage us to ask whether that commonplace is well founded. The evidence can be recapitulated as follows:

180

1. Perhaps already when Jerusalem observed a prepaschal fast of but six weeks, the Epiphany octave seems to have included a station at the Lazarium on the fifth day, commemorating the raising of Lazarus.

2. The extension of the fast by Egeria's time (evidently to eight weeks) does not reflect such a distinction between Lent and Holy Week as does *Ap. Const.* V.13. Nonetheless, independent of the normal liturgical regimen, there is a dramatic reenactment of the raising of Lazarus in the afternoon of the Saturday before Great Week, the bishop met by the monks representing Christ met by Lazarus' sister (Egeria, 29.4). After a short synaxis at that spot, the procession continues to the Lazarium. There the older synaxis of the fifth day of Epiphany is celebrated, at least up to the gospel. The pericope appointed in the Epiphany octave (John 11.1–45), if read at all, would have been abbreviated, much of it having just been read at the previous station. At the dismissal there is another gospel reading, John 11.55–12.11, a reading that has the effect of relating this day to the coming Great Week.

3. In the early fifth century the Saturday visit to Bethany was not clearly linked to the raising of Lazarus. The preliminary synaxis at which the first part of the gospel was read had been discontinued. The gospel at the Lazarium itself was that formerly read at the dismissal, John 11.55–12.11. The gospel account of the raising of Lazarus was read only in the Epiphany octave, now on the sixth day. In the Armenian lectionaries the Saturday before Great Week bears the title, "The Sixth Day before the Passover of the Law, Saturday."

4. In the later lectionaries preserved in Georgian, there is no synaxis at Bethany in the Epiphany octave, and the gospel on "the Sabbath of the Day of Palms" remains John 11.55–12.11. The rubric indicates *Commemoratio Lazari*, but it is not clear to what that refers. There is a new commemoration of Lazarus on September 7, and that is the only occasion on which the gospel of the raising of Lazarus by Jesus is read.

As we shall see shortly, this evolution stands in stark contrast to the steady Byzantine tradition, which still presents the celebrations of the resurrection of Lazarus and of Christ's triumphal entry into Jerusalem as two closely interrelated festal days separating Lent from Holy Week. From this, we may conclude, I believe, that the visit to Bethany and the similar procession from the Mount of Olives on the two afternoons before Monday of Great Week represent excursions demanded by other liturgical calendars, not new liturgical days "invented" at Jerusalem. That observance at the Lazarium proved too ephemeral and began to fade into something other than the celebration of the raising of Lazarus almost as soon as we see it in Egeria.

Why was the visit to Bethany on the Saturday before Great Week undertaken in the first place? Why did the church at Jerusalem duplicate on this day, albeit with elaboration, the older celebration (itself probably derived) on the fifth day of Epiphany? I can find but one answer to such questions: the Saturday of Lazarus and Palm Sunday were already being observed somewhere else and the brief appearance of the first of those at Jerusalem was due to an influence from without. The second, the Palm Sunday that proved more sturdy, was, I believe, similarly grafted onto the tradition of Jerusalem, and from the same source. Jerusalem's Matthean tradition offers no support for a celebration of the entry into Jerusalem at that point in the year.

What was the source that made these excursions seem appropriate on these days? That cannot be ascertained with certainty. However, given the intimate bond between Constantinople and Jerusalem in consequence of the imperial building program, it is easiest to imagine that the impetus for the visit to the Lazarium on that Saturday came from Byzantium, where that day seems to have been established already as the celebration of the raising of Lazarus. That Saturday, we will argue, was already followed at Constantinople by the feast of Palms prior to any visit to the scenes of those commemorations at Jerusalem. Those visits to significant sites constitute a second stratum of the Jerusalem liturgy in response to the expectations of visitors, most probably from Constantinople, to the Holy City.

Lest such a claim for the priority of those celebrations at Constantinople seem too gratuitous, we shall introduce below the testimony of a sermon of John Chrysostom showing both those observances at Constantinople, although, of course, without visits to historical sites. The visits to those sites were what Jerusalem had to offer. The origin of the liturgical days that made those visits seem not only appropriate but highly significant must have another explanation.

5. LENT AT CONSTANTINOPLE

The first two parts of our study should have established already that our information on Constantinople in the fourth century is limited. Further, we have learned well by now that years of claims of fixity in Byzantine liturgical tradition were overstated, to say the least. That tradition has continued to evolve as every other, and still continues to do so. We have been able to give close consideration to the liturgy of Jerusalem in the fourth and following centuries because our sources for that city are uncommonly rich, but that is not true of Constantinople. This is particularly the case in questions concerning the liturgical year, since our earliest manuscript evidence for the Byzantine liturgy is a *euchologion*, and, unlike western sacramentaries, the *euchologion* is only occasionally sensitive to liturgical time.

Our best source for the liturgical year at Constantinople is the typikon of Hagia Sophia edited by Juan Mateos. In addition to his principal manuscript, the tenth-century *Hagios Stavros 40* at the Jerusalem patriarchate, Mateos presented variant readings from *Patmos 266*, a monastic manuscript of the preceding century, as well as some from later manuscripts. *Hagios Stavros 40* is a copy of an older manuscript, taken down from dictation, as can be seen, for example, from the spelling of *baptistērion* as *vaptistērion* on folio 224ᵛ. The text from which it was copied, however, would be difficult to date since the tradition represented abounds in anachronisms. We have already noted, for example, that September 23 is still identified there as the New Year (*to neon etos*), even though the beginning of the civil year was set at September 1 in the fifth century. In light of that, the absence of the feast of the Triumph of Orthodoxy (instituted in 843) from both the Patmos and Jerusalem manuscripts seems a less than secure test of date.[26] The assessment of the age of the appointments found in the typikon of Hagia Sophia must be undertaken more patiently, on a case by case basis, and with a large tolerance for ambiguity.

We have noted that *Ap. Const.* V.13 separates Lent and the six days of the paschal fast, and that the Saturday and Sunday between those fasts belong to neither. We encounter that tradition in the Byzantine rite still today. Lent, in the narrower understanding of it, is an unbroken period of forty days beginning on a Monday and ending at vespers of Friday six weeks later. At the office for Friday before Great Week, the present *Triodion* appoints a troparion attributed to Andrew the Blind, a monk of Mar Saba in the eighth century.

"Having completed the forty days that bring profit to our soul, let us cry: Rejoice, city of Bethany, home of Lazarus. Rejoice, Martha and Mary, his sisters. Tomorrow Christ will come, by his word to bring your dead brother to life. . . ."[27]

Here we see the earlier understanding of the fast of forty days as a continuous period, not counting the number of days of fasting. For such an accounting of the number of fast days, Holy Week and, indeed, a further, eighth week must be included to bring the number to forty. In the text just cited, however, the forty days are completed in the afternoon of Friday before Holy Week, an understanding that was still active when Andrew wrote his troparion, even though by that time a week of mitigated forefast had been added before Lent to yield the total number of forty days of fasting. That preliminary week of lighter fasting, the "tyrophagy," during which dairy products are allowed to be eaten, was added during the reign of the emperor Heraclius in the seventh century.[28]

The celebration of the eucharist has always been disallowed on fast days in Byzantine practice. In Lent, therefore, the eucharist is celebrated only on Saturdays and Sundays (plus March 25, an exception ordered, we have seen, by the Council in Trullo). On those lenten Saturdays and Sundays the epistles represent a course reading of Hebrews, while the season is the principal period for the course reading of the gospel of Mark. Byzantine tradition is well known for its maintenance of the custom of course reading. Those Marcan readings for the Saturdays and Sundays of Lent are interrupted only on the first Sunday (i.e., the Sunday at the end of the first week). This Sunday is now the feast of Orthodoxy, but in the typika of Mateos it is an independently established feast of the prophets Moses, Aaron, and Samuel. Beyond that, the appointments in the ninth and tenth century typika reveal some displacement in the Marcan series, especially on the Saturdays. In spite of that, however, it is easy to see behind the present appointments a reading of the epistle to the Hebrews and the gospel of Mark as the scriptural content of the eucharistic liturgy at Constantinople since, quite possibly, rather early in the history of Lent there.[29]

The lenten scriptural appointments for the eucharist in the typika of the ninth-tenth centuries are as follows:

First Week of Lent
Sabbath: Hb 1.1–12; Mk 2.23–3.5
Sunday: Hb 11.24–26, 32–40; Jn 1.44–52

Second Week of Lent
Sabbath: Hb 3.12–14; Mk 1.35–44
Sunday: Hb 1.10–2.3; Mk 2.1–12

Third Week of Lent
Sabbath: Hb 10.32–38; Mk 7.31–37
Sunday: Hb 4.14–5.6; Mk 8.34–9.1

Fourth Week of Lent
Sabbath: Hb 6.9–12; Mk 8.27–31
Sunday: Hb 6.13–20; Mk 9.17–31

Fifth Week of Lent
Sabbath: Hb 9.24–28; Mk 2.14–17
Sunday: Hb 9.11–14; Mk 10.32–45

Sixth Week of Lent
Sabbath: Hb 12.28–13.8; Jn 11.1–45
Sunday: Phil 4.4–9; Jn 12.1–18

Here, as indicated, the first Sunday is a break in the *Bahnlesung*, being the feast of the prophets. Aside from that, the epistles are consistently from Hebrews; the gospels are consistently from Mark throughout Lent. It is only at the end of the forty days, on the Saturday of the sixth week, the Saturday of Lazarus, that the gospel shifts to John. Even so, the epistle on that day continues the reading of Hebrews. That is not true for the Sunday, where the epistle is from Philippians. We shall be concerned, however, to argue that the Johannine readings on those two days represent less of a break with the Marcan cursus than would appear at first glimpse.

All the sixth week of the fast is designated (freely translated)

"Palm Week" in the typika of the ninth and tenth centuries. This week, ending in the festal Saturday of Lazarus and Palm Sunday, is in its own right the conclusion of Lent. The term toward which it moves is the feast of Palms. "Palm Monday" is followed by "Palm Tuesday" and the rest, to the "Saturday of the Palmbearer, Memorial of the Holy and Just Lazarus," and, finally, "Sunday, the Meeting with Palms of our great God and Savior Jesus Christ."

Pierre-Marie Gy has concluded that the readings of the lenten Sundays, at least, were in place in the latter half of the sixth century. At about that same time, Severus of Antioch, defending himself against the charge of novelty for having introduced a new phrase into the Trisagion, observes that the feast of *Hypapantē*, the Presentation of Christ in the Temple, observed at Jerusalem, had but lately been adopted at Constantinople, without any charge of innovation, and that it was still unknown at Antioch. The same, he says, can be said of Palm Sunday, recently observed by only a few churches, though now spread to virtually all, with none complaining of a new invention.[30] If his words indicate, as they seem to do, that this observance was only recently established at Antioch, that would seem to resolve a significant question surrounding Chrysostom's *Homily on Psalm 145* (PG 55.519ff.). That sermon was preached on the Saturday of Lazarus and refers both to that day and to the celebration of Jesus' entry into Jerusalem on the day following. Montfaucon believed that we could not determine the place of its delivery, whether Antioch or Constantinople. If, however, Palm Sunday was a recent innovation at Antioch in the days of Severus, by contrast to Constantinople,[31] then this sermon could hardly belong to Chrysostom's preaching in Antioch. Rather, it must be a testimony for the celebration of those days at Constantinople in the time of his leadership of that church, from 398 to 403.

Chrysostom speaks in that sermon of the coming Great Week, explaining the meaning of that phrase, and speaks of the Sabbath on which he preached as the head of that week. He describes the crowds who came out from Jerusalem to Bethany in response to the news that Jesus had raised Lazarus (John 12.9), and observes that it is not from Jerusalem only, but from every city that we now go out to meet Jesus, bearing not palms but the works of piety, alms, fasting, and watchings. He, the preacher, goes out with them, proferring instead of palms the word of doctrine. They are gone out singing, "Hosanna in the highest. Blessed is he who comes in the Name of the Lord," but "we" crying, "Praise the Lord, O my soul! I will praise the Lord as long as I live" (Ps 146 [Heb.], verses 1–2). If, as one would suppose, this psalm figured in the liturgy of the day, it did not survive in the typika of the ninth and tenth centuries. While Chrysostom begins by contrasting his hearers with those who went out to meet Jesus, as he proceeds it becomes more and more difficult to resist the suspicion that he is rather concerned to contrast the present observance at Constantinople with that at Jerusalem, where the actual procession in the afternoon had achieved such fame that his hearers thought themselves impoverished by being unable to be there. It is clear that he sees the raising of Lazarus as closely related to the entry of Jesus, and that marks his gospel source as that of John. The Armenian lectionaries for Jerusalem provide the account from Matthew, now (in the fifth century) read at the Martyrium in the morning.

That still does not establish those observances in Constantinople prior to the testimony of Egeria for Jerusalem. However, even if Chrysostom's sermon is slightly later, we can say that the Byzantine Saturday of Lazarus remained stable, while its observance at Jerusalem appears to be an addition to the normal offices of the liturgy, an addition that began almost at once to fade into something other than the celebration of the raising of Lazarus. Indeed, Jerusalem's original celebration of that miracle was in the octave of the Epiphany (that itself a phenomenon in need of explanation). There, a lenten fast of six weeks became seven by the first half of the fifth century, but Egeria still insists in the late fourth century that it was eight weeks. Neither a six- nor an eight-week Lent would have reason to interpose these festal commemorations of Lazarus and the triumphal entry between Lent and Great Week as part of the original liturgical structure. Rather, Egeria's visit to the tomb of Lazarus, clearly intended to celebrate his miraculous deliverance from death by Jesus, becomes almost as soon as we see it an observance more concerned with the announcement of the coming Passover.

By contrast, at Constantinople the Lent of six weeks is, so far as we can tell, consistently distinct from the six days of the Paschal Fast. There, at the end of a six-week course reading of Mark, the two festal days that lie between the two periods are related to the raising of Lazarus and the entry into Jerusalem, and so, evidently, draw their gospel readings from John, our only source for the Bethany miracle and the only gospel in which the entry into Jerusalem is chronologically related to the passion. That would explain the celebration of the entry into Jerusalem, but the commemoration of Lazarus on the preceding day, while related to the entry already in Chrysostom's sermon, remains something of a puzzle even at Constantinople.

Jerusalem's tradition, rooted in the gospel of Matthew, does not account for the procession down the Mount of Olives on the following Sunday afternoon. That *procession* was evidently a genuinely hagiopolitan contribution to the celebration of Christ's triumphal entry into Jerusalem, but that contribution, like the visit to the tomb of Lazarus on the previous day, embellished liturgical days themselves coming from outside the tradition of the Holy City.

Only so can we understand, in these and probably some other instances, Egeria's insistence that everything was appropriate not only to the place, but also to the day. Those celebrations on the Saturday and Sunday before Great Week, so far as can be ascertained at present, represent excursions in Jerusalem to visit sites associated with those days in the liturgy of Constantinople. As we shall see, however, that is not to suggest that those days had their origin in the liturgy of Byzantium.

Before turning from the shape of Lent at Constantinople, there is a further oddity reported in the typika of the ninth and tenth centuries that at least needs to be filed for future reference. This is the altogether astonishing fact that the Saturday of Lazarus, one week before the great paschal vigil, is a full initiatory liturgy.[32] A vestige of that remains today in the Byzantine rite where, as noted earlier, the baptismal troparion, "As many as have been baptized into Christ have put on Christ," is substituted for the entrance chant, Trisagion. In the typika, however, we confront the complete baptismal liturgy, accomplished by the patriarch in the little baptistry. At the conclusion of the morning office, Orthros, the reading of Acts is begun and the patriarch descends to the little baptistry and baptizes and anoints with chrism. A cantor begins there Psalm 31 [32] and continues that as he leads the neophytes into the basilica. On a signal from the deacon, the psalm is broken off and the reading of Acts resumes with the account of the baptism of the Ethiopian eunuch, which continues until the antiphons of the liturgy are begun. At the entrance, as noted, the baptismal troparion replaces Trisagion. The epistle is Hebrews 12, continuing the course reading of that book throughout Lent. The gospel is John 11.1–45.

There is yet in *Hagios Stavros 40* another provision for baptism at the end of Lent but outside the Paschal Vigil. This is at the conclusion of the morning office (Orthros) on Holy Saturday. There, a strangely laconic rubric notes, "after the dismissal, the patriarch performs the illuminations in the little baptistry." This, I believe, represents the actual time of baptism on Holy Saturday at the time of the copying of that manuscript, ca. 950–959. By that time there would have been few, if any, baptisms of adults, and paschal baptism could have held on only in a very reduced form. It is interesting to note that the earlier *Patmos 266*, being a copy of the cathedral typikon prepared for use in a monastic community, does not contain this rubric regarding baptism, the baptism of infants not being relevant to a monastic setting. Nonetheless, it does contain the formal baptismal liturgy on the Saturday of Lazarus, showing its much greater antiquity.

Liturgical manuscripts, by the very process of their production, are conservative of ritual patterns long fallen into desuetude. Mateos suggested that this baptismal liturgy, like the rubric on Holy Saturday morning, had as its purpose the reduction of the numbers to be baptized at the paschal vigil. I would suggest, rather, that the baptisms on Holy Saturday morning were the only paschal baptisms in the tenth century. As for the Saturday of Lazarus, it is difficult to know to what period that initiatory liturgy belongs. For the moment, we can only note the phenomenon of its inclusion in the medieval Constantinopolitan typika, observing that it places baptism at the conclusion of the fast of forty days, independent of that fast's relation to Pascha (with its own baptismal liturgy), an arrangement to which we shall have occasion to return.

6. THE ASSOCIATION OF LENT WITH THE FAST OF JESUS

Our lenten fast has been associated with the fast of Jesus in the wilderness of Judea for such a long time that it is surprising to find that our earliest explicit account of the Church's fast of forty days, as found in the second festal letter of Athanasius, makes no mention of the fast of Jesus at all, nor is that association made in any of his festal letters. Indeed, liturgical historians have long held that this association was made long after Lent had become established in the Church. Dom Gregory Dix, for example, wrote in *The Shape of the Liturgy*:

"The step of identifying the six weeks' fast with the 40 days' fast of our Lord in the wilderness was obviously in keeping with the new historical interest of the liturgy. The actual number of '40 days' of fasting was made up by extending Lent behind the sixth Sunday before Easter in various ways. But the association with our Lord's fast in the wilderness was an idea attached to the season of Lent only *after* it had come into existence in connection with the preparation of candidates for baptism. (An historical commemoration would strictly have required that Lent should follow immediately upon Epiphany, after this had been accepted as the commemoration of our Lord's baptism.)"[33]

Here we see reflected again Dix's conviction that historical interest in connection with liturgical celebration was a late development. Since we have been concerned at several points to take issue with Dix's point of view, his understanding of the association of Lent with Jesus' fast seems likely to be still another point at which we should examine his conclusions closely and critically.

We need not look far from our earliest description of Lent to discover that the situation is more complex than Dix recognized. One of Athanasius' predecessors in the see of Alexandria, the revered Bishop Peter, Patriarch of Alexandria at the beginning of the fourth century, issued ca. 305 a series of canons regulating the restoration of penitent apostates. It is a document reflecting sensitive pastoral concern and a liberal spirit. Noting that many of those who had capitulated in the persecution had not easily denied their faith but had suffered severe and prolonged torture before the severity of their pain led them finally to deny Christ and worship the gods, Peter orders in his first canon that such persons, having demonstrated their penitence for three years, should perform a quadragesimal fast in imitation of Christ, "for they did not come to this of their own will, but were betrayed by the frailty of the flesh; for they show in their bodies the marks of Jesus, and some are now, for the third year, bewailing their fault: it is sufficient, I say, that from the time of their submissive approach, *other forty days* should be enjoined upon them, to keep them in remembrance of these things; those forty days during which, though our Lord and Saviour Jesus Christ had fasted, He was yet, after He had been baptized, tempted of the devil. And when they shall have, during these days, exercised themselves much, and constantly fasted, then let them watch in prayer, meditating upon what was spoken by the Lord to him who tempted Him to fall down and worship him: 'Get thee behind me, Satan; for it is written, Thou shalt worship the Lord thy God, and Him only shalt thou serve' " (emphasis added).[34]

It has been usual to understand the "other forty days" as having no reference to the liturgical year, and that would not be unreasonable in the context. However, we must wonder whether that understanding of the text is conditioned by our supposition that there was no liturgically established season corresponding to that expression. Whatever its reference to this text of Peter of Alexandria, the association of the fast of Jesus with the liturgical season is reflected in a text of fourth-century Egypt other than the festal letters of Athanasius. This is the pseudepigraphal *Canons of Hippolytus*, preserved in Arabic. The twentieth of those canons speaks of the ascetical fasts of Wednesday and Friday and the Forty Days:

"The days of fast which have been established are the Wednesday, the Friday and the Forty Days. One who adds to these will receive a recompense and whoever transgresses these, save for sickness, constraint or necessity, such departs from the rule and disobeys God *who has fasted for us*" (emphasis added).[35]

That final phrase can only be understood as a reference to the fast of Jesus. Here, it is clear, the "Forty Days" refers to an established annual period of fasting in imitation of Jesus' fast. That we should have such a text from Egypt, probably from the second quarter of the fourth century, only underscores the oddity of the absence of such association in the festal letters of Athanasius. The context prompts further question, presenting the Forty Days as a disciplinary, ascetical practice not explicitly related to preparation for Easter. This linking of the quarantine with the weekly station days becomes more significant when we realize that the Paschal Fast is not included in that list of the days of fast. The following Canon 21 has to do with the daily synaxes in the church and it is only in Canon 22 that the Paschal Fast is discussed.[36] That fast of a week is clearly considered to commemorate the sufferings of Christ, and Canon 22 makes no reference to any longer fast of which these six days are a part. This arrangement seems peculiar if, as we saw in the festal letters of Athanasius, this Paschal Fast is as well the final week of the quarantine. The two fasts in Canons 20 and 22 are so distinct that the editor of the canons, René-Georges Coquin, considered that we have here an evidence of a significant separation of the two, and an even wider separation of the two than that which we have discussed as characteristic of Syria and Constantinople.[37]

In another work of about the same time,[38] Coquin showed that this same distinction between Lent and the weekly stations, on the one hand, and the six-day Paschal Fast, on the other, is indicated in the tenth of Origen's homilies on Leviticus.

"They fast, therefore, who have lost the bridegroom; we having him with us cannot fast. Nor do we say, however, that we relax the restraints of Christian abstinence; for we have the forty days consecrated to fasting, we have the fourth and sixth days of the week, on which we fast solemnly."[39]

There the "restraints of Christian abstinence" are the forty days' fast and the weekly fasts on Wednesday and Friday. That homily is preserved only in the Latin of Rufinus, and it has long been common to reject the reference to the forty days as an interpolation by Rufinus. In fact, it would be very unlike Rufinus so to violate the text. On the other hand, it is generally agreed that the fast before Easter in Origen's time lasted only six days. That fast we have already documented for Syria in *Didascalia Apostolorum* and for Alexandria in a "festal letter" of Dionysius. It is certain that it could not have been different for Origen, even if we suppose that his homily reflects the life of the church in Caesarea rather than Alexandria. If Origen did know of a fast of forty days, we may be sure that such a fast was not a preparation for Easter.

192

Baumstark, however, called attention to an alternative location for that fast in the liturgical year in ante-Nicene Egypt, which continues to live in the memory of the Coptic church today.[40] This has been known to western scholars since the seventeenth century, when J. M. Vansleben brought from Egypt a manuscript of *The Lamp of Darkness* (now Paris, B.N. arab. 203), an important encyclopedia of Coptic church practice by a highly respected fourteenth-century scholar of that church, Abu 'l-Barakat. We shall be concerned shortly to examine that work more closely, but it will suffice at the moment to observe that it is asserted there that prior to Nicea (much earlier, in fact), the Fast of Forty Days began on the day following the Epiphany, the celebration of the baptism of Jesus. Alexandrian practice, according to this tradition, followed the chronology of the gospel of Mark, the baptism of Jesus on January 6, the beginning of the year, and the imitation of the fast of Jesus beginning, as Dix said it should, on the following day, January 7.

This tradition seems to have been carried into western monasticism, especially in this instance Celtic monasticism, most probably by monks trained in the monasteries of Scete in the Wadi Natrum. Art historians have frequently noted the close similarity between Coptic and Celtic manuscript illumination, and one of them has called attention to the assertion of the Antiphonary of Bangor that the rule of that Irish abbey came from Egypt.[41] In any case, although some scholars have rejected the Coptic evidence for a post-Epiphany Lent, to be examined shortly,[42] they have not had the opportunity, evidently, to take account of the Félire (martyrology) composed by Oengus, a Celtic monk, ca. 800. There a quadragesima beginning on the day after the Epiphany is mentioned specifically.[43] January 6 celebrates no other Epiphany theme than the baptism of Jesus, and the fast of Jesus ("Jesu's Lent") begins on the following day, January 7. As we noted in Part Two, this is one of three quadragesimal fasts in that work, the others being the fast of Elijah before Christmas and the fast of Moses following Pentecost. Are we to understand that in Irish monastic practice, at least as that was familiar to Oengus, the season imitating the fast of Jesus, begun on January 7, did not extend to Easter?

For the Celtic practice behind the martyrology of Oengus that question must go unanswered. Having received his monastic formation elsewhere, he wrote that work at the abbey of Tallaght, but the roughly contemporary martyrology of Tallaght, based closely on the Roman martyrology, suggests no such similarity to Egyptian practice. Some light on the matter is offered, perhaps, by a still earlier monastic document from Campania, *Regula Magistri*, an important source for later monastic rules best dated to the first quarter of the sixth century. There, while the standard ecclesiastical Lent precedes Easter (and is extended to Sexagesima), a longer period of fasting begins immediately after the Epiphany, spoken of as the hundred days' fast, *centesima paschae*. The singing of Alleluia ceases after vespers on the Epiphany, to be resumed only at Easter.[44]

It is possible that what we encounter here in the *Regula Magistri* reflects a monastic tradition that has been adapted to the standard prepaschal Lent, but that still reflects the Egyptian roots of the Fast of Forty Days beginning on the day after the Epiphany. Such, Coptic tradition insists, was the early practice of the church of Alexandria, where the fast was from the beginning just such an imitation of the fast of Jesus as later tradition has claimed it to be. Indeed, Coquin has suggested,[45] the failure of Athanasius to associate the Fast of Forty Days with the fast of Jesus can well be an indication that that imitative period still followed on the Epiphany, an entrenched tradition that would explain the resistance of the Egyptians to the prepaschal Lent urged by Athanasius from 330. That possibility might also suggest that the first disciplinary canon of Peter I, associating the forty days of fasting with the fast of Jesus, did, in fact, have a setting in liturgical time, following immediately after the Epiphany.

7. A PREBAPTISMAL FAST OF FORTY DAYS IN ALEXANDRIA

The passage cited above from Gregory Dix faithfully reflects the common understanding of the origins of Lent as a period for final catechetical preparation of candidates for paschal baptism. It is more questionable when it opposes that understanding of the origins of the great fast to the imitation of the fast of Jesus, as we have tried to show in the preceding section. If, however, we are to think of that imitation of the fast of Jesus as immediately following the Epiphany, what is to be said of the time of baptism in such a scheme?

The oddity of the festal letters of Athanasius lies not only in their silence regarding the association of the Fast of Forty Days with the fast of Jesus, an association already made by Athanasius' predecessor, Peter I, but also in their silence regarding the administration of baptism. One of the more generally agreed upon findings of liturgical scholarship is the recognition that the administration of baptism at Easter was a primary element in the celebration of that festival. As we noted in Part One, however, Raniero Cantalamessa has expressed some reservations in that matter. Cantalamessa suggests, in fact, that we have no firm data regarding paschal baptism prior to Tertullian, and little more than Hippolytus' *Commentary on Daniel* to add to that in the third century. Still, it seems clear that by the end of the third century paschal baptism was rather widely practiced, and in the following century it became precisely the standard element in the paschal celebration that scholarship has come to take for granted.

There seems to be significant agreement, however, that Alexandria was one important exception to that common pattern of practice. We have a particularly fascinating account of the first paschal baptism at Alexandria, accomplished in the first year of the patriarchate of Theophilus in 385. This account is contained in a papyrus codex of the sixth or seventh century, formerly number 18833 in the Phillipps Library in Cheltenham. The present location of the manuscript seems to have passed from public knowledge with the sale of that library, but it was, happily, published in an edition by Crum in 1915 with an appended note by A. Ehrhard defending the fundamental historicity of the core of the narrative, the materials for which he took to have been preserved in monastic records.[46]

The document gives an account of a meeting between Theophilus and Orsisius, hegoumen of Tabennis and third abbot general of the Pachomian foundations. This meeting was in consequence of a letter of invitation sent to Orsisius by Theophilus at the hands of two of his deacons, Faustus and Timotheus. Having located the abbot after wandering and searching through several communities, the two deacons escorted him back to Alexandria by boat. The trip, we are told, lasted six days, and they arrived in Alexandria just before Pascha. On meeting Orsisius, and after an exchange of felicitations, Theophilus explains the reason for his request that the abbot come to Alexandria.

"After this he declared to him the mystery, namely: from time immemorial when my Fathers came to confer baptism *on the appropriate day* there used to come, as they prayed still at the font, a beam of light and sign the waters. However, in this year we were not worthy of seeing this; and since I was frightened and upset, I revealed the matter to the clergy. And in the night of Saturday I went to present the oblation, and I heard a voice out of the sanctuary which said, 'If Orsisius does not come, you will not see that which you desire' " (emphasis added).[47]

Theophilus, our account continues, then invited Orsisius to come with him to the church, and they arrived there on "the great parasceve of the Great Pascha, early in the morning on the Sabbath." Theophilus then undertook once again to consecrate the font, and, now that Orsisius was included in the ceremony, the prodigy occurred as it had under Theophilus' predecessors. Then, after the baptisms, they proceded to the Catholikon for the eucharistic liturgy. "In this wise," says the author of the account, "the feast was doubled: the Resurrection and the baptism; and thus it is done until this day."[48] While this account can make the paschal baptism seem accidentally coincidental with the arrival of Orsisius, there is some evidence that baptism was performed at Easter in some of the Pachomian Tabennesiot communities. In any case, it seems clear that behind this account there lies a rapprochement between the patriarchate and the Pachomians.

This account, related also in the *History of the Patriarchs of Alexandria* by the tenth-century historian, Severus of El Asmunein,[49] shows that it was only in the first year of Theophilus' reign (385) that paschal baptism became the custom of the church in Egypt. We are not told what day it was that Theophilus had previously known as "the appropriate day" and on which he unsuccessfully undertook to consecrate the font. It must have been some weeks prior to Holy Week, however, since the deacons Faustus and Timotheus took some time in locating the abbot. Their search led from one monastery to another and is referred to as a "wandering." Having located him finally, they took a boat down the Nile and that trip took six days. Crum, indeed, questioned whether so short a time would suffice for what must have been a journey of between 550 and 800 kilometers.

The fourteenth-century encyclopedia of Coptic church practice by Abu 'l-Barakat, mentioned above, gives a somewhat more precise notion of what that "appropriate day" was. Regrettably, there is still no complete edition of that work, and the more extensive partial editions present only the Arabic text. We are fortunate, however, that the sections most relevant to our study were published in French translation by Dom Louis Villecourt in volumes 36–38 of *Le Muséon*,[50] although his own analysis of the text is not free from confusion. It is chapters XVIII and XIX that particularly concern us. In chapter XVIII, having said that the present time of Lent is determined by the computation of the epact that was established by the Patriarch Demetrius (189–232), Abu 'l-Barakat says of the fast:

"The holy fast was made previously from the second day of the Epiphany, according to the word of the holy gospel: When Jesus came up from the water, immediately the Spirit made him go out to the desert to be tempted by the devil, and he fasted 40 days and 40 nights. And the week of the Passion was then made separately at the time which is proper to it, because it has a conditioned time and a determined limit that the Fathers have established and prescribed so that the glorious Pasch would be later than the feast of the Jews, so that it would never coincide with it."[51]

The following chapter (XIX) deals with the feasts of Christ. There are fourteen of these, among which is the feast of Palms, of which Abu 'l-Barakat writes:

"This is the seventh Sunday of the Fast, and it is the end of the holy quarantine. This was formerly the pasch [conclusion] of the Fast, this, and not the Pascha of the Resurrection, when the holy quarantine began its fast on 12 Tybi and its term was 21 Amshir, and the week of the Pascha was celebrated apart in the month of Nisan and one celebrated the feast of the Pascha of the Resurrection at the end of the week, on Sunday, taking care that it not coincide with the Pascha of the Jews; until the days of the Father, patriarch Anba Demetrius, the 23rd of the patriarchs of Alexandria, because he acquired, by the grace of the Holy Spirit, the knowledge of the sciences of the Church and established the calculation of the epact, that of which the wise philosophers had been incapable. And he joined the week of the Pascha to Lent and he established this in agreement with the patriarchs who, at his time, were over the other three sees. And the ordo of this feast has been given in the chapter on the Fast, because it is the conclusion of it."[52]

From these two passages we can see the Coptic tradition regarding the primitive shape of Lent. Before it was possible to project the date of Easter in such a way as to be sure that it would follow after the Passover, the Paschal Fast lasted but a single week. The Fast of Forty Days, on the other hand, began on the day following the Epiphany, in direct and conscious imitation of the fast of Jesus. That fast was brought to its conclusion (its *pascha*, in common Coptic parlance) with the feast of Palms on the Sunday after the sixth and final week of the fast.

Just prior to his discussion of the ordo of the feast of Palms in chapter XVIII, Abu 'l-Barakat notes that the preceding Sunday is called the Sunday of Baptism(s), as it is in Coptic use still today.[53] While paschal baptism was established in Alexandria under Theophilus, in the seventeenth century Vansleben said that baptism was not allowed from Palm Sunday to Pentecost, and that this Sunday before Palm Sunday affords the final opportunity for baptism until after Pentecost.[54] That is still the case, but it is not the reason given by Abu 'l-Barakat in the fourteenth century. He says, "the sixth Sunday is called the Sunday of Baptism. It is that on which one cooked the chrism, *and it is said that the baptism of the apostles took place then*" (emphasis added).[55]

This assertion of the time of the apostles' baptism is unusual in liturgical history, and puzzling. Whatever we are to make of it, however, the assertion regarding the sixth Sunday seems to be transferred from the Friday of the sixth week to that preceding Sunday. Abu 'l-Barakat claims only that that had formerly been the day for the consecration of the chrism, a rite that was surely performed on Maundy Thursday at the time of his writing. In fact, in the tenth century the consecration of the chrism was on the sixth day of the sixth week of the fast. We know this from a letter of Macarius, bishop of Memphis and secretary to the fifty-eighth patriarch, Cosmas. That letter is embedded in a series of documents presented in a memorial by an unknown Coptic prelate to the Mafryan of Mosul, James, the nephew of Michael, the patriarch of

Antioch. This memorial forms the first part of the *Book of the Chrism* contained in Arabic ms. 100 of the Bibliotheque Nationale in Paris.[56]

The purpose of Macarius' letter is to complain of the novel custom of consecrating the chrism on Thursday of Holy Week, an accommodation of Coptic tradition to that of the "Romans" (*Rum*) of Byzantium that was made in the tenth century, first under Cosmas' successor, the fifty-ninth patriarch, also (confusingly enough) named Macarius. The new custom, evidently, met with sufficient dissatisfaction to lead the sixty-first patriarch, Mennas, to return to the old date on alternate years. Finally, the sixty-second patriarch, Ephrem the Syrian (970–974), settled on Thursday of Great Week, also the Syrian date. With that the Coptic tradition, greatly revered by Macarius of Memphis, came to an end. His lament makes it clear that much more was involved than simply the day on which one consecrates the chrism.

"It was thus that there was introduced a custom to please the people and the rule of the see of Mark the Evangelist was changed. They knew not that touching this day, and on it, there were numerous virtues, mysteries and interpretations. And this because it is the consummation of the sacred quarantine and is the day of the fast. It is told that *this is the day on which the Lord Christ baptized his disciples.* This is the sixth day of the week, figure of the sixth millenary, on which God the Word was incarnate and delivered Adam and his posterity from the domination of the enemy over them and freed them from his enslavement. And it became the day of baptism. This is why the patriarch of Alexandria performed on it the consecration of the chrism, which is the oil of balm, and of the oil of gladness, which is the oil of olive, and of the water of baptism, and he baptized then the people of every land" (emphasis added).[57]

From this it is clear that the associations that Abu 'l-Barakat related to the Sunday before Palm Sunday previously belonged to the following Friday, two days before Palm Sunday. Vansleben considered this to be a reference to Good Friday, and much earlier discussion of the testimony of Macarius dealt with the spurious issue of whether the Copts had once baptized on Friday of Great Week.[58] In fact, by Macarius' time the Friday of the sixth week of the fast was no longer Good Friday. The shape of the Alexandrian Lent, which we have already discussed on the basis of the festal letters of Athanasius, did take root eventually, and continued to be documented in festal letters until late in the sixth century. From at least the time of Patriarch Benjamin (622–661), however, the total fast lasted eight weeks,[59] and the first of those, called "the Fast of Heraclius" today, was observed with the same stringency as the following six weeks of Lent, by contrast to the Byzantine tyrophagy (the forefast that allows dairy products). After the Fast of Heraclius, then, come the six weeks of Lent, the "forty days," and then the final Great Week. The day to which Macarius refers is the sixth day of the sixth week of Lent proper, the Friday preceding Palm Sunday. He speaks of this as the day on which Jesus baptized his disciples (Abu 'l-Barakat had "apostles").

While, as we have seen, the traditions associated with that Friday had been transferred to the preceding Sunday by the fourteenth century, it is worthy of note that the sixth day of the sixth week of Lent, called *Qandil*, is still distinguished as the "seal of the fast," and is the day on which there is performed the general anointing of the sick, a ceremony that the Byzantine rite observes on Thursday of Holy Week.[60] While this might seem to be the one element not transferred to Thursday of Great Week in the tenth century, I have been unable to discover anything of the history of this general anointing in either Coptic or Byzantine tradition. Macarius himself tells us that the baptism traditionally associated with that day had already vanished from practice, as had the scrutiny (*Fishishin*) on Wednesday of that week. After a long passage describing the conferral of baptism on this traditional day, a description heavily influenced by the *Apostolic Tradition*, he says:

"Such was the rite of the apostolic see in the city of Alexandria. But when the confusion and perturbation had overcome us, this rite was transferred to the monastery of Saint Abu Macarius. However, it was not complete. There was no scrutiny (*Fishishin*) on the day of Wednesday and no baptism on the day of Friday, but only the consecration of the chrism, which is the oil of balm, and of the oil of gladness, which is the oil of olive."[61]

The "confusion and perturbation" that required the transfer of these ceremonies to the monastery of St. Macarius in the desert of

Scete are probably to be identified with the establishment of a Melchite patriarchate in Alexandria following the Council of Chalcedon. By that time, baptism was being conferred almost exclusively on infants and the catechetical structure had fallen away. We may suppose, further, that few baptisms were performed at the monastery of St. Macarius.

How that ancient baptismal day, the sixth day of the sixth week after Epiphany, retained its value and its place in Egyptian tradition until it was vestigially restored in the sixth week of a Lent prior to Holy Week remains unclear. Egyptian Christianity was characterized by wide diversity, however, and it is quite possible that the old order was maintained at St. Macarius' well after the introduction of paschal baptism at Alexandria in the first year of Theophilus. This would be a possibility even if that new paschal baptismal day at Alexandria marked a closer relationship between the patriarchate and Tabennesid monasticism, given the significant difference between those communities and the monasteries of Scete. We have seen reason to believe that monks trained in the Wadi Natrun carried to Ireland, at some time between the sixth and the ninth centuries, the tradition of a Lent that began on the day after the Epiphany.

Nonetheless, at Alexandria in the patriarchate of Benjamin I, the sixth week of Lent was the week before the Paschal Fast. The sixth day of that sixth week was once again the day on which the chrism was consecrated, because it had been the day on which the patriarch of the see of St. Mark baptized the people (although that was no longer the case). He had baptized on that day because, in turn, it was said to be the day on which Jesus baptized. During the intervening century or more between the desuetude of the single baptismal day in the fifth century and the distinction of Lent from Holy Week after 577, the relationship of that traditional day to Pascha, and the nature of the rites performed on it, are hidden in the history of St. Macarius' monastery. Memory, however, is long in Scete. Those who visit St. Macarius' today are shown the domed pavilion in which the chrism was prepared and consecrated, although that rite has not been performed at the monastery for over four hundred years. We must content ourselves with the existence of the tradition that identifies the sixth day of the final week of Lent (not Holy Week) with the time of baptism in the earliest history of the see of St. Mark, a conclusion to Lent associated with the performance of baptism by Jesus.

In his letter, the bishop of Memphis, obsessed with the antiquity of the associations surrounding the "sixth day of the sixth week of the blessed fast," still did not speak of that fast as having originally fallen following the Epiphany. That was asserted, however, by a contemporary, and a Melchite at that, one not inclined to promulgate the peculiar antiquities of a see derelict from imperial orthodoxy. This testimony to the post-Epiphany Lent we find in the *Annals* of Eutychius:

"At this time, Demetrius, Patriarch of Alexandria, wrote to Agapius, Bishop of Jerusalem, to Maximos, Patriarch of Antioch and to Victor, Patriarch of Rome, on the subject of the calculation of the Pascha of the Christians and the fast, in what manner it is deduced from the Pascha of the Jews, concerning which thing they wrote many books and epistles, until they established the Christian Pascha in the form in which it is now observed; and that because, after the Ascension of the Lord Christ into heaven, Christians, when they had celebrated the feast of the baptism, began to observe the fast of forty days on the next day, which they observed then as did the Lord Christ, who after he was baptized in Jordan went out into the desert and remained there fasting for forty days. Furthermore, when the Jews celebrate Pascha they [the Christians] observe the same festival. Therefore, the patriarchs thus established this computation of the Pascha so that Christians fast forty days and then observe the fast day of the Pascha." (PG 111.989)

While we may hope that Eutychius' Arabic was less ambiguous than this translation of Edward Pococke's Latin version, it is nonetheless clear that Eutychius accepts and subscribes to the tradition that makes Lent follow immediately upon Epiphany prior to the patriarchate of Demetrius. At the same time, roughly, Macarius of Memphis insists that the sixth day of the final week of that fast was considered to be the day on which Jesus baptized.

Looking at this tenth-century evidence, it is difficult to doubt that these references to the commemorative fast of forty days following immediately after the Epiphany and also to the conferral of baptism on the sixth day of the sixth week of the fast are to be understood in relation to each other. It is so that the matter appears in Abu 'l-Barakat (albeit with the baptisms on the previous Sunday), and the earlier sources generally support the various elements of that tradition. What this stream of Coptic tradition asserts is that in the earliest period the baptism of Jesus was observed on 11 Tybi, and, in imitation of him, the Fast of Forty Days began on the following day. That fast continued for six weeks, and on the sixth day of the sixth week baptism was conferred, that being considered the day on which Jesus baptized his disciples. The fast came to its festal conclusion on the following Sunday with the feast of Palms. All that was independent of the celebration of Pascha, itself determined in relation to, but following, the Jewish Passover in the month of Nisan. Pascha, several weeks after the feast of Palms, was observed with a fast of six days, Monday through Saturday, and concluded with the celebration of the resurrection, without the conferral of baptism, on Sunday.

For that early tradition, there was no conflict between Lent as imitation of the fast of Jesus and as period of baptismal preparation. It was both of those in ante-Nicene Alexandria, if we can believe the sources we have examined. The direct sources are late, coming from the tenth and following centuries, but they are supported strongly by the testimony of the martyrology of Oengus, which shows the post-Epiphany Lent still active in the eighth century. Further, these Coptic documents are consistent with and explain many earlier texts, the sixth- or seventh-century Phillipps Papyrus Codex, the fourth-century Canons of Hippolytus, and the third-century tenth homily on Leviticus of Origen. While one must recognize that behind the third century we are hardly speaking of a consciously observed cycle of seasons and festivals called "the liturgical year," we shall see, nonetheless, that this Coptic tradition even throws valuable light on a recently revealed source from the second century, a source which, in turn, seems to validate dramatically this hypothetical reconstruction.

8. THE DAY ON WHICH JESUS BAPTIZED AND THE SATURDAY OF LAZARUS

We have noted above that two of the medieval sources, the *Lamp of Darkness* of Abu 'l-Barakat and the letter of Macarius, identify the day on which the chrism was confected as associated in legend with the conferral of baptism by Jesus. The fourteenth-century writer, Abu 'l-Barakat, makes that the sixth Sunday of the fast, the day at the head of the final week, and says, "it is said that the baptism of the apostles took place then." Four centuries earlier, Macarius wrote of the following Friday, "It has been told that this is the day on which the Lord Christ baptized his disciples."

If both writers seem somewhat diffident about this testimony, it is not surprising. None of the gospels provides an account of Jesus' baptism of the inner circle of his followers, although one might read John 4.2 in that sense. John 3.22 seems to assert rather more boldly that Jesus did baptize. Later sacramental theology, however, would be hard put to assign a content to such baptism prior to his passion. It would be difficult, moreover, to bring those Johannine texts into any sort of relation to Jesus' fast in the wilderness, since the fourth gospel says nothing at all of that fast. Only the synoptic gospels recount the story of his retreat in the wilderness of Judea following his baptism, and these say nothing at all of the performance of baptism by Jesus.

In a paper read at the Liturgical Week of the *Institut Saint-Serge* in 1965, René-Georges Coquin puzzled over this particular aspect of the Coptic tradition he had so thoroughly examined, finally confessing,

"We have not been able to discover the source of that Coptic tradition touching the baptism of the Apostles after the temptation in the desert, but it is evident that the Coptic church primitively adopted an organization of that part of the liturgical year calculated on the historical unfolding of the life of Jesus, at least as that was given in its own traditions."[62]

That brilliant surmise, as I believe it to be, has been dramatically vindicated since M. Coquin offered it, but not without slightly recasting his statement of the problem. The sources that speak of the day on which Jesus baptized place that day at the end of the church's fast of forty days. If, however, those forty days are given to "the historical unfolding of the life of Jesus," it is unlikely that the account of baptism by Jesus was located in the traditional text immediately following his fast in the wilderness. Whatever the narrative of the life of Jesus being unfolded, we may suppose that the reading of it continued during the forty days of the church's fast. It is highly unlikely that a narrative would provide an account of the fast in the wilderness so detailed as to provide liturgical readings for six weeks. We should, therefore, look for the account of Jesus' performance of initiatory rites at some later point in the narrative of his ministry, not immediately at the conclusion of the presumably brief account of his fast in the wilderness. The account of his fast, we may suppose, would be read at the outset of the church's imitation of it, but during the six weeks of that commemorative fast the narrative of Christ's ministry would continue to unfold, coming to some sort of climax at the end of those six weeks. Abu 'l-Barakat, indeed, says that the concluding festival was the feast of Palms. That would suggest a proximity of the account of Jesus' baptizing to that of his entry into Jerusalem.

Such, in fact, is precisely what we find in the most likely source at Alexandria for the life of Jesus, the gospel of Saint Mark. The canonical Mark, of course, contains no reference to the conferral of baptism by Jesus. However, since 1973 we have had access to information concerning an expanded text of Mark, which, according to an important ante-Nicene source, was used at Alexandria in connection with the rites of initiation. This document is commonly referred to today as the "Mar Saba Clementine Fragment," and has been included by Ursula Treu in her recent second edition of the first part of volume 4 of Stählin's standard text of *Clemens Alexandrinus* in the Berlin Corpus.[63]

Thanks to the meticulous literary analysis of Professor Morton Smith of Columbia University,[64] this fragmentary copy of what purports to be a letter of Clement of Alexandria is now widely accepted as being just that. There are some who doubt its Clementine authorship, but would yet place it early in the third century. Nonetheless, what is surely by now the majority opinion among patrologists was voiced by R.P.C. Hanson when he wrote, "Patristic scholars can agree that a new letter of Clement of Alexandria has been identified," although he gave that judgment in the context of a generally negative review of Professor Smith's book.[65]

The fragment was discovered by Professor Smith at Mar Saba, near Jerusalem, in 1958. It formed two-and-a-half pages of manuscript in an eighteenth-century cursive hand written on the end pages of a seventeenth-century printed edition of the letters of Ignatius of Antioch. The copying of the letter was interrupted, and the manuscript ends in the middle of a sentence. What remains, however, has profound significance for the study of New Testament tradition and its relation to liturgical tradition. We must prescind from the lively discussions of the *Sitz im Leben* for the putatively Marcan material cited in the letter, and satisfy ourselves with examining the light it throws on liturgical history, its *Sitz in Gottesdienst*.

Without wishing to suggest that the discussion is closed, we shall for convenience accept the authorship imputed by the manuscript and refer to its writer as "Clement." He addresses a certain Theodore, congratulating him on having resisted the blandishments and lies of the Carpocratians, a libertine gnostic sect centered in Alexandria in the second century. Clement does respond to one of the Carpocratian claims regarding the gospel of Mark read in the church of Alexandria, however, and it is at that point that our citation begins.

"Now of the things they keep saying about the divinely inspired Gospel according to Mark, some are altogether falsifications, and others, even if they do contain some true elements, nevertheless are not reported truly. For the true things being mixed with inventions, are falsified, so that, as the saying goes, even the salt loses its savor.

"As for Mark, then, during Peter's stay in Rome he wrote an account of the Lord's doings, not, however, declaring all of them, nor yet hinting at the secret ones, but selecting what he thought most useful for increasing the faith of those who were being instructed. But when Peter died a martyr, Mark came over to Alexandria, bringing both his own notes and those of Peter, from which he transferred to his former book the things suitable to whatever makes for progress toward knowledge. Thus he composed a more spiritual Gospel for the use of those who were being perfected. Nevertheless, he yet did not divulge the things not to be uttered, nor did he write down the hierophantic teaching of the Lord, but to the stories already written he added yet others and, moreover, brought in certain sayings of which he knew the interpretation would, as a mystagogue, lead the hearers into the innermost sanctuary of that truth hidden by seven veils. Thus, in sum, he prepared matters, neither grudgingly nor incautiously, in my opinion, and, dying, he left his composition to the church in Alexandria, where it even yet is most carefully guarded, being read *only to those who are being initiated into the great mysteries* [emphasis added]. But since the foul demons are always devising destruction for the race of men, Carpocrates, instructed by them and using deceitful arts, so enslaved a certain presbyter of the church in Alexandria that he got from him a copy of the secret Gospel, which he both interpreted according to his blasphemous and carnal doctrine and, moreover, polluted, mixing with the spotless and holy words utterly shameless lies. From this mixture is drawn off the teaching of the Carpocratians."[66]

It is against this introductory material that Clement will cite two passages from what is here translated as "the secret Gospel." There is no doubt that this correctly renders the Greek *mystikon evangelion*, but given the richness of Clement's use of "mystical" language, we should not allow that phrase to be deprived of other, more cultic nuance. Particularly important for our purpose is his indication that this special material is to be "read only to those who are being initiated into the great mysteries." While Clement's words here have been subjected to less obvious interpretations, the clear meaning is that this special material in the *mystikon evangelion* was read in connection with the conferral of baptism. Such information regarding a liturgical pericope at such a central rite at such an early period is precious indeed. Clement tells Theodore and us what that mystical teaching is:

"To you, therefore, I shall not hesitate to answer the questions you have asked, refuting the falsifications by the very words of the Gospel. For example, after 'And they were in the road going up to Jerusalem,' and what follows, until 'After three days he shall arise,' [i.e., Mark 10.32–34] the secret Gospel brings the following material word for word: 'And they come into Bethany. And a certain woman whose brother had died was there. And, coming, she prostrated herself before Jesus and says to him, "Son of David, have mercy on me." But the disciples rebuked her. And Jesus, being angered, went off with her into the garden where the tomb was, and straightway a great cry was heard from the tomb. And going near Jesus rolled away the stone from the door of the tomb. And straightway, going in where the youth was, he stretched forth his

207

hand and raised him, seizing his hand. But the youth, looking upon him, loved him and began to beseech him that he might be with him. And going out of the tomb they came into the house of the youth, for he was rich. And after six days Jesus told him what to do and in the evening the youth comes to him, wearing a linen cloth over his naked body. And he remained with him that night, for Jesus taught him the mystery of the kingdom of God. And thence, arising, he returned to the other side of the Jordan.'

"After these words follows the text. 'And James and John come to him,' and all that section [i.e., Mark 10.35–45]. But 'naked man with naked man,' and the other things about which you wrote, are not found.

"And after the words, 'And he comes into Jericho' [Mark 10.46.], the secret Gospel adds only, 'And the sister of the youth whom Jesus loved and his mother and Salome were there, and Jesus did not receive them.' But the many other things about which you wrote both seem to be and are falsifications.

"Now the true explanation and that which accords with the true philosophy . . . "[67]

It is at that point that the fragment ends. The long citation of special material seems to be clumsily inserted into the canonical Mark. Jesus and his disciples, having been "beyond Jordan" (Mark 10.1), are "in the road going up to Jerusalem" (Mark 10.32), and, in the added material, arrive as near as Bethany. After six days there, Jesus abandons his progress toward Jerusalem and departs back across Jordan. Then, after the special material, Mark 10.46 picks him up again just coming out of Jericho, arriving back at Bethany at 11.1. This zig-zag path in which a lengthy journey is reversed, only to be reversed again, is not visible in the canonical text of Mark. However, Professor Smith has shown that a very similar complex path surrounds the parallel material in John 10.41–12.19.[68]

The long passage inserted following Mark 10.34 is clearly related to the raising of Lazarus in John 11. Yet here the story does not end with Lazarus' restoration to life. Rather, after six days "the youth" comes to Jesus in what seems clearly to be some sort of initiatory costume (cf. Mk 14.51), and is introduced by Jesus into the mystery of the kingdom of God. That this initiatory encounter is of a baptismal character is not stated in the text, but the use of this pericope in connection with baptism must have established such an understanding.

Abu 'l-Barakat made the sixth Sunday to be the day on which (it was said) Jesus baptized his apostles, and, as we have noted, that Sunday before Palm Sunday is still a major occasion for baptism in the Coptic church today. Of the baptism of the apostles we still have no record at all. Four centuries earlier, Macarius of Memphis made the following Friday, the sixth day of the sixth week, to be the day on which (it was said) Jesus baptized his disciples. That expression is, given the terminology of the time, somewhat less specifically focused on the twelve. It is still plural, while the Mar Saba fragment offers us only a single disciple, the unnamed youth of Bethany whom the fourth gospel identifies as Lazarus.

Nonetheless, we must propose this Mar Saba fragment as the otherwise unknown source of the Coptic tradition associating the traditional baptismal day with the day on which Jesus baptized. It is true that the subject of the narrative is but a single individual in the Mar Saba fragment, and that the text does not even say that Jesus baptized him. Yet it was this text that was read, Clement says, "only to those who are being initiated into the great mysteries," and it is virtually certain that those disciples of Christ were being baptized.

Any number of questions have surrounded and continue to surround the Mar Saba fragment, but those questions, I believe, are at least set in a new context by the recognition that this forgotten and strange text provides an answer to a question that had not been asked, to my knowledge, until well after the discovery of the fragment in 1958, but was asked by Coquin in 1965, years before its publication in 1973, viz., Where did medieval Copts get the idea that Jesus had baptized on the day on which baptism was conferred at the end of their primitive Lent?

Of the origins of that strange version of the raising of Lazarus we have no clue, though it seems most likely that it originated in Egypt. Nonetheless, the clumsiness of its insertion between verses 34 and 35 of Mark 10 suggests that it was put there for a reason, perhaps because it was already associated with baptism or because its reference to "six days" made its initiatory quality seem appropriate to the baptisms already established on the sixth day. In any case, that clumsy insertion into Mark 10 had already occurred when Clement wrote to Theodore, and it was already the pericope read to those who were being initiated into the great mysteries. If the author who regarded it as an authentic part of the gospel tradition was indeed Clement of Alexandria, that would probably date its inclusion between 70 and 170.

In his smaller study of the text, Professor Smith reported the suggestion of Cyril Richardson that it had been the pericope at the paschal vigil.[69] That was wrong, of course, and Richardson subsequently retracted the suggestion. But Richardson's major error was in supposing that ante-Nicene Alexandria baptized at Pascha. That the "secret Gospel" was the baptismal pericope seems clear, and that gives totally unexpected support to the insistence of Macarius of Memphis that the primitive practice of the church of Alexandria was to baptize on the sixth day of the sixth week of the blessed fast, the day on which Jesus baptized. For that reason the patriarchs of Alexandria considered that to be "the appropriate day" for baptism until 385, the first year of Theophilus, when, for the first time, the Pascha came to have a double meaning, baptism and the resurrection.

Prior to that, we may hypothesize, the course reading of Mark, begun at the Epiphany with the account of Jesus' baptism, was read through six weeks during the commemoration of the fast of Jesus. At some point in the sixth week, that reading reached Mark 10.32–34, and in conjunction with the conferral of baptism, most probably on the Friday of that week, the story of the raising of the young man at Bethany was read. On that day and on the following day, Saturday, the reading of chapter 10 was completed. The next day, Sunday, had the reading of Mark 11, Christ's entry into Jerusalem, the "feast of Palms" Abu 'l-Barakat called it, the festal day that brought the fast to its conclusion.

Such a hypothesis, while reasonable, is likely to seem no more than that. In fact, it seems, we find this hypothesis verified in the current practice of the Byzantine rite, a practice in place, in its main outlines, already in the typika of the ninth and tenth centuries and probably preserving a pattern that was then centuries old. We must suppose that the peculiar text of Mark at Alexandria, a text of which we had no notice at all before its publication by Professor Morton Smith, had been suppressed as the texts of the gospels became standardized. It is difficult to know exactly when that suppression occurred, but it seems that when it did occur the secret gospel had already achieved a place of such significance in the liturgical tradition that it was replaced with the only canonical parallel to its story of the miracle at Bethany, the raising of Lazarus in John 11.1–45. I would suggest that what Smith calls the "longer text" of Mark provides following Mark 10.34 the origin of the Saturday of Lazarus, the major baptismal day preceding Palm Sunday at Constantinople.

A comparison of the lenten course reading of Mark, which we have suggested for ante-Nicene Alexandria and the gospel appointments of the ninth-tenth century Byzantine typika will illustrate the point.

	Alexandria (hypothetical)	*Constantinople*
	[Epiphany: Mk 1.1–11]	
First Week of Lent	Mk 1.12ff.	Sabbath: Mk 2.23–3.5
		Sunday: Jn 1.44–52
Second Week of Lent	Continuation of Mark	Sabbath: Mk 1.35–44
		Sunday: Mk 2.1–12
Third Week of Lent	Continuation of Mark	Sabbath: Mk 7.31–37
		Sunday: Mk 8.34–9.1
Fourth Week of Lent	Continuation of Mark	Sabbath: Mk 8.27–31
		Sunday: Mk 9.17–31
Fifth Week of Lent	Continuation of Mark	Sabbath: Mk 2.14–17
		Sunday: Mk 10.32–45
Sixth Week of Lent	Friday: Mk 10.32–34, the secret gospel, Mk 10.35–45	
	Sabbath: Mk 10.46–52	Sabbath: Jn 11.1–45
	Sunday: Mk 11.1–11	Sunday: Jn 12.1–18

The column for Alexandria merely suggests the beginning of the first week of the fast with the account of Jesus going into the wilderness, and picks up in the sixth week what our sources have suggested regarding the reading at baptism on the sixth day of that week. In this hypothetical reconstruction, I have conjectured that the passages cited by Clement in the Mar Saba fragment to locate the added material for his correspondent (Mark 10.32–34 before the added material and Mark 10.35–45 after it) were read together with the added pericope. In the Bohairic Coptic New Testament manuscripts, Mark 10.32–45 is an integral chapter (chapter 31). I have also conjectured that the following Coptic chapter 32, Mark 10.46–52 (with minor additions from the secret gospel) was read on the following day; some old Coptic lectionaries do in fact appoint this reading for that day. That would lead into the reading of Mark 11 and the entry into Jerusalem on the Sunday after the baptisms, the feast of Palms, which concluded the fast.

As noted previously, the typika of Hagia Sophia from the ninth and tenth centuries show signs of considerable transposition of appointments, especially on the Saturdays. Further, the first Sunday has a reading from John for the feast of the Prophets. Nonetheless, behind these developments it is still easy to see the remains of a course reading of Mark on all Saturdays and Sundays in Lent, the only lenten days on which the eucharist was celebrated. All proceeds in a fairly orderly fashion through the Sunday of the fifth week. On that day the gospel reading is Coptic chapter 31, in which the story of the raising of the young man at Bethany was embedded, Mark 10.32–45. But at the next liturgy on the following Saturday the course reading of Mark is abruptly abandoned in favor of John 11.1–45, the raising of Lazarus, the only canonical parallel to that material added in the secret gospel, and this *Saturday of the Palmbearer, Memorial of the Holy and Just Lazarus*, although but a week from the paschal vigil, is observed as a major baptismal liturgy. On the following day as well, it is from the fourth gospel that the entry into Jerusalem is read, the only account of that event that relates it chronologically to the passion. The Marcan account does not connect the two chronologically, nor was there such a connection in early Alexandria between the feast of Palms, which concluded Lent, and the Pascha observed apart in the month of Nisan. In both instances, however, the Fast of Forty Days stretches from the Monday of the first week through the Friday of the sixth, and its conclusion celebrates the triumphal entry into the Holy City on the Sunday following the conferral of baptism, itself associated with Jesus' miraculous raising from the dead of a young man at Bethany.

At Constantinople, separated from the Epiphany and situated instead prior to Holy Week, we see the remains of the Alexandrian

212

evangelical regimen for Lent from a time when that still began on the day after Epiphany and ended with the conferral of baptism on a day on which the candidates heard the story of the miraculous raising from the dead of a young man in Bethany. That baptismal tradition, represented fully in the medieval typika, is remembered still today in the substitution of the baptismal troparion, "As many as have been baptized into Christ have put on Christ," for the regular entrance chant, Trisagion, on that day when the memorial of the raising of Lazarus marks the lasting influence of the secret gospel of Mark on the liturgical tradition.

No other consideration that I know of would account for the abrupt shift to the fourth gospel for the commemoration of Lazarus as a baptismal festival on that day. As we observed above, both the Saturday of Lazarus and Palm Sunday seem to have been kept at Constantinople in the time of Chrysostom. Given the relation of those days to this lenten program, and its evident derivation from the early Alexandrian Marcan cursus, we may suppose that these Johannine gospel readings fell already in Chrysostom's time at the end of a Marcan lenten cursus.

There being no sign of such a Marcan cursus nor any developed and stable lenten program at Jerusalem, we have suggested that the visit to Bethany and the procession down the Mount of Olives on the Saturday and Sunday before Great Week, functions already in place in Jerusalem by 383, represent the retracing in Jerusalem of events celebrated in the liturgy of another city at the insistence of visitors from that city. That city, it would appear, was Constantinople, and its visitors to the Holy City in the Theodosian age were not without influence. Constantinople derived its Great Week gospels from Jerusalem, the passion of Matthew, as can be seen from the close correspondence between *Hagios Stavros 40* and *Jerusalem arm. 121*, but the Saturday of Lazarus and Palm Sunday come to Jerusalem from Constantinople, and to Constantinople from ante-Nicene Alexandria.

Such an influence from Alexandria on early Constantinople has not characterized our standard understanding of the sources of the Byzantine liturgy. In the standard view, the most common influence on Constantinople (as on Cappadocia and all of Asia) was Antioch. Antioch, however, does not show the strong preference for course reading that we see at Constantinople.[70] Although there are late evidences from Syria and Armenia that the tradition of a post-Epiphany Lent was known, the separate conclusion of such a fast with Palm Sunday, which appears to have characterized the Byzantine Lent in the time of Chrysostom, is unknown before Nicea, save in this tradition for primitive Alexandria. Nor is there any sign elsewhere of a Saturday of Lazarus (derived from the secret gospel) as a separate concluding baptismal day. If, as we have argued, the Byzantine lenten program had its origins following the Epiphany in Alexandria, we must confess that we do not know how that program came to be adopted in the imperial city, but it would suggest a relationship between those two sees to which liturgiology has given little attention.

9. THE RECKONING OF THE FORTY DAYS BEFORE EASTER

In the light of the Coptic evidence for a fast of forty days following immediately upon the Epiphany, and the signs of such a tradition also in the West in the Martyrology of Oengus, we can see that there is less question of whether the Fast of Forty Days commemorated the fast of Jesus than there is of the circumstances under which that commemoration came to be attached to Pascha. We have noted already the evidences of a prepaschal program for the final preparation of candidates for baptism at Rome, and have examined the suggestion that this was once a period of three weeks, although followed by Holy Week in our later evidences. After Nicea, as early as 340 by implication (from Athanasius' letter to Sarapion) and overtly in 385 (in Siricius' decretal to Himerius) at Rome, that period is spoken of as forty days. Such an understanding of forty days as the appropriate duration would seem to have come from the Alexandrian ante-Nicene practice, while its prepaschal location is a dimension of the paschal baptismal practice first visible in Tertullian and Hippolytus.

Eutychius, the tenth-century Melchite patriarch of Alexandria, ascribes the reorganization of Lent, its attachment to Easter, to the late second- and early third-century patriarch, Demetrius,[71] and this same claim is made for Demetrius twice in the Alexandrian *Synaxarium*.[72] This attribution of the reorganization of the fast to

Demetrius is always related to his computation of the epact, the mathematical relation of lunar and solar movements. Marcel Richard believed that Demetrius may, in fact, have discovered the epact, but he joined Coquin in rejecting the notion of such an early establishment of the prepaschal Lent.[73] Indeed, we have seen in the Phillipps papyrus codex reason to believe that the old Alexandrian baptismal day, weeks before the paschal fast, was still active in the first year of Theophilus, 385. That would explain both Athanasius' silence regarding baptism in his festal letters and his failure to associate the prepaschal fast of forty days with the fast of Jesus, even though an earlier patriarch of Alexandria, Peter I, had so associated the notion of a quadragesimal fast with the imitation of Jesus. The perdurance of a forty-day fast after Epiphany would explain also the difficulty encountered by Athanasius in establishing such a fast prior to Easter, a difficulty documented by the letter to Sarapion in 340, a decade after his first announcement of that fast in the festal letter of 330.

In his paper at the Liturgical Week of the Insitut Saint-Serge in 1965, Coquin suggested that the reform attributed to Demetrius in the medieval sources, resulting in the transposition of the fast of forty days from the six weeks following the Epiphany to the six weeks preceding Easter, was rather an initiative of Athanasius, pursued with diplomatic caution in the light of the tradition attaching to the old arrangement of the year. However, in 1967, the same year in which Coquin's paper was published, he presented a further study of the matter to the Académie des Inscriptions et Belles-Lettres in which he argued that the situation of the fast prior to Pascha was a dimension of the settlement of the paschal question at the Council of Nicea.[74]

The tenth-century historian, Severus of El-Asmunein, in his *History of the Patriarchs of Alexandria,* notes such an action of Nicea in his accounts of the patriarchates of both Athanasius and his immediate predecessor, Alexander.[75] These texts simply assert that Nicea "fixed the orthodox faith, the days of the fast and the day of Pascha." Eutychius also asserts that the decision of Demetrius was confirmed by the fathers at Nicea.[76] Coquin also reported a similar assertion in a Syriac liturgical commentary of the ninth or tenth century, *Exposition of the Offices of the Church,* attributed (pseudonymously) to George of Arbela. That writer, having mentioned a tradition that set the fast of Jesus following Pentecost, then explains the practice of the Church.

"The holy Fathers, having seen that the three evangelists mentioned the fast immediately after the baptism, then from the beginning of the economy, fixed the fast immediately after the celebration of the Epiphany, but they made the week of the Passion in the days of the 14 Nisan.—However, they observed the days of the Passion in different ways: some fasted the first day of Unleavened Bread, breaking the fast the second and third days and taking no account of the Sunday; others fasted all the week of Unleavened Bread and broke the fast on Sunday; still others fasted the days on which our Lord suffered, i.e., the Friday and Saturday, and broke the fast on Sunday.—But when the synod of Nicea was assembled, (the Fathers) decided unanimously that the fast should be joined to the Passion, i.e., to Pascha, so that the resurrection of our Saviour should be at the end of the fast."[77]

A less precise assertion of the Nicene fixing of the fast in connection with the settlement of the paschal question is found in the somewhat later (before 1036) Nestorian *Chronicle of Se'ert*.[78]

We do not, of course, possess the formal *Acta* of the council, the known "Canons of Nicea" having been edited by a later fifth-century historian, Gelasius of Cyzicus, from such historical sources as Eusebius and Rufinus. It is widely doubted today that such a documentary record of the council's work ever existed. Eusebius makes it quite clear that, alongside the Arian question, the fixing of a common paschal date loomed large in the agenda of the council.[79] Beyond that, we must be satisfied that it is only after that council that we encounter the situation of a Fast of Forty Days prior to Pascha. It is interesting to note, nonetheless, that the six weeks of that quarantine are variously arranged. Callewaert considered the terms of Lent to be the Sunday of Quadragesima and Thursday of Holy Week, the day before the old triduum. It is the six weeks before Easter at Milan and Athanasius' Alexandria. By contrast to those very similar arrangements, Lent occupies the six weeks before Holy Week in the Syria of *Apostolic Constitutions* and, evidently, at Constantinople, the arrangement that eventually became general in the East. This difference reflects an ambiguity in the understanding of Pascha, whether it be the fast of the Passion or the concluding feast, an ambiguity that is common throughout early Christian history. It is not difficult to imagine that this almost simultaneous appearance of different patterns for the same forty-day fast was due to the general concern to conform to a synodal agreement, which was itself unintentionally ambiguous.

What is common in this post-Nicene appearance of Lent is the understanding that it lasts for forty days, in spite of the variations in practice. We do not know why it was that within a generation of Nicea all the Church agreed that the major fast of Christians lasts forty days, even while undecided on just which forty days those were. Given that uncertainty we can hardly sweep aside the considerable evidence that such a fast, following the Epiphany and commemorating the fast of Jesus, had already existed before the council.

Such a tradition, fused with other patterns of preparation for paschal baptism, could easily present the agreement and the variety found after Nicea. All are agreed that the fast is for forty days. All are agreed that it is preparation for Pascha. It is preparation for baptism at Rome and Milan, but in the latter city the enrollment for that final preparation took place on the Epiphany. At Alexandria, where (it is argued) such a fast began on the day after Epiphany, the forty days commemorated the fast of Jesus and led toward the conferral of baptism. As promoted by Athanasius, it leads to Easter, but it neither commemorates the fast of Jesus nor prepares for baptism (until, at least, the time of Theophilus).

Still, although the testimony of Athanasius remains an exception, it seems most likely that the establishment of the principal fast prior to Pascha is a reflection of the ever-growing custom of conferring baptism at that principal festival. Already established in North Africa and at Rome in the early third century, during the third and fourth centuries paschal baptism became the norm in all of the Church and, with that, the weeks before Pascha were dedicated to the final preparation of the candidates. The six-week duration of that preparation, modeled on the forty-day fast of Jesus, can be understood as Alexandria's contribution to the post-Nicene patterns.

More was involved, however, than preparation for baptism. Already in *Didache* 7, the prebaptismal fast is urged upon the entire community insofar as possible. As important as such exercises were, we see little of Lent as a season of interest to baptismal candidates alone. By the time the prepaschal season becomes visible, it is urged as an ascetical exercise for the whole people in preparation for the celebration of Pascha, whether that be understood as the Sunday of the resurrection or as the six-day fast ending in that festival.

Even if, as it appears, Alexandria was slow in making that change in its baptismal day, its old custom of observing the forty days in commemoration of the fast of Jesus was extended to the fast before Pascha everywhere. Athanasius, in exile in Rome in 340, found that the Egyptians were made a laughing-stock because they, of all the world, did not fast during the forty days before Pascha. Given his commitment to Nicea, Athanasius would find such neglect particularly embarrassing if the prepaschal position for the Fast of Forty Days had been ordered by the council.

The manner of observing the forty-day fast, as we have seen, varied considerably. There seems little reason for us to assume that this was viewed in the fourth century as forty days of actual fasting, the solitary and problematic testimony of Egeria being the exception. The forty days as described in the festal letters of Athanasius would have included thirty fast days, to which would be added the Sabbath of Holy Week. In the West, there were six fast days per week, and so the total number of fast days was thirty-six. John Cassian speaks of this as "the tithe of the year."[80] Where the Fast of Forty Days was clearly distinct from the Paschal Fast, as at Constantinople, Lent yielded but thirty fast days (five in each of the six weeks), and six more days were provided in the Paschal Fast. Such is the picture afforded by *Apostolic Constitutions* V.13. From the end of the fifth century, perhaps, and probably from another part of Syria than Antioch, the lectionary published by Burkitt shows a pattern reminiscent of Socrates' bewilderment at the varieties of lenten praxis. In this Syriac lectionary only the first and middle weeks of Lent and the Great Week are assigned readings.[81] From this liturgical pattern alone it is probably impossible to know whether these were the only weeks observed with fasting, as Socrates believed, but this seems likely.

Whatever we are to make of the testimony of Egeria, there can be no doubt that the practice she described, eight weeks with five fast days in each, was followed in Antioch in the time of Severus in the sixth century.[82] In the following century, that same pattern is encountered at Alexandria in the festal letters of Benjamin I. Both of these sources are Monophysite, and Rahlfs has argued persuasively that it was an ecumenical initiative of Heraclius that urged a similar eight-week total at Constantinople, seeking to forestall a further ground of disagreement with the Jacobite traditions. At Constantinople, however, the added week at the beginning of the period called for abstinence from flesh only, allowing the continued use of cheese and other dairy products, from which it is called *Tyrophagia* ("cheese-eating"). Later at Alexandria also a distinction between the first week and the six weeks of Lent will be found, although there the first week, called the "Fast of Heraclius," is observed with the same stringency as the six weeks of Lent and the Paschal Fast, a variation from the orthodox practice that the Melchite Eutychius relates to a shameful vow made to Heraclius.[83]

Extensions of the fast are found in the West also in the sixth and following centuries. We have already noted the appearance of the *Regula Magistri* in the first quarter of the sixth century, probably in Campania. There a *centesima paschae* began on the day after the Epiphany, extending to Pascha, during which no meat was served. Lenten fasting intensified during the last six weeks, further restrictions being introduced at *Tregesima* and *Vigesima*. Further, the rule recognizes that the Quadragesima itself fails to fulfill the "forty days," therefore, it orders,

"From Sexagesima on, moreover, let the meal always be taken after Vespers on Wednesday, Friday and Saturday, but on the other days until Lent let it be taken at the ninth hour, so that what the Sundays of Lent subtract from the forty fast days may be made up by the prolongation of fasting until evening on Wednesday, Friday and Saturday from Sexagesima on, and the number of forty fast days may be complete."[84]

In secular fast practice, too, the forty days were observed over the six weeks just prior to Pascha, the Sunday at the head of the first week being called *Quadragesima*. Callewaert, we noted, believed that Sunday to be the day from which the unbroken period of forty days was counted, so that the fortieth day was the Thursday before Easter and the *triduum pascale* (Friday, Saturday, and

Sunday) followed the forty days.[85] Elsewhere it seems clear that the forty days were reckoned from Monday through Friday (e.g., *Ap. Const.* V.13), but if we accept Callewaert's understanding of the Roman reckoning, then it is even more similar to the Byzantine than our earlier reconstruction would suggest, the difference being that Rome had not yet accepted the notion of a six-day Paschal Fast, but only the two days ordered already in the *Apostolic Tradition*. In any case, Callewaert is quite correct in observing that it is the Sunday *in capite ieiunii* that is called *Quadragesima*, the fast extending through six weeks from that point.

In *Liber Pontificalis* the collection of papal biographies first compiled under Hormisdas (514–523) with further additions under Vigilius in 538, the notice of the second-century bishop Telesphorus says, "he ordered that a fast of seven weeks be celebrated before Pascha." While this tells us little of historical value about Telesphorus, it suggests that a further week had been added by the time that notice was written, giving the name *Dominica in Quinguagesima* to the seventh Sunday before Easter. While that extension was opposed by two councils in Orleans in 511 (Canon 24) and in 541 (Canon 2), still a further week's extension, noted already in *Regula Magistri*, yielded a *Sexagesima* also in the old Gelasian Sacramentary and the Epistolary of Victor of Capua in 546. In the early seventh century, still another week was added before *Sexagesima*, and to this *Dominica in Septuagesima* there was finally assigned (by Gregory I, according to Callewaert[86]) the cessation of Alleluia that the *Regula Magistri* had assigned to the day following the Epiphany. Between those stands the *Holy Rule* of Benedict, where chapter 15 simply states that Alleluia is omitted from the *caput quadragesimae*, the beginning of Lent. Nor does Benedict reveal any concern to make up the days taken from the forty by the Sundays in Lent, as did the earlier rule.

While there seems no way to present a very coherent picture of all these developments, it does appear that in their totality they represent an attempt to harmonize two traditions, one that had known a fast of forty days after Epiphany and another that had, as early as 340, situated that fast before Easter. The latter predominated in secular spirituality, perhaps being the extension of an earlier preparation for baptism. The situation of the forty days after the Epiphany seems to be rather a monastic tradition, reported in the West only in the *Regula Magistri* and the equally monastic Martyrology of Oengus, the Irish monk who wrote ca. 800. This latter tradition was less significant in the main stream of western tradition, especially as concerns the ordering of the liturgy. Still, by the seventh century, from the *Dominica in Septuagesima*, three weeks before Lent, the Alleluia was "locked up," as *Regula Magistri* had said of the day after the Epiphany.

Given the importance of Egyptian monasticism, it is tempting to suppose that the beginning of the fast after Epiphany came into the West from that monastic tradition. Were that the case, however, we should expect to hear something of that from Cassian. In fact, he seems to know rather little of Lent in Egypt, as variable as that must have been. He gives no indication that he has heard of any institutionalized fasting from the Epiphany, nor, on the other hand, does he reveal any awareness of a fast of six weeks in which but five days a week are fasted. That, we know, was the case at both Alexandria and Milan in the later fourth century. He nowhere argues that the lenten *Quadragesima* is an unbroken period of forty days rather than the sum of the days actually fasted. Rather, he takes with full seriousness the fact that where the fast is lifted on Sundays, the six weeks of six fast days in each will yield thirty-six days of fasting, while the same result will be achieved where but five days a week are fasted for seven weeks, to which the paschal Sabbath is added. In either case, we offer to God the tithe of the year, and that is for Cassian the real rationale of Lent. It is nonetheless called *Quadragesima*, and this may, he says, be an imprecise allusion to the forty days fasted by Moses, Elijah, and Jesus.[87]

After Egeria's testimony about Lent at Jerusalem in 383, this passage in Cassian is the first to lay such emphasis on the number of days actually fasted. It was followed in the sixth century by Severus of Antioch. Beyond the six- and seven-week patterns discussed by Cassian, Severus speaks of eight weeks of five days each, to yield the number of forty, the same computation as that mentioned by Egeria.

In the West, that number of forty fast days was accomplished by the assignment of the title, *caput ieiunii*, to the Wednesday before *Quadragesima* Sunday, but it is difficult to know from what time that title was attached to that day. Gregory I repeats the position of Cassian, with more attention to Roman practice, viz., that we have six weeks of Lent in each of which six days are fasted, yielding thirty-six days, the tithe of the year.[88] From as early as Amalarius in the ninth century, therefore, it was common to assert that the first four days were an addition to Lent made in the seventh century. That was the accepted view until Tomassi, in the early eighteenth century, challenged it on the basis of the continuity of the first four days with the liturgical patterns of the following weeks. The first four days begin the cycle of regional stations and also the assignment of the psalms in order as communion chants. He concluded that the four days had belonged to the fast since before Gregory I.

That was true for some already in the fifth century, according to Maximus of Turin, who reports that many began the fast on the Wednesday before *Quadragesima*, noting that the gospel was already that which is still assigned to Ash Wednesday, "When you fast, be not, like the hypocrites, of a sad countenance" (Matthew 6.16). Nonetheless, by contrast to that *caput ieiunii*, the following Sunday continued to be called *initium quadragesimae*, and its gospel was that of the fast of Jesus in the wilderness. The Lent of forty days begins with that sixth week before Easter, but if one would count forty days of actual fasting, it is necessary to begin counting from the preceding Wednesday. That distinction between *caput ieiunii* on the Wednesday in Quinquagesima and *initium quadragesimae* on the following Sunday was carefully maintained in Roman liturgical books. Yet in the closing years of the eighth century, an opusculum prepared in Gaul to aid in the promulgation of the Roman liturgy betrays the atrophy of that distinction, opening with the words, *Feria IV initium quadragesimae*.[89] While monastic documents such as the Martyrology of Oengus continued to present a more complex picture, the duration of Lent would finally follow *Ordo Romanus* XXII throughout Europe, Milan alone excepted. There, as still today, Lent begins only with the sixth week, the Sunday at the head of that week bearing the title, *Caput Quadragesimae*.

10. LENT AND PENITENCE

Cabrol suggested that the four days of the week preceding Lent were included through having become the time for admission to the order of penitents. The first week of Lent was distinguished as an Embertide, evidently, already in the time of Leo I, and the vigil on that Saturday was designated by Gelasius as one of the appropriate times for ordination of deacons and presbyters. The rites peculiar to admission to the penitential class, Cabrol suggests, were set in the preceding week.[90]

That Lent was a time for the public exercises of penitents may be implied already in the second decade of the fifth century when Innocent I describes to Decentius of Gubbio the reconciliation of penitents on Thursday of Holy Week,[91] but in fact he says nothing of the time of the beginning of their penitence. That had been associated with the forty-day fast of Jesus, we have seen, in the first of the disciplinary canons of Peter I of Alexandria at the opening of the fourth century, but it is not certain that this had to do with a liturgical season.

Josef Jungmann believed that the enrollment of penitents at Rome had first taken place on the Monday and Tuesday of the first week of Lent, the days immediately following *Dominica in Quadragesima*, calling attention to the duplication of the stational churches appointed in that week and on the Monday and Tuesday following Pentecost.[92] These are St. Peter *ad vincula* on the Mondays and St. Anastasia on the Tuesdays. While he believes such to have been the case in the fifth century, he does not assign a precise time to the reassignment of that ceremony to the preceding Wednesday. Perhaps we can say no more of this matter in the early fifth century than that at Turin, according to Maximus, the gospel that continued to accompany the exclusion of penitents was already assigned for this Wednesday before *Quadragesima*, and that many (other than penitents, evidently) began their lenten exercises on that day.

We have rather less information regarding the admission to public penance on that Wednesday than we do concerning the reconciliation on Maundy Thursday. The Gelasian Sacramentary, in one of its more primitive elements, according to Chavasse, provides a series of prayers to be said over the penitents, and a following rubric indicates that the *cilicium*, the hair-shirt, was given.[93]

There is no mention there or in later Roman documents of any ceremony involving ashes. Ashes had been associated with penance earlier in other places, although not in conjunction with the beginning of Lent. The first clearly datable liturgy for this opening day of Lent that provides for the sprinkling of ashes on the penitents is the Romano-Germanic Pontifical, issued at Mainz in 960.[94] From still earlier in the tenth century we have a text from Reginon of Prüm (PL 132.235), which indicates that the imposition of ashes was characteristic of admission to the penitential state. Still earlier, from the sixth century, but not related to the liturgical year, is the mention of a signing of the forehead with ashes in a Mozarabic rite for the admission of one gravely ill to public penance.[95] At what time the sprinkling with ashes became a dimension of admission to public penance on the Wednesday following *Quinquagesima* is not known. What does seem clear is that the ceremony had its origins in western Europe, not at Rome.

At the opening of the eleventh century, Aelfric, abbot of Eynsham, in his *Lives of the Saints*, reveals that it was customary in his experience for all the faithful to participate in a ceremony on this day that included the imposition of ashes.[96] At the end of the eleventh century, at a council at Benevento in 1091,[97] Pope Urban II ordered the general imposition of ashes on this day. How widespread the practice of Aelfric was by that time we do not know, but it is only well after even Urban that the day will become known as "Ash Wednesday."

The history of Lent shows what seems to be a shift of emphasis from preparation for baptism to a general public penitential observance predicated upon what were once exercises for penitents seeking formal reconciliation with the Church in Holy Week. That shift, however, is not as radical as it might seem. If we read this shift of meaning in the context of developments in the rites of Christian initiation, it will appear that it was not Lent alone that underwent change. The ascendancy of infant baptism as normal, if not "normative," and the no more than purely formal significance of the vestigial baptismal scrutinies left the reconciliation of penitents as the major concern of Lent. In both instances, however, the participation of all the faithful in these rites of passage surely represents an authentic stratum in Christian piety, which recognized that in either case it is the redemption not of some but of all that is at hand in the death and resurrection of the Lord. In the face of that promise, those reaching toward faith in the initiatory process, those lost to the community of faith seeking reconciliation, and all who have learned in faith that both new birth and reconciliation are but sacraments pointing to realities that rush toward us from the future, all alike know the time that moves toward Pascha as the time of metanoia, the time of conversion, the time of repentance, the time that identifies our human lives and all our human history as the process of conversion moving now and always to meet the coming of the Lord at the consummation of the age.

NOTES

1. B. Yebamoth 47.
2. J.-P. Audet, *La Didaché, Instructions des Apôtres* (Paris 1958).
3. For the initial studies, see Joan Hazelden Walker. "A Pre-Marcan Dating for the Didache: Further Thoughts of a Liturgist," *Studia Biblica 1978*. III: *Papers on Paul and Other New Testament Authors* (Sheffield 1980); idem, "Reflections on a New Edition of the Didache," *Vigiliae Christianae* 35 (1981) pp. 35–42.
4. Raniero Cantalamessa, *Ostern in der alten Kirche. Traditio Christiana* IV (Frankfurt am Main 1981) p. 79 (no. 48, note 1).
5. Jerome, *Epist. XXIV* (CSEL 54.216); Siricius, *Epist. I ad Himerium ep. Tarraconensem* (PL 13.1131-1147). In fact, the forty-day Lent at Rome is even earlier (see above, p. 170).
6. Gel. I.xxvi–xxviii. C. Mohlberg, ed., *Liber Sacramentorum Romanae Aeclesiae Ordinis Anni Circuli. Rerum Ecclesiasticarum Documenta*, Series Maior, Fontes IV (Rome 1960) pp. 32, 36, 39. For the scrutinies themselves, see pp. 42–53.
7. A. Chavasse, "La structure du carême et les lectures des messes quadragésimales dans la liturgie romaine," *La Maison-Dieu* 31 (1952) pp. 89–90. For a more recent assessment of this question, see Maxwell E. Johnson, "From Three Weeks to Forty Days: Baptismal Preparation and the Origins of Lent," *Studia Liturgica* 20 (Fall, 1990).
8. M. F. Lages, "Etapes de l'évolution du carême à Jerusalem avant le Ve siècle," *Révue des études arméniennes* 6 (1969) pp. 67–102; Lawrence A. Hoffman, "The Jewish Lectionary, the Great Sabbath, and the Lenten Calendar: Liturgical Links Between Christians and Jews in the First Three Christian Centuries," in J. Neil Alexander, ed., *Time and Community: in honor of Thomas J. Talley* (Washington, D.C. 1990) pp. 3–20.
9. C. L. Feltoe, ed., *Dionysiou Leipsana: The Letters and Other Remains of Dionysius of Alexandria* (Cambridge 1904) pp. 101f.
10. L.-Th. Lefort, "Les Lettres festales de saint Athanase," *Bulletin de la Classe des Lettres de l'Académie Royale de Belgique* 39 (1953) pp. 643-656; idem, *Athanase, lettres festales et pastorales en copte*. CSCO 150 (Louvain 1955). Unfortunately, some otherwise important work of A. Chavasse

[*op cit.* (n. 7 above); "La préparation de la Pâque, à Rome, avant le Ve siècle," *Memorial J. Chaine. Bibl. de la Faculté Cath. de Théol. de Lyon*, vol. 5 (Lyon 1950) pp. 61–80] antedates Lefort's critical correction and so continues to follow the distorted dating of E. Schwartz.

11. *The Festal Letters of S. Athanasius* (Oxford 1854) p.21.

12. Lefort, "Les lettres festales de saint Athanase," pp. 654–656.

13. *The Festal Letters of S. Athanasius* (Oxford 1854) p. 100.

14. Callewaert, "La durée et le caractère du Carême ancien dans l'Eglise latine," *Sacris Erudiri* (1940) pp. 478–481.

15. The classic text is the Epistle 25 of Innocent I to Decentius of Gubbio, dated 416. Robert Cabié, *La Lettre du pape Innocent Ier a Décentius de Gubbio* (Louvain 1973) pp. 28–29.

16. C. Callewaert, "La Quaresima a Milano al tempo de S. Ambrogio," *Sacris Erudiri* (1940) pp. 549–560.

17. The Lent of 387 at Antioch is sometimes considered to have had eight weeks on the basis of Chrysostom's eighteenth sermon *Ad populum Antiochenum* (PG 49.719ff.). On the whole matter of Egeria's description of Lent, see Renoux, *Le Codex*, II, p. 183; cf. Deconinck, *Revue Biblique Internationale* 7 (1910) pp. 433ff. The Severus fragments are appended to the *De sacris ieiuniis* of John Damascene (PG 95.76), the first of them coming from 513.

18. See Alfred Rahlfs, "Die alttestamentlichen Lektionen der griechischen Kirche," *Mitteilungen des Septuaginta-Unternehmens der K. Gesellschaft der Wissenschaften zu Göttingen*, Band 1 (Berlin 1909–1915) p. 176.

19. Sozomen, HE 7.19. (NPNF II.II, p. 390)

20. These appear in English translation by E. H. Gifford in NPNF II.VII, pp. 1–143.

21. *Procatechesis* 9 (NPNF II.VII, 3).

22. So Dom Cabrol observed in DACL8².2087.

23. Renoux, *Le Codex*, p. 265 [127], n. 3.

24. Michel Tarchnischvili, *Le Grand lectionnaire de l'Église de Jérusalem*, I. CSCO 189 (Louvain 1959) p. 80.

25. Michel Aubineau, *Les Homélies festales d'Hésychius de Jérusalem. Subsidia Hagiographica* 59 (Brussels 1978) p. 388.

26. Mateos, *Le Typikon*, I, p. x–xiv.

27. Mother Mary and Archimandrite K. Ware, trans., *The Lenten Triodion* (London and Boston 1978) pp. 465f.

28. Alfred Rahlfs, op. cit. (n. 18 above), pp. 202–205.

29. By contrast to this opinion, the reasons for which will appear below, see Enrica Follieri and Oliver Strunk, *Triodium Athoum. Monumenta Musicae Byzantinae* 9, *pars suppletoria* (Copenhagen 1975) pp. 4–5. Pointing to the dependency of the Byzantine stichera on a Palestinian gospel lectionary, the authors say that this, "implies finally, although it cannot be said to prove, that the Constantinian Gospel lectionary is a relatively late construction." (I am indebted to Prof. Peter Jeffery of the University of Delaware for this reference.)

226

30. Sermon 125 (PO 29.247–249).

31. Such seems to be the understanding of P.-M. Gy, "La Question du système des lectures de la liturgie byzantine," *Miscellanea Liturgica in onore di sua eminenza il cardinale Giacomo Lercaro.* II (Rome 1967) p. 257: "non seulement la fête des Rameaux est de diffusion récente, mais celle de l'Hypapantè, d'origine hiérosolymitaine, vient d'être introduite à Constantinople sans l'avoir été pour autant à Antioche."

32. Mateos, *Le Typikon*, II, pp. 62–65.

33. Gregory Dix, *The Shape of the Liturgy* (London 1945; reprint with notes by Paul V. Marshall, New York 1982) p. 354.

34. ANF VI, p. 269.

35. PO XXXI.2, p. 387 [119].

36. Ibid., p. 389 [121].

37. Ibid., pp. 328f. (60f.).

38. René-Georges Coquin, "Les origines de l'Épiphanie en Égypte," *Noël, Épiphanie: retour du Christ. Lex Orandi* 40 (Paris 1967) pp. 147f.

39. *Hom. in Lev.*, X.2 (GCS 29, p. 445): "Illi ergo ieiunent, qui perdiderunt sponsum; nos habentes nobiscum sponsum ieiunare non possumus. Nec hoc tamen ideo dicimus, ut abstinentiae christianae frena laxemus: habemus enim quadragesimae dies ieiuniis consecratos, habemus quartam et sextam septimanae dies, quibus sollemniter ieiunamus."

40. A. Baumstark, *Comparative Liturgy*, trans. F. L. Cross (Westminster, Md. 1958) p. 194.

41. Harry Bober, "On the Illumination of the Glazier Codex: A Contribution to Early Coptic Art and Its Relation to Hiberno-Saxon Interlace," *Homage to a Bookman: Essays on Manuscripts, Books and Printing Written for Hans P. Kraus on His 60th Birthday, Oct. 12, 1967* (Berlin 1967), pp. 31–49; Françoise Henry, *Irish Art in the Early Christian Period to 800 A.D.* (London 1965), pp. 64f. Note 3 on p. 64 gives the text in the translation of F. E. Warren, *The Antiphonary of Bangor*, II, p. 28:

House full of delight
Built on the Rock
And indeed true vine
Transplanted from Egypt. . . .

42. Hansjörg Auf der Maur, *Feiern im Rhythmus der Zeit I: Herrenfeste in Woche und Jahr. Gottesdienst der Kirche: Handbuch der Liturgiewissenschaft.* Teil 5 (Regensburg 1983) p. 145, writes: "Sehr unwahrscheinlich scheint die neuestens wieder von Th. J. Talley formulierte, jedoch wenig überzeugend unterbaute Hypothese, die Quadragese habe sich in Aegypten unmittelbar in Anschluss an das Tauffest Jesu (Epiphanie) entwickelt." Strangely, he does not mention the postulation of just that view by Coquin (*op. cit.*, n. 38 above), although he appeals to the authority of that essay on Epiphany in other contexts (e.g., p. 156). By contrast, cf. P. Jounel, in A. G. Martimort, ed., *The Church at Prayer: Vol. IV, The Liturgy and Time* (Collegeville, Minn. 1986) p. 66.

43. Whitley Stokes, ed., *The Martyrology of Oengus the Culdee. Henry Bradshaw Society*, vol. xxix (London 1905) p. 34. Stokes translates the difficult verse texts for January 6 and 7 as follows:

6. Ran to his King, right noble choice! Julian, rock with purity: the great baptism of Mary's Son—perfect gladness! deserves not outrage.

7. The martyrdom of Lucianus with a great host that was higher: I have commemorated what is nobler, the beginning of Jesu's Lent.

44. Luke Eberle, trans., *The Rule of the Master* (Kalamazoo, Mich. 1977) chapter 45, verses 8–11 (p. 204).

45. "Les origines de l'Épiphanie en Égypte," pp. 151f.

46. W. E. Crum, ed. and trans., *Der Papyruscodex saec. VI-VII der Phillippsbibliothek in Cheltenham. Koptische theologische Schriften. Schriften der Wissenschaftlichen Gesellschaft in Strassburg*, 18. Heft (Strassburg 1915).

47. Ibid., pp. 67–68.

48. Ibid., p. 69.

49. B. Evetts, *History of the Patriarchs of the Coptic Church of Alexandria.* PO I, p. 427.

50. Louis Villecourt, "Les Observances liturgiques et la discipline du jeûne dans l'Église copte," Mus. 36 (1923) pp. 249–292; 37 (1924) pp. 201–280; 38 (1925) pp. 125–320. Dom Villecourt undertook, with E. Tisserant, a critical edition of *La Lampe des tenebres* for *Patrologia Orientalis*, but only a single fascicle containing the two opening chapters appeared (PO XX.4 [Paris 1928]). Earlier comments on this Coptic tradition by Baumstark, *Comparative Liturgy* (Oxford 1958) p. 194, n. 2, and J.-M. Hanssens, *La Liturgie d'Hippolyte*. OCA 155 (Rome 1959) p. 449, rest ultimately on the chapters published in *Le Muséon*.

51. Mus. *38* (1925) p. 266.

52. Ibid., pp. 314–315.

53. Ibid., p. 269. Cf. Gérard Viaud, *La Liturgie des Coptes d'Égypte* (Paris 1978) p. 44.

54. Quoted by Villecourt, Mus. 38 (1925) p. 269, note 1.

55. Ibid.

56. L. Villecourt, "La Lettre de Macaire, évêque de Memphis, sur la liturgie antique du chrême et du baptême à Alexandrie," Mus. 36 (1923) 33–46.

57. Ibid., p. 39.

58. So, e.g., Dom de Puniet in DACL 2[1], 258. Baumstark, *Nocturna Laus*. LQF 32 (Münster Westfalen 1957) pp. 30–31 and note 110, supposes the reference to be to the Friday before Easter. E. Lanne, "Textes et rites de la liturgie pascale dans l'ancienne Église copte," *L'Orient Syrien* 6 (1961) pp. 288f., understands the reference to be to the Friday before Palm Sunday.

59. The latest date for which the six-week total can be documented is

577. For the history of Lent in Alexandria, see A. Rahlfs, op. cit. (note 18 above), pp. 178–179.

60. G. Viaud, *La Liturgie des Coptes d'Égypte*, pp. 44–45.

61. Mus. 36 (1923) pp. 38.

62. R.-G. Coquin, "Les origines de l'Éphiphanie en Égypte," *Nöel, Épiphanie: retour du Christ. Lex Orandi* 40 (Paris 1967) p. 146.

63. O. Stählin, ed., *Clemens Alexandrinus*, Bd. IV, Teil I. (2. Aufl., U. Treu, ed.) GCS (Leiden 1980) pp. xvii–xviii. I undertook to relate this document to the medieval Coptic tradition first at the Oxford Patristic Conference in 1979: "The Origin of Lent at Alexandria," *Studia Patristica* XVII (Oxford and New York 1982) pp. 594–612.

64. Morton Smith, *Clement of Alexandria and a Secret Gospel of Mark* (Cambridge, Mass. 1973). Prof. Smith published in the same year a less technical work on the document, *The Secret Gospel* (New York 1973). I reported on the state of the manuscript as of January 1980 in "Liturgical Time in the Ancient Church: The State of Research," *Liturgical Time: Papers Read at the 1981 Congress of Societas Liturgica*, W. Vos and G. Wainwright, eds. (Rotterdam 1982) p. 45. This volume also appeared as *Studia Liturgica* XIV.2–4 (1982).

65. JTS, n.s. 25 (1974) p. 515.

66. The translation is that of Morton Smith, op. cit., pp. 446f.

67. Ibid., p. 447.

68. Ibid., pp. 159–161.

69. M. Smith, *The Secret Gospel*, pp. 64f.

70. P.-M. Gy, "La Question du système des lectures de la liturgie Byzantine," *Miscellanea Liturgica in onore di sua eminenza il cardinale Giacomo Lercaro*, II. pp. 257–258.

71. PG 111.989. M. Coquin, in a personal communication, has indicated an independent tradition known to a thirteenth-century writer: "L'historian chrétien Girgis b. 'Amid al-Makin (1205–1273) rapporte la même tradition pour le jeûne de 40 jours qu'Eutychius, mais attribue le rattachement à Pâque au patriarche Agrippinus—au lieu de Démétrius—il a donc sans doute une autre source qu'Eutychius, comme ont dit généralement."

72. J. Forget, trans., *Synaxarium Alexandrinum*. CSCO, Arab. 18. (Rome 1921) pp. 64f., 111f.

73. M. Richard, "Le comput Pascal par Octaététris," *Le Muséon* 87 (1974) pp. 307–339.

74. R.-G. Coquin, "Une Réforme liturgique du concile de Nicée (325)?," *Comptes Rendus, Académie des Inscriptions et Belles-Lettres*, 1967, pp. 178–192.

75. B. Evetts, *History of the Patriarchs of the Coptic Church of Alexandria*. PO I, V, X.5, Tome I (Paris 1904–1915), pp. 402, 407.

76. PG 111.1007. I am indebted to M. Coquin for this reference.

77. Translated here from the French of Coquin, "Une Réforme litur-

gique du concile de Nicée?,'' p. 180. He presents the text from the version of R. H. Connolly, CSCO 71, p. 51.

78. Mgr. Addai Scher, *Histoire Nestorienne inédite (Chronique de Séert)*, Part I. PO IV (Paris 1907) pp. 280–281.

79. *Vita Constantini*, 3.3.

80. *Conference* XXI.25.

81. F. C. Burkitt, *The Early Syriac Lectionary System* (From the *Proceedings of the British Academy*, Vol. XI). (London n.d.) pp. 6–8.

82. The fragments are appended to the *De sacris ieiuniis* of John Damascene, PG 95.75.

83. PG 111.1090. After Heraclius' conquest of Jerusalem, the Jews there were put to death, according to Eutychius, although Heraclius had promised them safety. The Fast of Heraclius is kept as a substitutionary penance for Heraclius.

84. *Requla Magistri* 28.9–12. Luke Eberle, trans., *The Rule of the Master* (Kalamazoo, Mich. 1977) pp. 187f.

85. C. Callewaert, ''La durée et le caractère du Carême ancien dans l'Église latine,'' *Sacris Erudiri* (1940) pp. 651–653.

86. C. Callewaert, ''L'oeuvre liturgique de s. Grégoire. La Septuagésime et l'Alléluia,'' *Sacris Erudiri* (1940) pp. 651–653.

87. John Cassian, *Conferences* XXXI.28.

88. C. Callewaert, ''La durée et le caractère du Carême ancien dans l'Eglise latine,'' *Sacris Erudiri* (1940) p. 450, n. 2.

89. M. Andrieu, *Les Ordines Romani du haut moyen age*, III, pp. 253–262.

90. F. Cabrol, art., ''Caput ieiunii,'' DACL 2¹, 2134–2137.

91. Innocent I, Epistle 25, caput 7. (PL 20.559)

92. J. Jungmann, *The Early Liturgy to the Time of Gregory the Great* (Notre Dame, Ind. 1959) pp. 245–246.

93. Gel. I.xv. A. Chavasse, *Le Sacramentaire Gélasien* (Tournai 1958) pp. 147–149.

94. C. Vogel and R. Elze, *Le Pontifical Romano-Germanique du dixième siècle*, II (Città del Vaticano 1963) p. 21.

95. M. Férotin, ed., *Le Liber Ordinum* (Paris 1904) cols. 87–88.

96. H. Thurston, s.v., ''Ash Wednesday,'' *The Catholic Encyclopedia*, I (New York 1913) p. 775.

97. Mansi 20.739.

Conclusions and Prospects

At this point in such a study one would like to present a summary of its demonstrated findings, its "incontestable achievement." However, in the study of the early liturgy the "incontestable achievement" is a chimera, and one must be satisfied with the opportunity to present a confession, an overview of the topic which has grown out of the research only partially reported. As is ever the case, that research has opened fresh vistas for further study, and that, in turn, reinforces the suspicion that one's present overview is but a glimpse at a landscape through which we are always moving, a landscape certain to be transformed by new and unexpected features at any moment, yielding a vastly altered view of the whole. So the present always molds the past as it is accessible to us. At the moment, nonetheless, my own present view of the beginnings of the liturgical year would include the following elements.

From the earliest days of the mission to the Gentiles the question of the relationship between "Law" and "Gospel" loomed large and generated tensions. Some of the more pressing questions were settled at the "Council of Jerusalem," but that did not prevent differences in assessment of the continuing importance of other religious traditions inherited from Judaism. The preaching to the Gentiles did not demand the inculcation of Jewish festivals, but the significance of those for Jewish Christians was not obliterated by the passion and resurrection. On the contrary, the death of Jesus at the time of the slaying of the lambs for Passover (reflected already in 1 Cor 5.7) supplied a new focus for that festival, perhaps from its next celebration after the resurrection.

Driven from Jerusalem by the mounting troubles there surrounding the destruction of the temple, Christians of Jewish background settled elsewhere, the cities of Asia Minor being significant centers for the continuing life of that community. There the celebration of Pascha as the memorial of the death of Jesus represented a continuity with Judaism foreign to the practice of other communities, which observed only the first day of each week as celebration of the resurrection. Pascha was observed in Asia with a fast and vigil on the accustomed date, the fourteenth of Nisan, the first spring month, and was concluded with the celebration of eucharist at cockcrow on the fifteenth. From the outset, Christian paschal rejoicing took place only at a time after the rejoicing of the Jews. When it became impossible to observe the traditional lunar date for the fast, due to the lunar calendar's need for periodic intercalation, the date was adjusted to the solar Julian calendar of Asia, and Pascha was kept on the fourteenth of Artemisios, the first month of spring. That date was equivalent to the Roman April 6. Elsewhere, on the basis of supposedly historical data, the actual historical date of the passion was set on March 25, the Julian equivalent to 14 Nisan in the year of our Lord's death, and some kept that as the fixed date of Pascha. These two traditions perhaps came into conflict at Laodicea around 165, but by that time a more significant alternative for the setting of the paschal date had appeared in Palestine and at Alexandria.

In Palestine, the building of a new Roman city over the ruins of Jerusalem brought Gentile bishops to that city from around 135. Encountering there the continuing expectation of the observance of Pascha, they maintained their own tradition of observing only the weekly cycle, the cycle sanctified by the covenant, and began to keep Pascha in such a way as to terminate the fast only in the night from Saturday to Sunday. The Paschal Fast itself was kept on Saturday, an exception to the otherwise general prohibition of fasting on the Sabbath. The juxtaposition of that fast with the older weekly fast on Friday soon led to the observance of a two-day fast in many places. In the third century that two-day fast was extended to six days under the influence of a chronology of the passion that put the Last Supper on Tuesday evening and Judas' treasonous compact on Monday. That chronology, encountered still in the fourth century, did not prevail, but its extension of the Paschal Fast to six days did. The Holy Week evident in Syria and Egypt in the middle of the third century was established throughout the Church during the following century.

That very early Pascha, observed as the memorial of Christ's death, celebrated the entire mystery of Christ, including not only his resurrection and glorification, but also the incarnation, a unified celebration with parallels in the identification of the birth and death dates of the patriarchs in rabbinic literature. Under influences that are still less than clear, but perhaps related to the break in the Johannine community, the incarnation came to sharper focus in the early second century. While the prologue of the fourth gospel can be read as identifying the baptism of Jesus as the point of the incarnation (a reading supported by the text of Luke 3.22 in Codex Bezae), further christological development placed increasing emphasis on the conception and birth of Jesus. We may see a glimpse of this development in 1 John 5.6. One consequence of this, I believe, is that the incarnational content of Pascha was increasingly identified with the conception of Christ. Where, as in Asia, that paschal date was April 6, the nativity could be set nine months later, on January 6. That date for the nativity was known also to Clement of Alexandria, while Basilidians and Marcionites placed the baptism of Jesus at the same time, a concurrence that would encourage us to place the identification of January 6 as the beginning of the gospel rather early in the second century.

While this date was computed as that of the nativity, nine months after the paschal date for the conception, it functioned as the beginning point for the reading of the gospel, and the beginning of the local gospel would color the content of the festival. The Ephesian use of the gospel of John would identify, perhaps, the nativity and the baptism on the same day, leading quickly to the miracle at Cana in which Jesus manifested his glory. At Jerusalem the preference for Matthew would closely identify that beginning of the gospel as the nativity in Bethlehem, a content for the festival of January sixth that Jerusalem maintained with notorious tenacity. The Alexandrian devotion to Mark would focus the beginning of the gospel on the baptism. The common theme that united all these was the *Manifestation of God in Man*, a common theme in the religions of antiquity, designated by the term *ta epiphania*.

Alexandria affords a particularly compelling example of this understanding of the nativity date as the beginning of the course reading of the gospel. There, the reading of the account of Jesus' baptism on January 6 was followed at once by an imitation of his forty days of fasting in the wilderness, a six-week period given to the final preparation of catechumens for baptism. That conferral of baptism at the end of the fast was associated with the raising from the dead (and subsequent initiation) of a young man at Bethany, recounted in the Mar Saba Clementine fragment (where it is inserted following Mark 10.34), and sealed with the celebration of Christ's entry into Jerusalem on the following Sunday, weeks before the beginning of the six-day Paschal Fast. It is interesting to observe that between Jesus' entry into Jerusalem in chapter 11 and the passion narrative ordained for that paschal observance (chapters 14 and following), the gospel of Mark gives only a body of Jesus' teachings with no chronological narrative line.

That peculiar Alexandrian baptismal day, maintained through most of the fourth century, gave way finally to what had become common throughout most of the Church, the celebration of baptism at Pascha, preceded always by some period of fasting in final preparation. Quite possibly as a dimension of the paschal settlement at Nicea, the prepaschal time was wedded with the Alexandrian imitation of the fast of Jesus, and such a forty-day duration of the fast became characteristic of Lent throughout the Church. From Constantinople to Antioch that fast preceded the Paschal Fast of six days, and Byzantine tradition preserved the old Alexandrian Marcan cursus, transposed from its time following the Epiphany. This has been maintained to our own day, the noncanonical "secret Gospel of Mark" at the climax of the Markan cursus replaced with its only canonical parallel, John 11.1–45. Nothing tells us the time of that substitution and one would suppose that it was made rather early in the process of the canonization of the New Testament. Nonetheless, medieval Coptic writers remember the old baptismal day in the sixth week of the fast as the day on which Jesus baptized, and Byzantine typika of the same period present the Saturday of Lazarus as a major baptismal day, even though its new place in the year puts it but one week before the paschal vigil.

Such an ante-Nicene Alexandrian background for the Saturday of Lazarus and Palm Sunday shows that these were not first instituted at Jerusalem as has been believed. Our reading of such a fourth-century account of Jerusalem as that provided by Egeria can no longer take functions first reported there to be hagiopolitan innovations. Rather we must seek to distinguish between the original Jerusalem tradition, preserved in the normal liturgy of the hours and the eucharist, and those visits to sacred sites arranged to meet the expectations of pilgrims, expectations often based on their native liturgical experience.

By the early fourth century the projection from April 6 to yield the date of the Epiphany on January 6 was replicated in North Africa and at Rome to give December 25 as the nativity date, based on March 25 as the date of the passion. Later in the fourth century that nativity festival on December 25 was adopted at Constantinople, throughout Cappadocia, and at Antioch, while the Epiphany was adopted in the West, albeit with an unfortunate limitation of its meaning to "the manifestation of Christ to the Gentiles," at least at Rome and in Africa.

The festivals of the liturgical year, like other ecclesiastical structures, have interacted with pagan traditions in ways that have enriched the Church's experience at many points. Nonetheless, the tendency to take similarities to pagan observances as affording insight into the origins of the liturgical year has too long closed our eyes to the intimate relation that exists between the gospel tradition and its liturgical employment. The gospels, we may believe, were shaped by the expectation that they would be proclaimed in public assemblies over a certain period. That period, shaped by those narratives and by the response of Christian life to their proclamation, is the liturgical year.

The conflation of traditions has brought to the early history of liturgical time those complications that we have sought to examine and unravel, at least in part. Behind that conflation, however, lies a thing of utter simplicity, the telling of a story, one story, its temporal anchor and goal the Passover, at which the Redeemer accomplished his *transitus* into the eschatological kingdom and on which the Church, making the memorial of his death, proclaims the oldest materials in the tradition of the gospel, the passion of our Lord Jesus Christ. For much of the Church still in the early decades of the second century, that memorial was not tied to the annual Passover of the Jews, but was a weekly observance made on the first day of the week, that day beyond the Sabbath that was also called the Eighth Day. That weekly observance was probably universal in the later first century, while the annual was not. It is only to that extent that we can say that the liturgical week is older than the liturgical year.

From that early telling of the story of the Redeemer's coming and of his life among us, so as to arrive at the telling of the story of his passion at Passover, to the present—with its Advent wreaths, the Christmas creche, Epiphany water, imposition of ashes, the procession with palms, and all the rest—we see not just a series of encounters with surrounding cultures nor even a series of ecclesiastical enactments, but simply the imaginative and affective response of the People of God to that story that has shaped the years of their lives, all the centuries of them, to his life, and made history itself the path of the Redeemer.

The memory of the Cross has been renewed in every generation not only in the sacraments through which we are incorporated into his Paschal Mystery, but even more poignantly in the passions of the martyrs whose witness has been perfected by participation in his passion. From Stephen to the present their deaths have revealed the power of the resurrection, and from as early as the martyrdom of Polycarp (and probably much earlier) those death-dates have been observed as triumphs of Christ, adding new skeins in every generation to the fabric of memory that reveals the continuing presence of Christ in history.

The effect of such a fabric of memory is to open the future to hope, to reveal all the time that remains as promise of the coming of the Lord, which is already tasted proleptically. That hope is a function of sacred memory, born of it and bound to it. Passover celebrated the memories of history's beginning in Creation, of Isaac and of the Exodus, but it celebrated also the final coming of Messiah, and that same interaction of memory and hope characterized the Christian celebration of Pascha. The memorial of the Cross included the expectation of the parousia, and that expectation marked the festival as also celebration of the first parousia. As we encounter a second date, at nine months' distance, for the "manifestation" of that parousia, it, too, came to be characterized by the expectation of the final parousia. Something of that rich interplay is with us still today in a liturgical year that remembers the beginning of the incarnation in the conception of Christ both on the ancient

236

date of the Passion, March 25, and on the final Sunday of Advent as we approach the end of this world's times.

Festival is a time of heightened religious consciousness, and the principal theme of any festival—the conception or birth or baptism of the Redeemer, his presentation in the temple or transfiguration on the mountain top, his triumphal entry into Jerusalem, or that of a martyr into the New Jerusalem—will always evoke other memories and awaken hope for the coming of the Lord that is the goal of history. Nonetheless, every festival, every Sunday, is rooted primarily and finally in that paschal mystery that is the center of it all, the eucharist, which from the beginning and always proclaims the Lord's death until he comes.

That paschal mystery does not afford redemption from the terrors of history in the manner of the gnostics, but rather reveals the meaning of history itself. The early proclamation of the resurrection could suggest such a deliverance from history, and, in a sense, the opposition of history and eschatology that some have found in Gregory Dix reflects the durability of such a misunderstanding. Paul's epistles themselves show that he could be so misunderstood by some, and the response of the primitive Church to that possibility was a heightened attention to the "historical Jesus," which led to the composition of the gospels.

Archbishop Philip Carrington (*The Primitive Christian Calendar*, 1952) sought to relate the genesis of the gospel of Mark to the readings of the synagogue, and his work has been refined by M. D. Goulder in *The Evangelists' Calendar: A Lectionary Explanation of the Development of Scripture* (London 1978). Goulder argues that the gospels grew out of Midrash on the synagogue readings beginning from *Simḥat Torah* at the end of the celebration of the feast of Tabernacles. While there is much that is uncertain regarding the synagogue lectionary (and therefore regarding such an appeal to it), that possibility might shed some light on the gnawing persistence of hints connecting Tabernacles with Epiphany, the point from which we see the beginning of the course reading of the gospels later. Those hints, too vague to afford even a basis for a hypothesis, suggest that the relationship of Epiphany to Tabernacles should at least be accorded a place in the unaddressed agenda of this study that may merit future attention.

Regrettably, not all the unaddressed agenda are so because of the vagueness of the material. Much has been omitted for considerations of space, and much remains to be done. The feast of the Presentation of Christ in the Temple, *Hypapantē,* appears in Egeria's Jerusalem as only the *quadragesima* of Epiphany and seems to mark the closing of an Epiphany quarantine that, while not a fast, is perhaps not unrelated to that at Alexandria that was closed with the feast of Palms. This deserves an examination that it has not received here. The same must be confessed of many other observances that have been omitted because of limitations of space or of knowledge. We may hope that these will have in the future the study they deserve, or that someone more widely read will call to our attention the scholarly treatment they have already received. In the meantime, I hope that the line of argument presented here, however hypothetical, will encourage further examination of the boundaries between the formation of the gospels and their liturgical employment, for it is along those boundaries, I believe, that we must seek the origins of the liturgical year.

Bibliography

Andrieu, Michel. *Les Ordines Romani du haut moyen âge. Spicilegium Sacrum Lovaniense* 11, 23, 24, 28, 29 (Louvain 1931–1961).

Aubineau, Michel. *Les Homélies festales d'Hésychius de Jérusalem. Subsidia Hagiographica* 59 (Brussels 1978).

Audet, J.-P. *La Didachè, Instructions des apôtres* (Paris 1958).

Auf der Maur, Hansjörg. *Die Osterhomilien des Asterios Sophistes. Trierer theologische Studien* 19 (Trier 1967).

———. *Feiern im Rhythmus der Zeit I: Herrenfeste in Woche und Jahr. Gottesdienst der Kirche: Handbuch der Liturgiewissenschaft.* Teil 5 (Regensburg 1983).

Bacchiocchi, Samuele. *From Sabbath to Sunday* (Rome 1977).

Bainton, Roland. "Basilidian Chronology and New Testament Interpretation," *Journal of Biblical Literature* 42 (1923).

———. "The Origins of Epiphany," *Early and Medieval Christianity. The Collected Papers in Church History*, I (Boston 1962).

Baldovin, John, S. J. *The Urban Character of Christian Worship: The Origins, Development, and Meaning of Stational Liturgy. Orientalia Christiana Analecta* 228 (Rome 1987).

Baumstark, Anton. *Comparative Liturgy*, revised by B. Botte, English ed. by F. L. Cross (Oxford 1958).

———. *Nocturna Laus.* LQF 32 (Münster Westfalen 1957).

Beatrice, Pier Franco. *La lavanda dei piedi. Contributo alla storia delle antiche liturgie cristiane. Bibliotheca "Ephemerides Liturgicae" Subsidia* 28 (Rome 1983).

Beck, Edmund. *Des Heiligen Ephraem des Syrers Hymnen de Nativitate (Epiphania).* CSCO 186, 187 (Louvain 1959).

———."Le baptême chez Saint Ephrem," *L'Orient Syrien* 1 (1956) 111–130.

Bertonière, Gabriel. *The Historical Development of the Easter Vigil and Related Services in the Greek Church.* OCA 193 (Rome 1972).

Bickerman, E. J. *Chronology of the Ancient World* (London 1968).

239

Bober, Harry. "On the Illumination of the Glazier Codex: A Contribution to Early Coptic Art and Its Relation to Hiberno-Saxon Interlace," *Homage to a Bookman: Essays on Manuscripts, Books and Printing Written for Hans P. Kraus on His 60th Birthday, Oct. 12, 1967* (Berlin 1967), pp. 31–49.

Botte, Bernard. *Les origines de la Noël et de l'Épiphanie. Textes et études liturgiques* 1 (Louvain 1932).

————. *La Tradition Apostolique de saint Hippolyte: essai de reconstitution.* LQF 39 (Münster Westfalen 1963).

Botte, B., Melia, E., et al., eds. *Noël, Épiphanie: retour du Christ. Lex Orandi* 40 (Paris 1967) pp. 25–42.

Brock, Sebastian. "Studies in the Early History of the Syrian Orthodox Baptismal Liturgy," JTS, n.s. 23 (1972) pp. 16–64.

Broek, R. van den. *The Myth of the Phoenix according to Classical and Early Christian Traditions* (Leiden 1972).

Brunner, G. "Arnobius ein Zeuge gegen das Weihnachtsfest?," JLW 13 (1936) 178–181.

Burkitt, F. C. *The Early Syriac Lectionary System. Proceedings of the British Academy*, XI (London 1923).

KHS-Burmester, O.H.E. *A Guide to the Ancient Coptic Churches of Cairo* (Cairo, n.d.).

Cabié, Robert. *La Pentecôte: L'évolution de la Cinquantaine pascale au cours des cinq premiers siècles* (Tournai 1964).

————. *La Lettre du pape Innocent Ier a Decentius de Gubbio* (Louvain 1973).

Callewaert, C. *Sacris Erudiri: Fragmenta Liturgica Collecta* (Steenbrugge 1940).

Campenhausen, Hans von. "Ostertermin oder Osterfasten? Zum Verständnis des Irenäusbriefs an Viktor," *Vigiliae Christianae* 28 (1974) pp. 114ff.

Cantalamessa, Raniero. *L'Omelia "In S. Pascha" dello Pseudo-Ippolito de Roma: Ricerche sulla Teologia dell'Asia Minore nella seconda metà del II secolo* (Milan 1967).

————. *Ostern in der alten Kirche. Traditio Christiana* IV (Bern 1981).

Casel, Odo. "Art und Sinn der ältesten christlichen Osterfeier," JLW 14 (1938).

Chadwick, Henry. *The Early Church* (Harmondsworth 1967).

Chavasse, Antoine. *Le Sacramentaire Gelasien* (Tournai 1958).

_____. "La Préparation de la Pâque, à Rome, avant le Ve siècle, jeûne et organisation liturgique," *Memorial J. Chaine. Bibliotheque de la Faculté Catholique de Théologie de Lyon,* vol. 5 (Lyon 1950) pp. 61–80.

_____. "La Structure du Carême et les lectures des messes quadragésimales dans la liturgie romaine," *La Maison-Dieu* 31 (1952) pp. 76–119.

_____. "L'organisation stationnale du Carême romain avant le VIIIe siècle. Une organisation 'pastorale,'" *Revue des sciences religieuses* 56 (1982) pp. 17–32.

Chilton, Bruce. "Isaac and the Second Night: A Consideration," *Biblica* 61 (1980) pp. 78–88.

Connolly, R. H. *Didascalia Apostolorum* (Oxford 1929).

Conybeare, F. C. *The Key of Truth* (Oxford 1898).

_____. *Rituale Armenorum* (Oxford 1905).

_____. "The Gospel Commentary of Epiphanius," *Zeitschrift für die neutestamentliche Wissenschaft* 7 (1906), pp. 318–332.

_____. "Ananias of Shirak upon Christmas," *The Expositor. Fifth Series* IV (1896) pp. 321–337.

Coquin, René-Georges. *Les Canons d'Hippolyte, édition critique de la version arabe, introduction et traduction française.* PO XXXI.2 (Paris 1966.)

_____. "Une Réforme liturgique du concile de Nicée (325)?," *Comptes Rendus, Académie des Inscriptions et Belles-lettres* (Paris 1967).

Coüasnon, Charles. *The Church of the Holy Sepulchre in Jerusalem. The Schweich Lectures of the British Academy, 1972* (London 1974).

Cross, F. L. *I Peter, A Paschal Liturgy* (London 1954).

Crum, W. E., ed. *Der Papyruscodex saec. VI–VII der Phillippsbibliothek in Cheltenham. Koptische theologische Schriften. Schriften der Wissenschaftlichen Gesellschaft in Strassburg,* 18. Heft (Strassburg 1915).

Cullmann, O. *The Early Church* (Philadelphia 1956).

Daly, Robert J. *Christian Sacrifice. Studies in Christian Antiquity* 18 (Washington, D. C. 1978).

Daniélou, Jean. "Grégoire de Nysse et l'origine de la fête de l'Ascension," *Kyriakon: Festschrift Johannes Quasten,* II (Münster Westfalen 1970) pp. 663–666.

Davis, Percival Vaughan. *Macrobius: The Saturnalia* (New York 1969).

Deddens, Karel. *Annus Liturgicus? Een onderzoek naar de betekenis van Cyrillus van Jerusalem voor de ontwikkeling van het 'kerkelijk jaar'* (Goes 1975)

Dekkers, Eligius. *Clavis Patrum Latinorum,* editio altera. *Sacris Eruditi* 3 (Steenbrugge 1961).

Deshusses, Jean. *Le Sacramentaire Grégorien*, Tome I^e. *Spicilegium Friburgense* 16 (Fribourg Suisse 1971).

Devos, Paul. "La date du voyage d'Égérie," *Analecta Bollandiana* 85 (1967) pp. 165–194.

————. "Égérie à Bethléem. Le 40e jour après Pâques à Jérusalem en 383," *Analecta Bollandiana* 86 (1968) pp. 87–108.

Dindorf, L. *Chronicon Paschale ad exemplar Vaticanum* (Bonn 1832).

Dix, Gregory. *The Shape of the Liturgy* (2nd ed., London 1945; reprint, with notes by P. Marshall, New York 1982).

Duchesne, Louis. *Origine du culte chrétien* (Paris 1889). English translation by M. L. McClure, *Christian Worship, Its Origins and Evolution* (London 1949).

Engberding, Hieronymus. "Der 25. Dezember als Tag der Feier der Geburt des Herrn," ALW 2 (1952) pp. 25–43.

Etheridge, J. W. *The Targums of Onkelos and Jonathan ben Uzziel on the Pentateuch, with the Fragments of the Jerusalem Targum from the Chaldee* (New York 1968).

Evetts, B. *History of the Patriarchs of the Coptic Church of Alexandria*. PO, I, V, X.5 (Paris 1904–1915).

Feltoe, C. L. *Dionysiou Leipsana. The Letters and Other Remains of Dionysius of Alexandria* (Cambridge 1904).

Fendt, Leonhard. "Der heutige Stand der Forschung über das Geburtsfest Jesu am 25.XII und über Epiphanias," TL 78.1 (January 1953) pp. 1–10.

Férotin, Marius. *Le Liber Ordinum. Monumenta Ecclesiae Liturgica* V (Paris 1904).

Floeri, F., and Nautin, P. *Homélies Pascales, III: Une homélie anatolienne sur la date de la Pâques en l'an 387*. SC 48 (Paris 1957).

Forget, Iacobus. *Synaxarium Alexandrinum*. CSCO, Arab. 3 Tom. xviii (Rome 1921), xix (Louvain 1926).

Frank, Hieronymus. "Zur Geschichte von Weihnachten und Epiphanie," JLW 13 (1936) pp. 1–38.

————. "Frühgeschichte und Ursprung des römischen Weihnachtsfestes im Lichte neuerer Forschung," ALW 2 (1952) pp. 1–24.

————. "Die Vorrangstellung der Taufe Jesu in der altmailändischen Epiphanieliturgie und die Frage nach dem Dichter des Epiphaniehymnus Inluminans Altissimus," ALW 13 (1971) pp. 115–132.

Funk, F. X. *Didascalia et Constitutiones Apostolorum* (Paderborn 1905).

Ginzel, F. K. *Handbuch der mathematischen und technischen Chronologie* (Leipzig 1906).

Goudoever, J. van. "The Significance of the Counting of the Omer," *Jewish Background of the New Testament* (Assen, n.d.).

———. *Biblical Calendars* (Leiden 1959).

Goulder, M. D. *The Evangelists' Calendar: A Lectionary Explanation of the Development of Scripture* (London 1978).

Guerrier, Louis. *Le Testament in Galilée*. PO IX.3 (Paris 1913).

Gy, Pierre-Marie. "La Question du système des lectures de la liturgie byzantine," *Miscellanea Liturgica in onore di sua eminenza il cardinale Giacomo Lercaro*, II (Rome 1967) pp. 251–261.

Hall, Stuart G., ed. *Melito of Sardis On Pascha and Fragments* (Oxford 1979).

Halsberghe, Gaston. *The Cult of Sol Invictus* (Leiden 1972).

Hamman, A. "Valeur et signification des renseignements liturgiques de Justin," *Studia Patristica* XIII.ii. TU 116 (Berlin 1975) pp. 364–374.

———. *The Paschal Mystery*, trans. T. Halton. (Staten Island, N.Y. 1969).

Hanssens, Jean-Michel. *La liturgie d'Hippolyte*. OCA 155 (Rome 1959).

Henry, Françoise. *Irish Art in the Early Christian Period to 800 A.D.* (London 1965).

Heylen, F., ed. *Filastrii Episcopi Brixiensis Diversarum Hereseon Liber*. CC Lat. IX (Turnholt 1957).

Higgins, Martin. "Note on the Purification (and Date of Nativity) in Constantinople in 602," ALW 2 (1952) pp. 81–83.

Hoffman, Lawrence A. "The Jewish Lectionary, the Great Sabbath, and the Lenten Calendar: Liturgical Links Between Christians and Jews in the First Three Christian Centuries," in J. Neil Alexander, ed., *Time and Community: in honor of Thomas J. Talley* (Washington, D.C. 1990) pp. 3–20.

Holl, Karl. *Gesammelte Aufsätze zur Kirchengeschichte*. II: *Der Osten* (Tübingen 1927).

Hunt, E. D. *Holy Land Pilgrimage in the Later Roman Empire AD 312–460* (Oxford 1982).

Janini, Jose. *S. Siricio y las cuatro temporas* (Valencia 1958).

Jaubert, Annie. *The Date of the Last Supper*, trans. by I. Rafferty (Staten Island, N. Y. 1965).

Johnson, Maxwell E. "From Three Weeks to Forty Days: Baptismal Preparation and the Origins of Lent," *Studia Liturgica* 20 (Fall, 1990).

Jullian, C., art. "Feriae," Daremberg et Saglio, *Dictionnaire des antiquités grecques et romains*, II² (Paris 1896) pp. 1042–1066.

Jungmann, Josef. *The Early Liturgy to the Time of Gregory the Great* (Notre Dame, Ind. 1959).

Khouri-Sarkis, G. and du Boullay, A. "La bénédiction de l'eau, la nuit de l'Épiphanie dans le rite syrien d'Antioche," *L'Orient Syrien* 4 (1959) pp. 211–232.

Kretschmar, Georg. "Himmelfahrt und Pfingsten," *Zeitschrift für Kirchengeschichte*, Folge IV, Band 66.3 (1954–1955) pp. 209–253.

———. "Beiträge zur Geschichte der Liturgie, insbesondere der Taufliturgie, in Aegypten," *Jahrbuch für Liturgik und Hymnologie*, Band 8 (1963).

———. "Die Geschichte des Taufgottesdienstes in der alten Kirche," *Leiturgia*, Band V (Kassel 1970).

Lages, M. F. "Etapes de l'évolution du carême à Jérusalem avant le Ve siècle," *Révue des études arméniennes* 6 (1969) pp. 67–102.

Lake, Kirsopp, trans. *The Apostolic Fathers. Loeb Classical Library*, 2 vols. (Cambridge, Mass. 1959).

Lanne, Emmanuel. "Textes et rites de la liturgie pascale dans l'ancienne église copte." *L'Orient Syrien* 6 (1961) 279–300.

LaPiana, George. "The Roman Church at the End of the Second Century," *Harvard Theological Review* 18 (1925) pp. 201–277.

Lawler, Thomas C., trans. *St. Augustine: Sermons for Christmas and Epiphany. Ancient Christian Writers*, no. 15 (Westminster, Md. 1952).

Ledwich, W. "Baptism, Sacrament of the Cross," *The Sacrifice of Praise*, B. Spinks, ed. (Rome 1981) pp. 199–211.

Lefort, L.-Th. "Les Lettres festales de saint Athanase," *Bulletin de la Classe des Lettres de l'Académie Royale de Belgique* 39 (1953) pp. 643–656.

———. *Athanase, lettres festales et pastorales en copte.* CSCO 150 (Louvain 1955).

Levy, J. and H. "The Origin of the Week and the Oldest West Asiatic Calendar," *Hebrew Union College Annual* XVII (1942–1943) pp. 1–152.

Lietzmann, Hans. *Petrus und Paulus in Rom* (Bonn 1915).

———. *A History of the Early Church* (Cleveland and New York 1953).

Lohse, Bernard. *Das Passafest der Quartadecimaner* (Gutersloh 1953).

Lohse, E., art. "Pentēkostē," TDNT VI (Grand Rapids, Mich. 1968) pp. 44–53.

Loi, Vincenzo. "Il 25 Marzo data pasquale e la cronologia Giovannea della passione in età patristica," *Ephemerides Liturgicae* 85 (1971) pp. 48–69.

Mateos, Juan. *Le Typikon de la Grande Église.* OCA 165, 166 (Rome 1962, 1963).

McArthur, A. Allan. *The Evolution of the Christian Year* (London 1953).

Meslin, Michel. *La fête des kalendes de janvier dans l'empire romain.* Collection Latomus, vol. 115 (Brussels 1970).

Meyer, Arnold. *Das Weihnachtsfest, seine Entstehung und Entwicklung* (Tübingen 1912).

Mohlberg, Cunibert. *Liber Sacramentorum Romanae Aeclesiae Ordinis Anni Circuli. Rerum Ecclesiasticarum Documenta.* Series maior: Fontes IV (Rome 1960).

Mohrmann, Christine. *Etudés sur le latin des chrétiens* (Rome 1958).

―――. "Le conflit pascal au IIᵉ siècle: note philologique," *Vigiliae Christianae* 16 (1962).

Morin, Germain. "L'origine des quatre-temps," *Revue bénédictine* 14 (1897) pp. 337–346.

Mosna, C. S. *Storia della domenica dalle origini fino agli inizi del V secolo. Analecta Gregoriana* 170 (Rome 1969).

Mossay, Justin. *Les fêtes de Noël d'Épiphanie d'après les sources littéraires cappadociennes du IVe siècle. Textes et études liturgiques* 3 (Louvain 1965).

Mutzenbecher, Almut. "Der Festinhalt von Weihnachten und Epiphanie in den echten *Sermones* des Maximus Tauriensis," *Studia Patristica* V, Part III. TU 80 (Berlin 1962) pp. 109–116.

Norden, Eduard. *Die Geburt des Kindes: Geschichte eine religiösen Idee. Studien der Bibliothek Warburg,* III (Leipzig/Berlin 1924).

Perler, Otmar. *Meliton de Sardes, Sur la Pâques.* SC 123 (Paris 1966).

Pettazzoni, Raffaele. *Essays on the History of Religions. Studies in the History of Religions (Supplements to Numen)* I (Leiden 1954).

Pocknee, Cyril E. *The Christian Altar* (London 1963).

Rahlfs, Alfred. "Die alttestamentlichen Lektionen der griechischen Kirche," *Mitteilungen des Septuaginta-Unternehmens der K. Gesellschaft der Wissenschaft zu Göttingen,* Band 1 (Berlin 1909–1915) pp. 119–230.

Regan, Patrick. "The Fifty Days and the Fiftieth Day," *Worship* 55 (1981) pp. 194–218.

Renoux, Athanase. "Les catéchèses mystagogiques dans l'organisation liturgiques hiérosolymitaine du IVe et du Ve siècle," Mus. 78 (1965) 355–359.

—. *Le Codex arménien Jérusalem 121.* I: *Introduction aux origines de la liturgie hiérosolymitaine, lumières nouvelles.* PO XXXV.1. N° 163 (Turnhout 1969); II: *Édition comparée du texte et de deux autres manuscrits.* PO XXXVI.2. N° 168 (Turnhout 1971).

Richard, Marcel. "La question pascale au IIe siècle," *L'Orient Syrien* 6 (1961) pp. 179–212.

—. "Le comput Pascal par Octaététris," *Le Muséon* 87 (1974) pp. 307–339.

Riedel, W. and Crum, W.E. *The Canons of Athanasius of Alexandria* (London 1904).

Rolfe, John C. *Ammianus Marcellinus. Loeb Classical Library* (Cambridge, Mass. 1963).

Rordorf, Willi. *Sunday* (London 1968).

Salaville, S. "La *Tesserakosté* au Ve canon de Nicée," *Échos d'Orient* 13 (1910) pp. 65–72; 14 (1911) pp. 355–357.

—. "La *Tesserakosté*, Ascension et Pentecôte au IVe siècle," *Échos d'Orient* 28 (1929) pp. 257–271.

Salmon, Pierre. *Le lectionnaire de Luxeuil* (Rome 1944).

Scher, Addai. *Histoire Nestorienne inédite (Chronique de Séert)*, Part I. PO IV (Paris 1907).

Schmidt, Carl. *Gespräche Jesu mit sienen Jüngern nach der Auferstehung.* TU 3.13 (1919).

Schmidt, Hermanus. *Hebdomada Sancta* (Rome 1957).

Schmitz, Josef. *Gottesdienst im altchristlichen Mailand. Theophaneia* 25 (Köln/Bonn 1975).

Schram, Robert Gustav. *Kalendariographische und chronologische Tafeln* (Leipzig 1980).

Schwartz, Eduard. *Christliche und jüdische Ostertafeln. Abhandlungen der K. Gesellschaft der Wissenschaften zu Göttingen. Philologisch-historische Klasse.* Neue Folge, Band VIII.6 (Berlin 1905).

Shepherd, Massey H. *The Paschal Liturgy and the Apocalypse. Ecumenical Studies in Worship* 6 (Richmond, Va. 1960).

————."The Liturgical Reform of Damasus I," *Kyriakon: Festschrift Johannes Quasten* (Münster Westfalen 1970) pp. 847–863.

Smith, Morton. *Clement of Alexandria and a Secret Gospel of Mark* (Cambridge, Mass. 1973).

————. *The Secret Gospel* (New York 1973).

Spiegel, Sholem. *The Last Trial* (New York 1967).

Stevenson, Kenneth. *Jerusalem Revisited — The Liturgical Meaning of Holy Week* (Washington, D.C. 1988).

Stokes, Whitley, ed. *The Martyrology of Oengus the Culdee. Henry Bradshaw Society*, vol. xxix (London 1905).

Strobel, August. *Ursprung und Geschichte des frühchristlichen Osterkalendars.* TU 121 (Berlin 1977).

————.*Texte zur Geschichte des frühchristlichen Osterkalenders.* LQF 64 (Münster Westfalen 1984).

Taft, Robert. "Historicism Revisited," *Liturgical Time: Papers Read at the 1981 Congress of Societas Liturgica* (Rotterdam 1982) pp. 97–109.

Talley, Thomas J. "History and Eschatology in the Primitive Pascha," *Worship* 47 (1973) pp. 212–221.

————. "The Origin of Lent at Alexandria," *Studia Patristica* XVII (Oxford and New York 1982) pp. 594–612.

————."Liturgical Time in the Ancient Church: The State of Research," *Liturgical Time: Papers Read at the 1981 Congress of Societas Liturgica* (Rotterdam 1982) pp. 34–51.

Tarchnischvili, Michel. *Le grand lectionnaire de l'Église de Jerusalem.* Tome I, CSCO 188–189, *Scriptores Iberici* 9-10 (Louvain 1959); Tome II, CSCO 204–205, Scriptores Iberici 204–205 (Louvain 1960).

Thornton, T. C. G. "Problematical Passovers," *Studia Liturgica* 20 (Leuven 1989) pp. 402–408.

Thurston, H., art. "Ash Wednesday," *The Catholic Encyclopedia*, I (New York 1913) p. 775.

Usener, Herman. *Das Weihnachtsfest* (Bonn 1911).

van Esbroek, Michel. "La lettre de l'empereur Justinien sur l'Annonciation et la Noël en 561," *Analecta Bollandiana* 86 (1968) pp. 351–371.

Vansleben, Johann Michael. *The Present State of Egypt or, A New Relation of a Late Voyage into that Kingdom* (London 1678).

Vaux, Roland de. *Ancient Israel: Its Life and Institutions*, trans. John McHugh (London 1961).

Viaud, Gérard. *Les Coptes d'Égypte* (Paris 1978).

Villecourt, Louis. "La Lettre de Macaire, évêque de Memphis, sur la liturgie antique du chrême et du baptême à Alexandrie," Mus. 36 (1923) pp. 33–46.

———."Les Observances liturgiques et la discipline du jeûne dans l'Église copte," Mus. 36 (1923) pp. 249–292; 37 (1924) pp. 201–280; 38 (1925) pp. 125–320.

Vogel, C., and Elze, R. *Le Pontifical Romano-Germanique du dixième siècle. Studi e Testi* 226, 227, 269 (Città del Vaticano 1963, 1972).

Vogüe, Adalbert de. *The Rule of the Master*, trans. Luke Eberle (Kalamazoo, Mich. 1977).

Walker, Joan Hazelden. "A pre- Marcan Dating for the Didache: Further Thoughts of a Liturgist," *Studia Biblica 1978. III: Papers on Paul and Other New Testament Authors* (Sheffield 1980) pp. 403–411.

———."Reflections on a New Edition of the Didache," *Vigiliae Christianae* 35 (1981) 35–42.

Ware, Kallistos, and Mother Mary, trans. *The Lenten Triodion* (London and Boston 1978).

Wilkinson, John. *Egeria's Travels to the Holy Land*, rev. ed. (Jerusalem 1981).

Wilmart, André, "Le Comes de Murbach," *Revue bénédictine* 30 (1913) pp. 25–96.

———."La collection des 38 homélies latines de Saint Jean Chrysostome," JTS xix (1917–1918) pp. 305–327.

Winkler, Gabriele. "The Original Meaning of the Prebaptismal Anointing and its Implications," *Worship* 52 (1978) pp. 24–45.

———."Einige Randbemerkungen zum österlichen Gottesdienst in Jerusalem vom 4. bis 8. Jahrhundert," OCP 39.2 (1973) 481–490.

Wissowa, G. *Paulys Real-encyclopädie der classischen Altertumswissenschaft* (Stuttgart 1894–1926).

Acknowledgements

The publishers are grateful to the following for permission to quote from copyright material:

Alba House for The Paschal Mystery by A. Hamman.

Columbia University Press for The Saturnalia translated by P.V. Davies. © 1969, Columbia University Press. By permission.

Faber and Faber Publishers for The Lenten Triodion by Kallistos Ware and Mother Mary.

Harvard University Press for Clement of Alexandria and a Secret Gospel of Mark by Morton Smith copyright © 1973 The President and Fellows of Harvard College. Reprinted by permission.

Lutterworth Press for The Paschal Liturgy and the Apocalypse by Massey H. Shepherd, Jr.

Methuen & Company, Ltd., for Irish Art in the Early Christian Period by Françoise Henry.

Oxford University Press for Didascalia Apostolorum (1929) by R. Hugh Connolly.

Paulist Press for St. Augustine: Sermons for Christmas and Epiphany translated and annotated by Thomas Comerford Lawler from the Ancient Christian Writers Series. © 1952 Rev. Johannes Quasten and Rev. Joseph C. Plumpe. Used by permission.

Penguin Books Ltd. for The Early Church by Henry Chadwick copyright © 1967 Henry Chadwick. Reprinted by permission.

Verlag Friedrich Pustet for Feiern im Rhythmus der Zeit I: Herrenfeste in Woche und Jahr by Hansjörg Auf der Maur.

SCM Press Ltd. for The Evolution of the Christian Year by A. Allan McArthur.

The Society for Promoting Christian Knowledge for Christian Worship by Duchesne translated by M.L. McClure.

Winston Press for The Shape of Liturgy by Dom Gregory Dix. Copyright © 1945 Dom Gregory Dix. Published by Winston Press, Minneapolis, Minnesota (formerly published by The Seabury Press). All rights reserved. Used with permission.

Index